THE POLITICS OF STORYTELLING

General series editor:
Michael Jackson, Harvard University

Vol. 1. *Matters of Life and Longing: Female Sterilisation in Northeast Brazil* by Anne-Line Dalsgaard
2004
ISBN 978 87 7289 901 5

Vol. 2. *Managing Uncertainty: Ethnographic Studies of Illness, Risk and the Struggle for Control,* edited by Richard Jenkins, Hanne Jessen, and Vibeke Steffen
2005
ISBN 978 87 7289 963 3

Vol. 3. *The Politics of Storytelling: Violence, Transgression, and Intersubjectivity,* by Michael Jackson
2002
ISBN 978 87 7289 737 0
2nd edition 2013, reprint 2019
ISBN 978 87 635 4036 0

Critical Antropology explores life
on the margins of the modern world,
and demonstrates the power of
ethnography to provide new insights
into the human condition.

Critical Anthropology
ISSN 1811 0665

The Politics of Storytelling

VARIATIONS ON A THEME BY HANNAH ARENDT

Second Edition

Michael Jackson

MUSEUM MUSCULANUM PRESS

Michael Jackson, currently Distinguished Professor of World Religions at Harvard Divinity School, is internationally renowned for his work in the field of existential anthropology. He is a leading figure in contemporary philosophical anthropology and widely praised for his innovations in ethnographic writing. His most recent books include *Being of Two Minds, Road Markings: An Anthropologist in the Antipodes, The Other Shore: Essays on Writers and Writing,* and *Lifeworlds: Essays in Existential Anthropology.*

The Politics of Storytelling: Variations on a Theme by Hannah Arendt
Michael Jackson
© 2013 Museum Tusculanum Press and Michael Jackson
Second edition, reprint 2019
First edition, 2002
Cover design by Erling Lynder
Printed in Denmark by Specialtrykkeriet Arco
ISBN 978 87 635 4036 0

Distrubuted in the UK and Ireland by Gazelle Book Services
Distributed in Scandinavia by Museum Tusculanum Press
Distributed in North America and the rest of the world by
The University of Chicago Press.

Museum Tusculanum Press
Dantes Plads 1
DK-1556 Copenhagen
www.mtp.dk

Compared with the reality which comes from being seen and heard, even the greatest forces of intimate life—the passions of the heart, the thoughts of the mind, the delights of the senses—lead to an uncertain, shadowy kind of existence unless and until they are transformed, deprivatized and deindividualized, as it were, into a shape to fit them for public appearance. The most current of such transformations occurs in storytelling...

—HANNAH ARENDT, *The Human Condition*

For Brijen K. Gupta

CONTENTS

ACKNOWLEDGMENTS

Over fifty years ago, when an undergraduate at Auckland University, I was awarded the annual anthropology prize and with my modest prize money bought a copy of Hannah Arendt's *The Human Condition*. In the decades since, I have returned to this book countless times, though still remember as though it were yesterday the leftwing basement store (Progressive Books) where I purchased it and the sense I had of having found something that might clear my way through the wilderness in which I was then lost—for *The Human Condition* gave me my first glimpse of how the questions of philosophy might be explored through the methods of ethnography, how a contemplative life might be integrated with a life of active and practical engagement in the world, and how ethnography and literature might be brought together in new and edifying ways.

In 1998, the Stout Research Centre at Victoria University of Wellington, New Zealand, gave me a calm and convivial fellowship year in which to pursue the research that inspired this book. I am deeply indebted to Vincent O'Sullivan, then Director of the Stout Centre, and Niko Besnier, then professor of anthropology at Victoria University of Wellington, for the warmth of their friendship, the generosity of their support, and the inspiration of their company during my time in Wellington. To Abdi Bihi, Les Cleveland, Ronda Cooper, Roya Jazbani, Eru Manuera, and Jennifer Shennan I also owe my thanks for their opportune and unstinting help. In Sydney, Australia, lively conversations with my friend, colleague, and neighbor, Ghassan Hage, helped me develop important insights into refugee and migrant experience, and at the University of Copenhagen, Denmark, where, thanks to initatives by Susan Reynolds-Whyte and Michael A. Whyte, I began a stint as Guest Professor at the Institute of Anthropology in 1999, I profited from numerous exchanges of ideas with colleagues and students alike. For critical comments on various sections of this work I am grateful to Nils Ole Bubandt, Sverker Finnström, Bruce Kapferer, Orvar Löfgren, Anh Nga Longva, Francine Lorimer, Maja Povrzanović, Nigel Rapport, and Vibeke Steffen. To Marianne Alenius, who embraced this work so wholeheartedly, and supervised its publication with such care, I owe an enormous debt of gratitude. Thanks are also due to Jordy Findanis, on whose meticulous editorial care I depended in preparing this second edition.

Last but not least, I acknowledge the intellectual magnanimity of Brijen K. Gupta, a dear friend, mentor and ally for over fifty years, to whom I dedicate this book.

PREFACE TO SECOND EDITION

Like many writers, I am as loath to go back to my earlier published work as I am reluctant to revisit earlier chapters in my life. Each work represents the best that I could achieve at the time, and rather than endlessly revise past endeavors I prefer to undertake new work in the hope that it will redeem the failings of the old. What, then, is the justification for a second edition of *The Politics of Storytelling*? One answer is that this book is still read and referred to—evidence, I like to think, of the enduring value of Hannah Arendt's insights into the universal human impulse to translate our disparate and often overwhelming personal experiences into forms that can be voiced and reworked in the company of others. In restoring the original subtitle to my book, I pay homage to Arendt's dialectical view that storytelling is a mode of purposeful action (praxis) that simultaneously discloses our subjective uniqueness and our intersubjective connectedness to others, as well as the environmental forces to which we are all subject. A second reason for re-issuing this book is to incorporate some of my more recent thinking on the subject of storytelling—inspired by the courses I have taught at the University of Copenhagen and at Harvard Divinity School over the last ten years, and by my use of life stories in my ethnographic work.

The Politics of Storytelling had its origins in fieldwork I did in Wellington, New Zealand, in 1998 with Iraqi and Somali refugees. When I embarked on this research I wanted people to tell me their stories; I wanted to understand where they were coming from, the kinds of experiences they had undergone in flight from war and persecution, in refugee camps, and in their country of asylum. But what I encountered was hesitancy, awkwardness, and suspicion. In part, this reflected the unspeakable experiences many of these refugees had undergone—events that not only resisted recollection but lay beyond their power to comprehend, interpret, or narrate. It quickly became clear to me that life stories often have less to do with speaking one's mind or sharing one's experiences than with saying what is safest or most expedient to say. To put it bluntly, in extremis one often finds that the truth will get you nowhere or get you into trouble. One has to learn to carefully select, censor, and misrepresent one's reality in order to get one's way—to escape from terror, to cross a border, to be selected for emigration, to avoid racist insults and condescending expectations in the country of asylum; and persuade state officials to look kindly on one's petition for family reunions. Stories are often cover stories, defences against danger and hurt. They downplay any disparity between the truth of one's own experience and the truths enshrined in the dominant narratives of the state, which expects gratitude from refugees, not grievances, conformity not criticism. Living as a citizen in a free country, I could indulge notions of verisimilitude and objective testimony. The refugees I met were struggling to survive spiritually and socially in what to them was an alien and often demoralizing environment. To share their experience with a New Zealand writer might cost them dearly, and so they censored, prevaricated, or withdrew.

All stories are, in a sense, untrue. They rearrange and transform our experiences. But these rearrangements, like the essays and explanatory models we produce in the academy, may serve very different *interests*— and it was this emphasis on discourse as *techné* rather than *epistemé* that came to inform my approach to storytelling. The critical point here is that strategies for acting on the world do not necessarily entail knowledge of the world, either as a script to be enacted or an end product to be possessed. As *techné*, storytelling can transform our experience, stir our emotions, and facilitate action without the mediation of conceptual thought and in *opposition to official narratives*. Thus, when a young woman was interviewed on CNN, ten years after what she called "the traumatic event" of 9/11 in which her fiancé perished, she made two compelling remarks. The first was to call into question the need to tell and retell a story of the event. "It's hard to put it into words," she said; "maybe one doesn't need to." Her implication: that silence may have as much therapeutic value as speech. Then, in explaining why she would not attend the public ceremonies on the tenth anniversary, she remarked, "I don't want 9/11 to define me," so disengaging her life from the life of the polis and the nationalistic narratives it insisted in constructing out of the raw experience of its citizens. A personal story redeems us "from alienation and impersonality, from the grip of stereotypes and prejudices," writes David Grossman. It restores our humanity in situations that reduce us to "one-dimensional creatures lacking volition" (Grossman 2008: 49, 51). Although Hannah Arendt emphasizes the power of storytelling to connect us with others, finding common ground and reclaiming a public world, there can be no doubt that she placed equal value on those who embraced the role of "conscious pariah" and spoke out against ideologies that enshrined the vested interests of power elites.

Hannah Arendt came to the United States in 1941 as a refugee. Much of what she wrote in the ensuing years bears the imprint of her experience of displacement and loss, and of the dilemma of preserving her own identity while proving herself to be a "prospective citizen" rather than "enemy alien"—giving the impression that she had sloughed off her previous identity and language, and left her past behind (Arendt 1943, 69–71). In *The Human Condition* (1958), Arendt addresses the question of how storytelling speaks to this struggle to exist as one among many, preserving one's unique character while fulfilling one's obligations as a citizen of a republic.

Basic to Arendt's thesis is the axiom of human plurality—that we are at once unique individuals (*ipse*) *and* members of a community, of a class, a nation and, ultimately, a single species, with capacities for speech and action that we have in common with every other human being who lives and who has lived (*idem*). Politics and power, for Arendt, are matters of how the private realm of individual experience is related to the public realm—the realm of transpersonal values, mercenary, and mundane interests, and dominant ideologies. There are echoes here of Walter Benjamin's distinction, in *The Storyteller*, between immediate experiences that have been directly undergone (*Erlebnis*) and experiences that have been thought through in ways that render them comprehensible to and shareable with others (*Erfahrung*). This entire field of experience is what Arendt calls the "subjective-in-between," since existence is never merely a matter of what I or you say or do but what *we* say and do together, interacting, conversing, and adjusting our interests, experiences, and points of view to one another. When one tells stories, therefore, one is never simply giving voice to what is on one's own mind or in one's own interests; one is realizing, or objectifying, one's own experience in ways that others can relate to through experiences of their own. Stories are like the coins of the realm, the currency we implicitly agree to make the means of exchange, and, as such, a means of creating a viable social world. Stories thus disclose not just "who" we are, but "what" we have in common with others, not just "who" we think we are but "what" shared circumstances bear upon our lives and our fate.

Clearly, Arendt is more concerned with the action, work, or process of storytelling, and the effects this has, than on the content of any story. Hers is an implicitly pragmatist view—that storytelling is a quintessentially intersubjective activity that brings the social into being. Her judgment of whether a story is good or bad, right or wrong, is not based on epistemological criteria—whether or not it reflects some absolute or abstract truth, or imparts true knowledge. It is based on a story's aftereffects, particularly whether it fosters the democratic ideal of a community of equals who are in constant conversation with one another, adjusting the interests of each to the interests of all.

Although Arendt's focus is on people acting together rather than any individual project of empowerment (1973, 30), it is useful to compare her perspective with object-relations theory in psychoanalysis. Wilfrid Bion (1975) postulated that we can only process and come to accept overwhelming life events ("beta elements") by working them through with a caring other—someone who can contain or safely hold us, and on whom we can rely in constructing a life-affirming rather than life-negating response to unbearable experiences. In the more recent work of Peter Fonagy and Mary Target (2003), this process of "working through" is construed as a form of play. With others, we play with reality—oscillating between a "pretend mode" in which images and ideas are allowed to take on a life of their own, and a mode of "psychic equivalence" in which ideas are made to stand for some external circumstance. For both Bion and Fonagy, concepts are equated with anything that helps a child objectify and vicariously control its relationship with the world—breast milk, food, toys, building blocks, paints, and found objects. Storytelling and conceptual thought, in this view, are means whereby a person, from early infancy, organizes and manages the life experiences that threaten to engulf, undermine, or nullify him or her. Since this work requires the presence of attentive others, the process of shaping and reshaping one's own subjectivity inevitably runs parallel to the work of shaping collective identity and solidarity. Stories enable us to live with ourselves as well as live with others.

In 1979 Joan Didion wrote, "We tell ourselves stories in order to live," a phrase whose full force she may not have recognized at this time. But there are two aspects to what we mean when we speak of stories enabling us to live. Stories are a way we recount and rework events that happened to us, that simply befell us. We do this firstly by sharing our experiences with others in a form that they can relate or respond to, thereby reaffirming and consolidating our sense of belonging to a family, a circle of friends, a community or even a nation. This covers the connection between storytelling and sociality. But we also tell stories as a way of transforming our sense of who we are, recovering a sense of ourselves as actors and agents in the face of experiences that make us feel insignificant, unrecognized or powerless. This covers the connection between storytelling and freedom—the way we recapture, through telling stories, a sense of being acting subjects in a world that often reduces us to the status of mere objects, acted upon by others or moved by forces beyond our control. As David Grossman puts it, storytelling counters the arbitrariness of existence; it allows one the freedom "to articulate the tragedy of [one's] situation in [one's] *own words.*" Writing affords us the same existential power, for "from the moment we take pen in hand or put fingers to keyboard, we have already ceased to be a victim at the mercy of all that enslaved and restricted us before we began writing" (Grossman 2008: 67, 68, emphasis in text).

Even a small child will, before falling asleep, want to go over the events of the day in his or her mind, getting things straight, putting things to right—vicariously relating a "story" that comes to a happy ending or recounting an event that happened during the day and caused perplexity or confusion. Here, for example, is a fragment of a crib monologue by Emily (21 months), recorded by Katherine Nelson:

> The broke, car broke, the ... Emmy can't go in the car. Go in green car. No. Emmy go in the car. Broken. Broken. Their car broken, so Mommy Daddy go in their car, Emmy Daddy go in the car, Emmy Daddy Mommy go in the car, broke, Da ... da, the car ... their, their, car broken (Nelson 1998, 162).

Nelson speaks of this as proto-narrative. It is the incipient form of what most of us do at the close of every day, and bears comparison with what Freud called the dream work—the process whereby the brain, during REM sleep, reorganizes the experiences of the day, translating these residues into a symbolic language that prepares us to embrace new experiences.

Although this process of collaborating in the creation of our own lives—or at least in composing the stories that make our lives seem coherent—is existentially imperative, Hannah Arendt insists that this notion of ourselves as makers and shakers is a necessary illusion. Although we recount our histories as we recount our lives—as narratives of visionary or villainous individuals—"the real story in which we are engaged as long as we live has no visible or invisible maker because it is not made" (1958, 186). In every historical *narrative* there are heroically or demonically powerful figures, to be sure—like Lincoln and Napoleon, Hitler and Churchill—but Arendt reminds us that these individuals were not the sole authors of the events we associate with their names. Although stories require agents, who make things happen and to whom things happen, in reality we act and speak without ever being sole authors of our destinies or lives, and history is "an endless new chain of happenings whose eventual outcome the actor is utterly incapable of knowing or controlling beforehand" (Arendt 1977, 59–60). Because our lives unfold in the indeterminate or potential space *between* ourselves and others, our original intentions are often confounded and our assumed identities eclipsed, leading us to do things we did not think we had it in us to do, and obliging us to constantly rethink the very notion of who we are. At the same time, all human action is conditioned by a plethora of often competing influences, interests, and persuasions that are the outcome of *previous* experience, and that have ramifications that go far beyond what any actor knows, desires, imagines, says, or does. The "simple fact," Arendt observes, is that "we don't know what we are doing when we are acting" and we can neither grasp, practically or intellectually, the manifold influences that bear upon us or the future implications of what we do (2000, 180). This is not to reduce human existence to contingency, for our lives would be unthinkable without at least the *ideas* of agency and design. What Arendt wants to emphasize is the fact that human action always involves more than a singular subject; it occurs within fields of *inter*action that she calls the "subjective in-between." Accordingly, whatever anyone does or says is immediately outstripped by what others do or say in return. Every action calls out a reaction that "strikes out on its own and affects others" (1958, 190). Obvious ethical questions are entailed by this view, since if one can never know exactly the extent to which one's actions make a difference to the ways things are, or the extent to which one is responsible for what one does, it becomes difficult to decide, for example, if or when one should be condemned for one's failings or praised for one's good deeds.

While it may be impossible to understand every antecedent cause or contingent factor that bears upon our actions, Arendt does not take the view that we are thereby in thrall to the past, for we may, through *forgiveness*, find release from the consequences of our past actions, or the effect of the actions of others upon us, and through the *promise* we make to ourselves and others, we may find redemption from "the chaotic uncertainty of the future" (1958, 237). These strategies, she says, reflect the fact of natality—the power of action to bring the new into being. Thus, when we recount a story about any event that has befallen us, we play down the boundless field of influences and consequences that impinge upon us, and create the impression that our lives and histories lie, at least to some extent, within our ken and control.

Although forgiveness and the promise, like storytelling and redressive rituals, offer the perennial possibility of redemption, suggesting that we are responsible for our actions and can change our course and transcend the past, Hannah Arendt avoids the question of whether such strategies are merely magical means of transforming the *appearance* of the world or *real* means of changing it. Arendt is not a fatalist, who sees us as playthings of the Gods (we might now say our history or our genes), for this would seem to imply that nothing we say or do can help us escape the mimetic and repetitive cycles of violence that have bedevilled us in the past, and that all our piety and wit cannot err the moving finger of history back to cancel half a line. She is not denying human freedom. She is simply pointing out that freedom is exercised in some domains, but not in others, and that it is important not to delude ourselves about the extent to which we are the authors and arbiters of our own lives. The problem, she observes, is our tendency to conflate "acting" (*praxis*) and "making" (*poesis*). Poesis, which is synonymous with what is nowadays called agency, suggests the sustained, self-conscious, goal-oriented way a person or persons work at making or producing something—researching a book, combating terrorism, building a house, having a family, treating a disease. Praxis, by contrast, denotes a field of human action and interaction that is largely beyond our comprehension and control, and which we simply suffer.[1] While Michel Foucault stripped history clean of heroic movers and shakers by reimagining it as a succession of different discursive formations, Hannah Arendt succeeds in getting rid of the notion of an agentive subject without, however, reducing history to anything as abstract as discourse. For her, the *vita activa* consists less in our intellectual conception of who we are, of what things mean, or the knowledge and moral precepts we espouse, than in our decisive interactions with others in a world that nonetheless exceeds our understanding and eludes our grasp. While our retrospective accounts and interpretations of these interactions in the *vita contemplativa* will almost certainly involve the ascription of intention and the allocation of blame, we *act*, for the most part, habitually and unreflectively, moved by deeply embedded dispositions that have far more to do with the struggle for being than the striving for meaning.[2]

One might cite, for example, in defence of this view, the way in which a war quickly outstrips the sociocultural conditions that brought it about or the political ideologies that gave it justification, running its course like a storm or a fever, possessing a life and logic of its own. In this vein, Lebanese refer to the civil war as "the events" (*al hawadith*), a "mild and faintly contemptuous understatement" that bears a close relation to the Arabic word for "accident" (Makdisi 1990, 65). Or one might remark the ways in which, despite our rational planning, our good intentions, and our care of self, markets pass through cycles of boom or bust, marriages go on the rocks, friends fall out, luck deserts or favors us, and "The best laid schemes o' mice an' men / Gang aft a-gley, / An' lea'e us nought but grief an' pain, / For promised joy." In mundane rituals and stories we seek to repair the damage to our shattered illusions of omnipotence. Monuments to the war dead, with their lists of specific names and battles, or Truth and Reconciliation hearings, with their stories of individual suffering, bear testimony to our human unwillingness to resign ourselves "to the brutal fact that the agent of the war was actually Nobody" (Arendt 2000, 179). Similarly, our perennial hope of enlightened leaders, and our search for gurus and saviors, testify to our inability to live without the illusion that we have, within our own hands and minds, the power not only to create history, but to create it as nature or God or reason determined it should be.

Sectarianism is perhaps the most ubiquitous and problematic example of this conviction that history, and not just the myths with which we make it intelligible, is largely a product of human agency and human will, for which we may be judged righteous or wrong-headed, heroic or villainous. Arendt's contrary view—that history has a life of its own that is beyond our complete control and comprehension—entails a non-judgmental attitude. For if human beings commonly "know not what they do," our intellectual task becomes less a matter of determining the causes of human action, or of deciding who is responsible for the way things turn out in this world, than of exploring the ways in which people struggle against the disadvantages of their circumstances and recover from the adversities of their histories. Knowing why things happen, or judging people for the errors of their ways, is thus less important than trying to understand how, in the face of hardship, human beings still find life worth living, and endure. But such research requires a method not of standing aloof and seeing the world from a disinterested, superior standpoint, but of actively engaging with others in their place, on their own terms. "Training one's imagination to go visiting," as Arendt (1982, 43) called this method of intellectual displacement, does not entail agreeing or even empathizing with the other, as her famous study of Adolf Eichmann makes clear. And though it repudiates Archimedean detachment, it does not imply the kind of suspension of ethical concern that would lead us to exonerate a person of a crime on the grounds that we understand what drove him to commit the offence. Rather, it simply asks that we do not invoke cultural, religious, or intellectual superiority in privileging received opinions, or our own particular point of view.

What, then, can be accomplished through storytelling? And can our stories be equated with our theories about the world—symbolic techniques of control and comprehension, born of our need to believe that we can grasp reality and determine the course of our lives? The answer to this question cannot be provided by philosophy alone, though a first step is to suspend our conventional notions about the essential differences between fact and fiction, science and myth, the real and the illusory, in order to explore, on a case by case basis, what consequences follow from any behavior, and what effects our actions have upon our lives and the lives of others.

In a recent essay, I argued that the questions of philosophy might be most productively explored through the methods of ethnography (Jackson 2009). Rather than habitually returning to the Greeks as our sounding board, I suggested that it might be more edifying to locate our thinking in the lifeworlds of our contemporaries, exploring their strategies—intellectual and practical, magical and imaginative, affective and objective—for making their lives viable and fulfilling.

Several lines of research demonstrate the value of moving beyond a logocentric tendency to polarize words and deeds in order to explore—and place on an equal footing—storytelling (and other verbal arts), ritual practices, emotional and mood changing techniques, and technologies of the body as forms of play rather than methods of knowing.

Consider Janet Hoskins's research among the Kodi of the eastern Indonesian island of Sumba. When Kodi speak about themselves and their lives they seldom do so directly—by telling life stories. When people spoke to Janet Hoskins about their personal possessions, however, they did so in accounts that were *implicit* life stories. Moreover, subjects that were not publicly spoken of in Kodi—such as sexual politics—would often find oblique expression in these accounts. "A young girl I knew well never confessed her feelings of romantic longing and later disappointment to me directly, but she was fascinated by the story of a magic spindle that flew through the air to snare a beloved. When later her own hopes were cut off, she sent a message to her lost lover through the secret gift of the object. A famous singer and healer who also wanted a female companion composed long ballads to his drum, introducing each ritual session with a history of efforts to cover the drum properly so it could be pierced by a male voice and travel up to the heavens … Another man, famed as a storyteller and bard, said he received his 'gift of words' in the simple, woven betel bag he carried with him at all times" (Hoskins 1998, 3). That objects are surrogates for people, metaphors for social relationships, and serve as objective correlatives of subjective moods and states may, Hoskins suggests, have a lot to do with the fact that, in Kodi ritual, objects often substitute for persons. Thus, in life-crisis rituals, a knife can substitute for a man, a cotton board, or gold pendant can take the place of a woman, a betel bag be buried in lieu of a person. Interestingly enough, Hoskins points out that the objects that stand for persons are very often containers: a betel pouch, a hollow drum, a porcelain vessel, a funeral shroud.

Sónia Silva's more recent research among Angolan refugees in northwest Zambia offers similarly profound insights into the ways in which divining baskets (*lipele*) have life cycles—from birth to death—and take on the properties of human being—thinking, hearing, judging, responding. Through their direct and constant engagement with these carefully crafted objects that belong in the public realm, yet are considered lifelong companions, alter egos, and means of counteracting the actions of the external world, individuals succeed in bringing a measure of control over their lives (Silva 2011, 140). Indeed, the lives of people and the lives of the *lipele* are inextricably linked. These are truly intersubjective relations; the story of a life and the story of a basket become one.

A second line of research addresses the recovery of agency and the limits of language.

In a brilliant study of war and ethnic conflict in the Balkans, Mattijs van de Port observes that everyone's autobiography contains turning-points (separations, illnesses, the death of beloved ones) when a story that had previously been unquestioned and accepted as a given is contradicted by reality. "And everyone knows those moments between stories when, through a temporary opening that soon closes up again, one catches a glimpse of non-fictional reality, reality *an sich*" (van de Port 1998, 32). Although stories are typically interrupted, broken, and rendered absurd by extreme experience, storytelling remains one of our most powerful techniques for healing ourselves and restoring order to a broken world.

The Politics of Storytelling explores this twofold human response to devastating loss—the first being a traumatic disorientation that may prove paralyzing and permanent, the second being a revised orientation to the world that may prove illuminating and liberating.

Let us first consider trauma. Trauma implies a radical loss of agency—of one's ability to act, to live in the present rather than the past, and to engage fully with others. Agency implies having a sense of existential power—and power, as Hannah Arendt reminds us, "arises only where people act together" (1973, 30). Storytelling, for Arendt, may mediate the recovery of this sense of being existentially empowered, as well as connected to the world around us. Storytelling is a form of restorative praxis—of sharing one's experience with others, of finding common ground, of coming out of the closet, of restoring one's place in the public sphere. But storytelling is also a way in which we act in the face of forces that render us inactive and silent. As Oliver Sacks notes, disease is never simply a loss or impairment of function; there is "always a reaction, on the part of the affected organism or individual, to restore, to replace, to compensate for and to preserve its identity" (1986, 4). The same principle of recruitment—whereby lesions are repaired and losses made good by new growth—obtains in social life.

Loss is always countermandered by actions—albeit imaginative, magical, and illusory—to regain some sense of balance between the world within and the world without.

Following a devastating stroke, Jean-Dominique Bauby awoke from a deep coma and learned how to dictate his memoir, using only his left eyelid (Bauby 1998). In *The Man with a Shattered World,* the great Russian neuropsychologist, A.R. Luria, describes a long-term patient of his who suffered massive damage to the left occipital-parietal region of his brain when hit by shell fragments in 1942. Alexandr Romanovich Luria was not only a pioneer in neuropsychological studies of memory, language, and cognition; he refused to allow the abstract models of science to eclipse the lived reality of human beings—the ways in which they saw their world and struggled to live even under the most debilitating circumstances. If science often gives the impression of writing off individuals in order to grasp the external forces that shape their lives, Luria's detailed case histories do justice to the individuals with whom he is concerned, illuminating the worlds of their experience. He therefore describes how, for twenty-five years, Zazetsky painstakingly filled volume after volume of notebooks with accounts of his fragmented world, even though he was unable to write connectedly about his life. Writing, observes Luria, "was his one link with life, his only hope of not succumbing to illness but recovering at least a part of what had been lost" (Luria 1987, xx).

Zazetsky was under no illusions that his scribblings would constitute a coherent narrative, help recover his memory, or be of much use to anyone else. Perhaps that is why he referred to his writing as "morbid," as though it was something he was compelled to do. "If I shut these notebooks, give it up, I'll be right back in the desert, in that 'know-nothing' world of emptiness and amnesia" (Luria 1987, 86). What sustained him was a primitive existential imperative—to act rather than be acted upon. "The point of my writing, he said, is to show how I have been, and still am, struggling to recover my memory ... I had no choice but to try" (84).

In *The Uses of Enchantment* (1978), Bruno Bettelheim shows how children unconsciously appropriate stories in the public domain—especially fairytales—as ways of working through and mastering the psychological problems of growing up—overcoming narcissistic disappointments, oedipal dilemmas, sibling rivalries, becoming able to relinquish childhood dependencies, gaining a feeling of selfhood and of self-worth, and a sense of moral obligation (1978, 3–19). Fairytales provide raw material for the imagination to work with—as well as models of existential struggle that help the child come to grips with the difficulties of life, including separation and loss, lovelessness and illness, unfairness, abandonment and lack of recognition. Through the dramatic story of Snow White, for example, a five year-old girl whose mother was cold and distant, could see that love and rescue did not always come from a female figure, and that men might offer care and protection—the hunter who spares Snow White's life despite the Queen's order that she be killed, the dwarfs who take her in, the prince whose kiss brings her back to life. In the story of Rapunzel, a five-year old boy found a way of rethinking a distressing situation—his mother at work all day, no father at home, and his grandmother and caregiver suddenly taken to hospital. In the image of retreating into one's own body—the tower in which Rapunzel was confined—he found consolation for the loss of support in the world around him, and a sense of security within himself.

More recently, Michael White has extended the insights of pioneers in narrative therapy like Freud, Jung, Janet, and Bettelheim, and developed a set of therapeutic techniques based on notions of *externalization* and *re-membering* (White 2007). These concepts are cognate with Arendt's ideas about the ways in which storytelling enables a deprivatization of experience and a recovery of sociality—but in Michael White's work the ideas are put into practice in compelling ways. For White, stories are cognitive maps that enable the client, with the therapist's guidance, to renegotiate, reimagine and reinvent the terms on which she is living her life, to reshuffle the deck of cards from which she has been dealt an unplayable hand, to be, in a sense, reborn.

White begins with an assertion that, for many of us, challenges a widespread assumption that many of the problems in our lives are a reflection of our own identity (there is something wrong with us), or the identity of others (I'm messed up because of my mother/father/family situation, etc.), or a reflection of the identity of our relationships (I'm in a bad marriage). White says that this kind of thinking—in which we locate the source of our problems within our nature, or in the nature of another, or in the nature of our situation, our history, our culture, our class—is counterproductive, and that externalizing or objectifying the problem that has been wrongly identified with an internal or subjective state is a productive therapeutic move. Consider this case as an example of the method of externalization. It concerned the parents of a boy called Jeffrey, who had been diagnosed with Attention Deficit Hyperactivity Disorder (ADHD). Michael White's strategy was to place this diagnostic label in brackets—to refuse to speak of it as an essence, or something that was inside Jeffrey, definitive of his nature, and to speak of it as something that could be played around with—that Jeffrey could regard as something external to himself, something that could, therefore, be manipulated by him, like a person or thing that had its own color, shape, and character. White enlisted the parents in this game of speaking of ADHD as an "it" that had been upsetting the family, giving them headaches, messing things up between Jeffrey and his teachers at school. As soon as Jeffrey and his parents agreed that the time had come to stop ADHD ruling their lives, Jeffrey could make his active and imaginative contribution to discussions about how best to get the monkey off their backs.

As an anthropologist, I find Michael White's work compelling, because in his search for ways of objectifying conditions that we assume to be internal or intrapsychic he not only calls into question a post-Enlightenment tendency to emphasize our inward or subjective *essence*—our character, personality, or nature—over our social *existence* in what Arendt calls the subjective-in-between; he throws light on modes of therapy that emphasize collective action over individual treatment, as well as processes of externalization or objectification, as in divination, where objects like charred bones, river stones, or texts are means of discovering new courses of action, or possession, meditation, and prayer, in which we are taken *out of ourselves* in order to be healed. This brings me to Michael White's second therapeutic technique: re-membering.

Many European theories of memory regard remembering as a function of our subjective or intrapsychic life. Remembering is a kind of intrapsychic hiccupping—a repetition, *within* the body-mind, of an event that originally involved our relation with others or our environment. Inspired by Barbara Myerhoff's ethnography (1982), Michael White speaks of re-membering as a process of reorganizing the events and persons that figure most prominently in our lives, much as we might reorganize the furniture in our homes to create a new and more liveable space. In other words, one thinks of one's self not as an autonomous unit with a distinctive internal character and external appearance, but as a part of a collectivity, a member of a family, lineage, or community in which there are many other members. Re-membering therefore "evokes the image of a person's life and identity as an association or a club. The membership of this association of life is made up of the significant figures of a person's history, as well as the identities of the person's present circumstances, whose voices are influential with regard to how the person constructs his or her own identity. Re-membering conversations provides an opportunity for people to engage in a revision of the membership of their associations of life, affording an opening for the reconstruction of their identity.

Finally, let us consider the relationship between storytelling, ethics, and critique.

In my 1982 study of ethics in Kuranko storytelling I showed how stories placed the everyday world in brackets in order to broach highly sensitive and refractory dilemmas in everyday life. Rather than confirm the conventional wisdom and dogmas in the public realm, stories placed these worldviews in brackets in order to explore the ethical quandaries of creating a just and fulfilling life.

Almost all Kuranko tales involve journeys between town (*suè*) and bush (*fira*). As such the moral customs (*namui* or *bimba kan*), laws (*seriye* or *ton*), and chiefly power (*mansaye*) associated with the town are momentarily placed in abeyance, and the wild ethos of the bush, associated with animals, shape-shifters, djinn and antinomian possibilities, comes into play. Moreover, Kuranko stories are told at night, or in twilight zones that lie on the margins of the workaday, waking world. There is a close connection, therefore, between the evocation of antinomian scenarios, states of dreamlike or drowsy consciousness, and the narrative suspension of disbelief. Kuranko *tilei* (fables, folktales, fictions) are make-believe; they are framed as occurring outside ordinary time and space (*wo le yan be la*—far-off and long ago); they play with reality, and entertain possibilities that lie beyond convention and custom. Typically, these tales begin with a dilemma or disturbance in the ideal order of moral relations: three sons of a chief, all born at the same time and on the same day, all claim the right to succeed their father; an elder brother maltreats his younger brother; a senior co-wife exploits a younger co-wife; a man betrays the trust of his closest friend; a chief abuses his power or imposes an unjust law on his people; a husband neglects his wife; a love affair jeopardizes a marriage. The ethical quandary lies in how to redress a situation in which there is considerable moral ambiguity, for there are always two sides to every story and several possible ways of restoring order, or seeing that justice is done. That is to say, ethical dilemmas are never resolved by simply laying down the law, invoking a moral principle that covers every situation, or passing a judgment; the dilemmas require collective *discussion*, in which people attempt to come up with the best solution possible, given the complex circumstances, even though it is understood that any solution may make matters worse, and that no one is ever in a position to know the repercussions of his or her actions. By not seeking consensus, and by suspending dogmatic patterns of thinking, Kuranko storytelling creates ethical ambiguity and inspires listeners to think outside the box. Accordingly, virtue is less a matter of achieving or exemplifying goodness than a relative question of doing the best one can, given the limits of any situation and considering the abilities and resources one possesses.

In more recent fieldwork, I have seen how the wider world has become, for young African migrants, a symbolic bush—at once a place of peril and of transformative possibilities, lying beyond the moral and legal space of the "town," and signifying a space for ethical questioning and bargaining, comparable to the space hitherto associated with bush spirits and the ancestral dead. Why should Africans languish in poverty when the Western world enjoys such abundance? Will a young woman's desire to marry for love jeopardize inter-family relations based on arranged marriage? How can one reconcile going abroad in search of one's fortune when this means losing touch with one's homeland and possibly neglecting one's obligation to family back home? By what right do politicians amass wealth for themselves and neglect the welfare of ordinary people (Jackson 2011).

Methodologically, then, storytelling implicates not only a politics but an ethics. As Fasching, Dechant, and Lantigua put it, "The study of ethics must be more than an 'objective' survey of abstract theories … The primary and most persuasive ways religious traditions shape ethical behavior are through storytelling and spiritual practices" (2011, 5). This implies a focus on "*the life stories* of [individuals] who have wrestled with questions of justice, non-violence, and ecological well-being in an age of racism, sexism, religious prejudice, nationalism, colonialism, terrorism, and nuclear war" (5). Although Fasching, Dechant, and Lantigua want to emphasize the life stories of "extraordinary persons" like Tolstoy, Gandhi, Martin Luther

King, Jr. and Malcolm X, my own focus is on the extraordinary stories of *ordinary* people whose experiences bring into sharp relief the ethical quandaries, qualms, and questions that all human beings encounter in the course of their lives, regardless of their religious, ethnic, cultural, or class identities.

In exploring storytelling as a form of ethical discourse, we must, however, resist wanting to extract moral lessons from the content of a story, for the ethical is always an open question that is never identical to moral formulae or legal codes. Rather than supporting the status quo, stories open up for discussion the ethical dilemmas not of perpetuating a given social order but of creating a more viable life. Michael Lambek has coined the term "ordinary ethics" to signal this departure from the Kantian tradition of Western moral thought—in which a priori assumptions about autonomy, agency, virtue, and community refer to particular situations cursorily, anecdotally, or not at all. For Lambek, ethics is "fundamentally a property or function of action rather than (only) of abstract reason" (2010, 14). There are echoes here of Veena Das's argument for a "descent into the ordinary" (2007, 15), and David Graeber's claim that "if we really want to understand the moral grounds of economic life, and by extension, human life," we must start not with cosmologies and worldviews but with "the very small things: the everyday details of social existence, the way we treat our friends, enemies, and children—often with gestures so tiny (passing the salt, bumming a cigarette) that we ordinarily never stop to think about them at all" (2011, 89). To this list, we might add storytelling.

INTRODUCTION

This book is an anthropological exploration of Hannah Arendt's view that storytelling is never simply a matter of creating either personal or social meanings, but an aspect of the "subjective-in-between" in which a multiplicity of private and public interests are always problematically in play (Arendt 1958, 182–84). Power relations between private and public realms imply a politics of experience. While storytelling may help us reconcile fields of experience that are, on the one hand, felt to belong to ourselves or our own kind and, on the other, felt to be shared or to belong to others, stories may just as trenchantly exaggerate differences, foment discord, and do violence to lived experience. For every story that sees the light of day, untold others remain in the shadows, censored, or suppressed.

In *The Human Condition* Hannah Arendt speaks of the public realm in two closely related ways. Phenomenologically, the public realm is a space of appearance where individual experiences are selectively refashioned in ways that make them real and recognizable in the eyes of others. Sociologically, the public realm is a space of shared *inter-est*, where a plurality of people work together to create a world to which they feel they all belong (Arendt 1958, 50–52, cf. Duby 1988, 4). For Hannah Arendt, the private realm denotes a conglomeration of singular and reclusive subjectivities "deprived of the reality that comes from being seen and heard by others." In so far as privacy suggests confinement to "the subjectivity of [one's] own singular experience," it spells "the end of the common world" (58). Two different senses of privacy are entangled here, for while the *res privata* defines domestic space—the domus, subject to the authority of the *pater familias*, a world within four walls—it also connotes the hidden, reserved, clandestine field of the personal in which certain thoughts, intentions, and desires are masked because they are not considered compatible with the *res publica*. Accordingly, privacy should not be equated with individuality, for the term may be used of any intimate or exclusive domain whose affairs are not open to, or legitimate in, the public gaze. As Habermas (1989) notes, the lifeworlds and voices of marginalized *classes* also tend to be "privatized" by being denied public recognition.

Behind Arendt's approach lies an unspoken ontological assumption that our individual humanity always has extension in space and time—hence the universality of metaphors of human existence as a net, a web, a branching tree, or a skein of roots. "To be rooted," noted Simone Weil, "is perhaps the most important and least recognized need of the human soul" (1952, 41). But rootedness is, Weil also observed, a *social* fact before it is anything else, inextricably linked to a person's "real, active and natural participation in the life of a community." To belong is thus to believe that one's being is integrated with and integral to a wider field of being, that one's own life merges with and touches the lives of others—predecessors, successors, contemporaries, and consociates, as well as the overlapping worlds of nature, the cosmos, and the divine. Although Hannah Arendt generally limits her discussion of storytelling to the political relationship between private and public realms, I will argue that this contrast gains greater comparative and anthropological force when it is assimilated to the relationship between microcosm and macrocosm, thereby embracing the relationship between the visible and invisible, the familiar and foreign, and the living and the dead. My second revision of Arendt's model seeks to avoid any inadvertent ontologizing of terms such as the private and the public, the individual and the communal, by placing a more existential emphasis on interexperience.[3]

As Arendt herself notes (passim 181–88), every person is at once a "who" and a "what"—a subject who actively participates in the making or unmaking of his or her world, and a subject who suffers and is subjected to actions by others, as well as forces of circumstances that lie largely outside his or her control. This oscillation between being an actor and being acted upon is felt in every human encounter, and intersubjective life involves an ongoing struggle to negotiate, reconcile, balance, or mediate these antithetical potentialities of being, such that no one person or group ever arrogates agency so completely and permanently to itself that another is reduced to the status of a mere thing, a cipher, an object, an anonymous creature of blind fate. The notion of home, I have argued elsewhere, is a matter of being-at-home-in-the world—of working out some kind of balance or adjustment between active and passive, autonomous and anonymous, modes of being (Jackson 1995, 123). In this existential view, being is never some fixed or intrinsic attribute, "an essence that one has or does not have" (Hage 1999, 20); in so far as being is being-in-the-world—tied to contexts of interaction with others—it is in continual flux. Not only is one's being affirmed or negated, bolstered or reduced, according to the social and physical circumstances in which one finds oneself; one's sense of being undergoes perennial redistribution in the course of one's strategic struggle to sustain and synthesize oneself as a subject in a world that simultaneously subjugates one to other ends. In psychoanalytic terms, one's being is cathected and recathected onto many others and many objects in the course of one's struggle to achieve a sense of security and viability. Thus, totemic species, inanimate objects—including prized personal possessions, dwellings, landscapes, and automobiles—as well as abstract ideas and ideals may become, by extension, aspects of oneself that one could not conceive of being without, while antisocial individuals and enemies may be derogated as subhuman, denied the attributes of moral being, and treated as though they had zero ontological value. Being is thus not only a belonging but a becoming. Like the Polynesian notion of *mana*, the Arabic *baraka*, and the Kuranko *miran*, being is a potentiality that waxes and wanes, is augmented or diminished, depending on how one acts and speaks in relation to others (cf. Jackson 1998a, 13). This is one reason why I set aside or bracket out all questions regarding the *essential* identity of individual persons or the definition of the terms that are often set up in opposition to them—the social, the natural, the supernatural, the global, the cosmic—in order to describe the strategizing and boundary crossing that goes on continually between human beings as well as between human and extrahuman worlds. The core of my argument is that an existential imperative underlies all these movements and strategies. In spite of being aware that eternity is infinite and human life finite, that the cosmos is great and the human world small, and that nothing anyone says or does can immunize him or her from the contingencies of history, the tyranny of circumstance, the finality of death, and the accidents of fate, every human being needs some modicum of choice, craves some degree of understanding, demands some say, and expects some sense of control over the course of his or her own life. However, I restrict myself to speaking of this existential imperative as a *sense* of agency, thereby setting aside the objective question as to whether human freedom of action actually exists, for what seems to me most compelling is the human need to *imagine* that one's life belongs to a matrix greater than oneself, and that within this sphere of greater being one's own actions and words matter and make a difference. As Nelson Mandela observed, reflecting on his years of confinement on Robben Island: "A garden was one of the few things in prison that one could control. To plant a seed, watch it grow, to tend it and then harvest it offered a simple but enduring satisfaction. The sense of being the custodian of this small patch of earth offered a small taste of freedom" (1994, 582–83).

In sum, while acknowledging the historical, biogenetic, cosmic, and genealogical forces that bear upon each human destiny, we ask ourselves, as the Greek dramatists and philosophers did, how much luck (*tuchē*) and happenstance can we humanly accept, how much agency and choice can we expect (Nussbaum 1986, 4).

The Narrative Imperative

Two theses, then, are brought together in this work. The first derives from Hannah Arendt's argument that storytelling is a strategy for transforming private into public meanings (though, as I shall show, this process cuts both ways); the second is existential, seeing storytelling as a vital human strategy for sustaining a sense of agency in the face of disempowering circumstances. To reconstitute events in a story is no longer to live those events in passivity, but to actively rework them, both in dialogue with others and within one's own imagination. This narrative imaginary involves an interplay of intersubjective *and* intrapsychic processes, since every transformation of inner monologue into social discourse—and every countervailing appropriation or subversion of this discourse in individual consciousness—depends as much on private reveries, fantasies, daydreams, and undeclared thoughts, as on public speech. In other words, while storytelling makes sociality possible, it is equally vital to the illusory, self-protective, self-justifying activity of individual minds. As Joan Didion observes, "We tell ourselves stories in order to live" (1979, 11).

The playwright Dennis Potter makes this point with considerable force, speaking of his lifetime struggle with a hereditary skin disease (psoriatic arthropathy) that ossifies the joints, causes the body to lose control of its temperature, and induces hallucinations. When first afflicted by this illness, he thought:

> The only way I can save my life is to invent my life. I hope I'm not being immodest, but I think there is a certain emotional power in my work which I become aware of *later*. And I think that power is actually the result of the contest between my real self and my invented self. My invented self overcomes my illness ... and keeps me sane (cited in Fuller 1993, 10–11).

Though many authors have argued that stories bestow order and coherence on events (e.g. Ochs and Capps 2001) we need to know how such reconstructions of reality are tied to existential imperatives, such as our need to be more than bit players in the stories of our own lives. In stories as in dreams, we take center stage. Nor is it particularly edifying to say that storytelling gives meaning to our lives, if by "meaning" we imply an intellectual grasp of events. For storytelling does not necessarily help us understand the world conceptually or cognitively; rather, it seems to work at a "protolinguistic" level, changing our *experience* of events that have befallen us by symbolically restructuring them. This is not simply a matter of contriving scenarios in which good prevails over evil. As a form of "mastery play" (Bruner 1976, 31, 1990, 78), storytelling reworks and remodels subject-object relations in ways that subtly alter the balance between actor and acted upon, thus allowing us to feel that we actively participate in a world that for a moment seemed to discount, demean, and disempower us. The great Danish writer Karen Blixen once said that "no one has a life worth thinking about whose life story cannot be told" (cited in Arendt 1973, 107). Though we may question the view that "stories are lived before they are told" (McIntyre 1984, 212; Mink 1970, 557–58), and disagree over the extent to which our lives are actually configured by the stories we tell, there is no denying that storytelling gives us a sense that though we do not exactly determine the course of our lives we at least have a hand in defining their meaning. Stories, like the music and dance that in many societies accompanies the telling of stories, are a kind of theatre where we collaborate in reinventing ourselves and authorizing notions, both individual and collective, of who we are. John Berger puts this nicely in his image of a French alpine village, deploying "words, spoken and remembered" and "opinions, stories, eyewitness reports, legends, comments and hearsay" to work on "a living portrait of itself, a communal portrait" that is never finished, but in which "everybody is portrayed and everybody portrays" (1979, 9).

As Berger also notes, no story is simply an imitation of events as they actually occurred. In changing the order of things, stories construe what happened adventitiously as somehow decided by the protagonists themselves. Stories are counterfactual or fictional, not because they aspire to mirror reality and fail, nor because they offer escapes from reality, but because they aid and abet our need to believe that *we* may discern and determine the meaning of *our* journey through life: where we came from and where we are going. In making and telling stories we rework reality in order to make it bearable. As Karen Blixen put it, "All sorrows can be borne if you can put them into a story or tell a story about them" (cited in Arendt 1973, 106). In this pragmatist sense the truth or falsity of a story cannot be decided by measuring it against some outside reality, for what matters is how stories enable us to regain some purchase over the events that confound us, humble us, and leave us helpless, salvaging a sense that we have some say in the way our lives unfold. In telling a story we renew our faith that the world is within our grasp.

A compelling example of this strategy is recorded by Keith Basso in his study of play and cultural symbols among the Western Apache. One late August day in Cibecue, Basso happened to observe a nine-year-old Western Apache child playing with a puppy. When the girl picked the puppy up by the tail, it reacted by yelping loudly and nipping her on the hand. The girl at once berated the dog in Western Apache, "You're nothing," she screamed. "You're nothing." Then she turned her back. A few moments later she admonished the dog again, this time in English phrases that mimicked an Anglo-American teacher's schoolroom manner. "Bad!" she cried shrilly. "You bad boy! Why you do that—make trouble for me? All time you want make trouble, want fight." As Basso points out, the child would ordinarily speak in Apache, but on this occasion she switches codes (conjuring and parodying schoolroom English) while at the same time *reversing the terms of the intersubjective encounter*. Initially, subject *to* the dog's biting and bad temper (an object of its behavior, a "nothing"), she recreates herself as subject *of* the situation, verbally controlling rather than merely suffering it, as a "someone." But also embedded in this play situation, in which the girl turns the tables on the puppy, is a more abstract and non-immediate relationship, for the intersubjective exchange between the girl and the dog is an oblique statement about, and an "indirect form of social commentary" on, cultural relations between Anglo-American schoolteachers and their Western Apache pupils, as well as the social history of inequality and disparagement these imply (Basso 1979, 9–13).

This sort of magical action is commonest when we are "blocked" from acting directly (Sartre 1948, 58–59). Ritualistic behavior comes into play when actions are thwarted, contradicted, or found to be ineffective. But it is not a question of individuals finding means of expressing *themselves*, for the key to understanding the kind of mastery play of which storytelling is one example is that a transformation is effected that switches the locus of action symbolically from one context of *relationship* to another. Story-telling is usually prompted by some crisis, stalemate, or loss of ground in a person's relationship with others and with the world, such that autonomy is undermined, recognition withheld, and action made impossible. Story-telling is a coping strategy that involves making words stand for the world, and then, by manipulating them, changing one's *experience* of the world. By constructing, relating, and sharing stories, people contrive to restore viability to their relationship with others, redressing a bias toward autonomy when it has been lost, and affirming collective ideals in the face of disparate experiences. It is not that speech is a replacement for action; rather that it is a supplement, to be exploited when action is impossible or confounded.[4]

The existential thesis I am advancing here should not be taken to mean, however, that "we *are* the stories we tell" (McAdams 1993, 5), or that sto-ries are somehow isomorphic with lives. Such mimetic assumptions are as flawed as the sociological view that stories embody the form of society. The error in both cases is to focus on fixed and finite meanings, usually of a conceptual kind, and thereby overlook the *action* of meaning-making. It is for this reason that I prefer to emphasize storytelling over stories—the social process rather than the product of narrative activity.

Consider for example the views that "life, as lived, is a story being told" (Berger 1984, 30), that "identity is a life story" (McAdams 1993, 5), and that "stories are lived before they are told" (MacIntyre 1984, 212). All such views tend to naturalize and fetishize the imagined parallels we draw between stories and lives—such as the tripartite structure of beginning, middle, and end—and assume that what is imaginatively necessary for some people "in order to live" constitutes a universally valid description of reality.

To clarify this issue, let us consider Sartre's argument that the power of the novel stems from its resemblance to life. Against the grain of Kafka and Beckett,[5] who repudiated the biographical fiction of absolute beginnings and determinable endings, Sartre argues that stories entrance us with the possibility that our lives may be as adventuresome, as orderly, and as rounded as our fictions make them appear to be. But as Frank Kermode observes in *The Sense of an Ending*, stories—at least in the modern world—cannot easily sustain this kind of consoling illusion of order and control. In the following passage, Kermode is speaking about Robert Musil:

> How good it would be, he suggests, if one could find in life the simplicity inherent in *narrative order*. "This is the simple order that consists in being able to say: "When that had happened, then this happened." What puts our mind at rest is the simple sequence, the overwhelming variegation of life now represented in, as a mathematician would say, a unidimensional order." We like the illusions of this sequence, its acceptable appearance of causality: "It has the look of necessity." But the look is illusory; Musil's hero Ulrich has "lost this elementary narrative element" and so has Musil. *The Man Without Qualities* is multidimensional, fragmentary, without the possibility of a narrative end. Why could he not have this narrative order? Because "everything has now become non-narrative." The illusion would be too gross and absurd (1967, 127).

It is not only the postmodern shattering and scattering of subjectivities—self, community, culture, and nation—that robs narrative of its credibility as a model of existential order. Nor can we entirely attribute the delegitimation of narrative to the abstract, denotative, non-narrative forms of understanding that permeate the postmodern world (Lyotard 1984). For the new technologies of communication that have virtualized reality in such manifold ways since the Second World War have, ironically, been countered by a resurgence of literary, journalistic, and cinematic realism during the same period, and it may well be that it is a desire to bear witness to the brute facts of human experiences "after Auschwitz," a desire to speak "without flippancy, about things that matter" (Wolff 1983, x), to do justice to lived experience by eschewing literary artifice, wishful thinking, and romantic stereotypes, that has, as much as anything, undermined the authority of traditional narrative. Though fiction provides us with ingenious ways of escaping reality into fantastic or virtual worlds where everything is predictable, simple, and resolveable, it is often the case that in times of *extreme* hardship people repudiate such legerdemain, spitting on language as a travesty of life, and seeing in silence the only decent way of respecting it. Though such silence is a far cry from the speechlessness that accompanies terror and trauma, deliberate silence is a familiar strategy among refugees, survivors of death camps, abused children, shell-shocked soldiers, victims of torture and rape, and the bereaved, and is often enjoined in ceremonies of remembrance for the victims of catastrophes.

In a poignant and powerful short story, Lorrie Moore goes straight to the heart of such experience. The story concerns a mother struggling to come to grips with the fact that her only child has a cancerous tumor on his liver. The mother is a writer. Throughout the crisis, her husband urges her to "take notes." She takes notes. She has recourse to narrative to cope with her confusion and stress. But she feels contemptuous of narrative. "I write fiction," she cries. "This isn't fiction." She says: "I mean, the whole conception of 'the story,' of cause and effect, the whole idea that people have a clue as to how the world works is just a laughable metaphysical colonialism perpetrated upon the wild country of time" (Moore 1998, 222). After her child has undergone surgery and is recovering, the mother renders her final angry judgment on the work of narrative:

How can it be described? How can any of it be described? The trip and the story of the trip are always two different things. The narrator is the one who has stayed home, but then, afterward, presses her mouth upon the traveler's mouth, in order to make the mouth work, to make the mouth say, say, say. One cannot go to a place and speak of it; one cannot both see and say, not really. One can go, and upon returning make a lot of hand motions and indications with the arms. The mouth itself, working at the speed of light, at the eye's instructions, is necessarily stuck still; so fast, so much to report, it hangs open and dumb as a gutted bell. All that unsayable life! That's where the narrator comes in. The narrator comes with her kisses and mimicry and tidying up.

The narrator comes and makes a slow, fake song of the mouth's eager devastation (237).

Though many people act, as Sartre puts it, *as if* the patterning of events in their fictions corresponded to the patterning of events in reality[6]— the truth is that our lives are for the most part, as Lorrie Moore notes, "unsayable," and emplotted only in our imaginations. "The trouble with life," observes Martin Amis in a more ironic vein, "is its amorphousness, its ridiculous fluidity. Look at it: thinly plotted, largely themeless, sentimental and ineluctably trite. The dialogue is poor, or at least violently uneven. The twists are either predictable or sensationist. And it's always the same beginning; and the same ending" (Amis 2001, 11). In the face of the idea that human lives are orchestrated and symphonic, we need to remind ourselves of Schönberg's atonality, with its rejection of classical harmonies and eternal formal laws. The idea that any human life moves serially and progressively from a determinate beginning, via a middle passage, towards an ethically or aesthetically satisfying conclusion, is as artificial as the idea of a river running straightforwardly to the sea. Lives and rivers periodically flood and run dry; rapids alternate with calm stretches, shallows with depths; and there are places where eddies, counter-currents, undertows, cross-currents, backwaters and dark reaches make navigation unpredictable.

The main problem, however, with the notion that stories can be equated with lives is the subjectivist assumption that a human life is essentially an individual life, an island in the stream, and that, moreover, we can refer back to this individual life, this originary, self-contained subjectivity, to determine the truth of the narrative that is constructed out of it. If, however, as I argue throughout this book, stories are neither the pure creations of autonomous individuals nor the unalloyed expressions of subjective views, but rather a result of ongoing dialogue and redaction within fields of intersubjectivity, then the very notions of selfhood and subjectivity that are brought into relief in the European tradition of storytelling are themselves creations of a *social* relation between self and other, and do not exist "outside of, or prior to," the narrative process (cf. Feldman 1991, 13). The same principle holds true of stories outside the European tradition, in which far less emphasis is given to the heroic career of individuals or the delineation of personal identity, and where lives are depicted as inescapably embedded in social, political, and historical affairs, as well as deeply integrated with worldviews and physical environments. Respecting this view, we may begin to see that stories, like memories and dreams, are *nowhere* articulated as purely personal revelations, but authored and authorized dialogically and collaboratively in the course of sharing one's recollections with others (Bakhtin 1981; Halbwachs 1980; Merleau-Ponty 1962, 354). This is why one may no more recover the "original" story than step into the same river twice. The fault is not with memory per se, but an effect of the transformations all experience undergoes as it is replayed, recited, reworked, and reconstrued in the play of intersubjective life. This is nicely demonstrated by Michael Gilsenan's account of the competitive, interactional dynamics of storytelling in rural Lebanon where narratives are "reworked, reauthored, retold to different audiences in different ways" that effectively "wrest control away from their original author" (1996, 64). The changing circumstances of history are, of course, critical to this process of narrative revision, as Anastasia Karakasidou's recent study of the history of Macedonian nation-building makes abundantly clear. Where, at one period or in one context or conversation, a multi-ethnic understanding of the past is accepted, in another time and place "the subtle and complex nuances of local history" are arrogantly dismissed, and any empirical evidence that flies in the face of the newly invented tradition is seen not only as untrue but as treasonable (1997, 228–37).

Thus, as Hannah Arendt puts it, though every story discloses an agent who initiated and suffered the events recounted, this particular subject never remains the sole *author* of his or her own life story, for the story comes into being within an "already existing web of human relationships" (1958, 184).

Lines in the Sand

I have suggested that though storytelling mediates our relation with worlds that extend beyond us, the important thing is not how we name these other worlds but how narrative enables us to negotiate an existential balance between ourselves and such spheres of otherness.

In every human society, the range of experiences that are socially acknowledged and named is always much narrower than the range of experiences that people actually have. By implication, no worldview ever encompasses or covers the plenitude of what is actually lived, felt, imagined, and thought. The vantage points from which we customarily view the world are, as William James puts it, "fringed forever by a *more*" that outstrips and outruns them (1976, 35). This *more* is also where language reaches its limits, a penumbral region where we are haunted by what words fail to cover, capture, conceive, and communicate. The contrast between what can be pinned down in words and what Michel de Certeau calls the "immense remainder" (1984, 61) that eludes language almost always entails an awareness of the shadowline between the living and the dead, the living and the unborn, and ourselves and unknown others. In Aboriginal Australia these fields of awareness suggest a contrast between the visible and the invisible. In Africa they find expression in the socio-spatial contrast between town and bush. In Freudian thought they are theorized in terms of an intrapsychic contrast between superego and libido. For Lévi-Strauss, the binary opposition of culture and nature is crucial. Nominally different though these distinctions are, they all share a common concern with how the line between categorically opposed domains may be understood, managed, and mediated through the performance of rituals and the telling of stories.

Conventionally, the workings of an either/or logic give the impression that these domains are antithetical and mutually exclusive—marked symbolically, as Mary Douglas has shown, by a contrast between purity and impurity. Operating both within the body-mind and within the body politic, censorship confirms the boundaries between an inclusive world that we learn to think of as synonymous with truth and humanity, and an excluded world that we regard as false, minatory, and alien. Although Michel Foucault has reminded us that these boundaries are redrawn periodically according to new epistemic criteria, censorship nonetheless ensures that any social universe will be conventionally defined through dialectic negation, with elaborate ground rules and formal regulations operating to segregate people on the basis of superficial or supposed differences, to police traffic across borders, to keep migrants and refugees from fully participating in the life of the state, to ritually outlaw "barbaric" practices and "superstitions," and to derogate a plethora of emotions, impulses, and drives as irrational, delusional, phantasmagoric, infantile, pathological, or primitive. But in enforcing "cleansing" operations that divide the world into Us and Them, censorship may blind us to the ways in which contrasted domains not only overlap, but are, paradoxically, as necessary as they are inimical to each other.

Storytelling defines one of the most vital of these crossing points, these sites of defilement and infringement. Although the stories that are approved or made canonical in any society tend to reinforce extant boundaries, storytelling also questions, blurs, transgresses, and even abolishes these boundaries.

As Lévi-Strauss has shown with considerable force and eloquence, stories are always structurally in-between. Whether considered in the light of their function, form, or performance, stories create indeterminate and ambiguous situations that involve contending parties, contrasted locations, opposing categories of thought, and antithetical domains of experience. In traversing the borderlands that ordinarily demarcate different social domains, or that separate any particular social order from all that lies at or beyond its margins, stories have the potential to take us in two very different directions. On the one hand, they may confirm our belief that otherness is just as we had imagined it to be—best kept at a distance, best denied—in which case the story will screen out everything that threatens the status quo, validating the illusions and prejudices it customarily deploys in maintaining its hold on truth. On the other hand, stories may confound or call into question our ordinarily taken for granted notions of identity and difference, and so push back and pluralize our horizons of knowledge. In the first case, storytelling seals off the possibility of critique; in the second, critique becomes pivotal, with the possibility glimpsed that there may be no human experience that does not exist *in potentia* within every human being and within every human society; that, as Montaigne put it, as much difference may be "found betweene us and our selves, as … between our selves and other" (1948, 298).

This dual potentiality of stories to either reinforce or degrade the boundaries that normally divide seemingly finite social worlds from the infinite variety of possible human experience is recognized in the Greek notion of narrative as *diegesis*. Stories both map out ideal itineraries (they "guide"), *and* they suggest how boundaries may be crossed (they "transgress") (de Certeau 1984, 129). This notion of transgression may be understood in two ways. Phylogenetically, the counter-factuality of stories reminds us that our evolutionary passage to humanity has depended heavily on a natural ability to lie—to use language not only to represent and communicate what *is* the case but to speak otherwise, in terms of what it is in one's interest and to one's advantage to say. For our hominid ancestors, hunting and foraging in a dangerous and contested environment, "fiction was disguise: from those seeking out the same water-hole, the same sparse quarry, or meagre sexual chance" (Steiner 1973, 224–25). To be able to misinform, mask, or misdirect gave hominids a vital edge in space or subsistence. Ontogenetically, this ability to contradict or deny reality is imperative for existential survival, for storytelling enables us to create the "necessary illusions" without which life becomes insupportable, e.g. making us appear central to events in which we were, in reality, only marginal. At the same time, these fictional reworkings provide us with a rhetorical means of exploiting the beliefs, sympathies, and desires of others, and so securing some *future* advantage. "Getting what you want very often means getting the right story" (Bruner 1990, 86).

Although both subjective and social viability may be said to depend on the counter-factual powers of storytelling, a distinction may be drawn between narratives whose "truth effects" serve and conserve the social order, and narratives whose "truth effects" are more blatantly tied to the struggles and tensions of personal existence. This distinction between what Michael Gilsenan calls "the exemplary and the extraordinary" (1996, 58) finds expression in a universal polarization of two categories of narrative, the first said to be sacrosanct, ancestral, and true, the second admittedly fanciful and fictional.

In his pioneering fieldwork, Malinowski noted that the Trobrianders make an important distinction between *liliu* ("sacred myths") on the one hand, and *kukwanebu* ("tales") and *libwogwo* ("legends") on the other. While myths are venerable and true, giving legitimacy to the existing social order, and legends fall within the range of things actually experienced, tales are merely makebelieve (Malinowski 1974, 102–7). A similar though only twofold distinction is drawn by Kuranko, between the charter myths that underwrite estate, age, and gender divisions (*kuma kore*, lit. "venerable speech") and antinomian tales (*tilei*). But this kind of typological splitting of stories into essentially different categories—like post-Enlightenment distinctions between science and religion—belies their interdependence.[7] It also obscures the instability of the epistemological contrasts between fact and fiction, real and imaginary, that inform such genre separations, for while folktales are fictions, they contain real moral truths, and though charter myths may have divine or ancestral backing, this does not prevent them from being used for antisocial ends. It is, moreover, well known that through migration and the vicissitudes of history, myths may atrophy and become mere tales.

For these kinds of reasons, I want to emphasize that the politics of storytelling concerns precisely these vexed and unstable contrasts between truth and untruth, articulated as an opposition between public and private domains, or, to borrow Gerd Baumann's terms, "dominant" and "demotic" discourses (Baumann 1996). As Michael Herzfeld has shown, stories involve disemia—a tension between the legitimate and the intimate: a "formal or coded tension between official self-representation and what goes on in the privacy of collective introspection" (1997, 14). At the same time that the ancestral legacy of "true" narratives lays down the law, reinforces respect for received values, and draws attention to the foundational principles of the social order, "fictional" narratives persistently address quotidian problems of injustice, revealing the frailty of authority, mocking the foibles of men, and shaming all those who mask their greed and ambition with the language of ideology and the trappings of high office. And while some stories create and sustain dehumanizing divisions between the powerful and the powerless—as in nationalist myths and fascist propaganda—others work to deconstruct such divisions and redress such imbalances, enabling the powerless to recover a sense of their own will, their own agency, their own consciousness, and their own being. In Bruce Kapferer's words, the "legends" of people undermine the "myths" of the state (1988). That is to say that if stories are lies, it is, as Camus reminds us, not because to lie is to say what isn't true; "it is also and above all, to say *more* than is true, and, as far as the human heart is concerned, to express more than one feels" (1970, 336). These references to the potentiality of personal stories to help us resist enslavement to stories promulgated by the state in defence of its own "special interests" remind us that Hannah Arendt never fully reconciled her democratic and totalitarian depictions of the public domain (Benhabib 1996: 22–30). Just as the private realm may become, at one extreme, a refuge from reality and a denial of the common weal so, at another extreme, it may generate critiques of the alienated, uniform, and totalitarian modes of mass society that Heidegger summarized in his notion of das Man. Arendt might well have understood these extreme possibilities as reflecting the paradox of human plurality, by which she meant that every person is at once a singular being and someone who shares common traits with every member of his or her species, class, or kind. We are, therefore, equally capable of identifying absolutely with others and acting as we were autonomous and unique. The tension between these existential poles generates the violent passions and opposing allegiances of political life.

In medieval Europe, the critical power of storytelling depended on a wealth of oral, anal, genital, and visceral imagery, drawn from bodily life (Bakhtin 1968). Through such commonplace yet universal images of eating, drinking, digesting, defecating, and sexual life, the lines between social classes could be crossed and the privileges of rank parodied. But the critical vitality of storytelling springs not from body imagery alone but from a direct, lived relationship between personal and social bodies. In exploring the ways in which storytelling contrives to cross and blur the line between different subjectivities, or between the space we call private and the space of the world, we must remember that these infringements are seldom simply conceptual or abstract. They are experienced and enacted in and through the body, and involve forms of mimetic play, gesture, intimacy, and phatic communion that challenge logocentric notions of meaning. In storytelling events, the effacement of the boundary between private and public space is commonly *lived through* as a physical, sensual, and vital interaction between the body of the storyteller and the bodies of the listeners, in which people reach out toward one another, sitting closely together, singing in unison, laughing or crying as one. Accordingly, the grotesque realism of continent and incontinent bodies, and of open and closed body boundaries, derives its discursive power not only from its analogical link to the opening and closing of boundaries in the social body, but from the fact that it is lived out in the context of the storytelling event itself.

In this perpetual counterpointing of hermeneutic openness and closure stories both release and contain great energy. Extrapolating from my African researches, I have argued elsewhere that the contrast between the social and the extrasocial implies a contrast between bound and free energy (Jackson 1978). According to this view, any social system tends toward stasis, entropy, and death, unless its field of bound energy—symbolized by inflexible rules, inherited roles, and fixed boundaries, as well as by psychophysical constraints on body movement, speech, and emotions—is periodically reinvigorated by the "wild" energies and fecund powers that are associated with extrasocial space and deep subjectivity. This vital two-way movement across the boundaries that normally enclose both the individual body and the body politic involves throwing open the social system to forces that, while necessary to its re-creation, are potentially destructive of its integrity. Among the Kuranko, the boundary crossings and blurrings that are essential to initiation, divination, and farming, are central to storytelling as well. Subject to strict controls that disengage them from the mundane world, stories not only transgress boundaries of age, gender, space, time, and being; they employ formal devices such as chiasmus ("crossing-over") that bring into conjunction normally separate spheres of life. This openness of African stories to crossing the rubicon between "town" and "bush" in order to contrive the semblance of a fit between determinate social positions and indeterminate or "wild" dispositions (Jackson 1998a, 61–68) is symbolically marked by the same leitmotifs that mark the blurring of boundaries—both personal and social—in all human societies: laughter, intoxication, music, song, dance, sexual intercourse, spirit possession, and ecstasy.

But this account of storytelling as an energy field in which social and extrasocial dimensions of reality are brought together is at once abstract and incomplete. Although stories may be implicitly concerned with conceptual problems (such as the relation between social positions and individual dispositions), and possess logical structure, they are grounded in *social* imperatives that cannot be understood either by subordinating sensible "experience" to unconscious "reality" (as Lévi-Strauss has advocated[8]), or by uncritically replicating individual rationalizations. Rather, our focus must be on the lived patternings of *intersubjective* life, for these underpin both the syntactic and strategic transformations that analysis sometimes persuades us to see as a self-sufficient field of symbolic logic. The source of the energy that both motivates and structures storytelling is the existential tension that informs every intersubjective encounter—a tension between being for oneself and being for another. Accordingly, the dialectic I alluded to earlier between opposed spheres of life, groups of people, and congeries of ideas, only has meaning in relation to the dynamic interplay of self and not-self that defines intersubjectivity. In stories, the energy that motivates the journeys and quests that articulate movements to and fro between contrasted fields of being arises from an *existential* imperative that compels human beings to transform the world as it is felt to bear upon them into a world in which they, both as individual subjects and as members of collectivities, feel they play a vital part.

Storying and Journeying

The notion that stories cross, breach, and blur the boundaries that demarcate crucial political and ethical spaces in our everyday lives is more than just a figure of speech. To say that storytelling moves us, transports us, carries us away, or helps us escape the oppressiveness of our real lives, is to recognize that stories change our experience of the way things are. But stories are not only like journeys because of the effects they have upon us; stories are so commonly and conspicuously *about* journeys—between such disparate realms as town/bush, heaven/earth, the land of the living/ the land of the dead—that one may see in journeying one of the preconditions of the possibility of narrative itself.

In all societies, stories echo the developmental cycle of the individual—a passage from dependency to independence in which one's departure from the microcosm of the natal family is a prelude to the creation of one's own life and the establishment of one's own family in the wider world. This journey has both temporal and spatial dimensions. It is often observed that both stories and lives are structured *temporally,* in terms of sequences of events aligned along a continuum from a beginning, through a middle, toward an end. As Paul Ricoeur has noted with deference to Heidegger, this structure reflects the force with which our lives are experienced as a modality of being-unto-death. But this progressive, lineal model of human existence may lose its analytical usefulness in societies where cyclical models of both human life and social time predominate, and where notions of individual finitude and millenial endings have minimal purchase. In such cases, the *emplacement* rather than the *emplotment* of stories becomes crucial, and suggests a model for cross-cultural analysis.

Against Heidegger's argument that being is primordially a mode of dwelling (1978, 145–61), one may just as plausibly view being as a mode of journeying. Etymologically, the Indo-European root of the word "experience" is *per* (to attempt, to venture), hence the Latin *experientia*, denoting experimentation, trial, proving, and test. But experience is also cognate with the Old English *faer* (danger, peril, fear), hence faring forth, ferrying, and, by implication, any peregrination in which the self is risked (cf. Turner 1985, 226). If stories are artefacts of dwelling, articulating relations of *identity* between people and places, they are just as obviously products of journeying, and thus sometimes depart from fixed itineraries, unsettle orthodox identifications, and open up horizons to new patterns of association.

In Aboriginal Australia, the landscape is storied. Abounding with "story places," the earth is said to embody the accreted and vital essence of ancestral lives, journeys, and creative actions. This phenomenal reality is, however, less an artefact of reflective thought than the cumulative effect of the intense and concentrated human *activity* that has been carried on in and around such places from time immemorial, so that every "sacred site" may be said to coalesce or interleave a sense of the effort, sweat, pain, and reproductive labor that has occurred there in the past as well as contemporaneously within each person's own specific experience and in the course of his or her own particular life (Jackson 1998a, 131–42, 175–76). Though Aboriginal Australia provides a paradigmatic example of the ways in which patterns of bodily movement to and fro within a humanized environment inform patterns of thought, the phenomenon is well-nigh universal. Thus, for peoples as diverse as the Yoruba of Nigeria (Drewall 1992), the Gypsies of Europe (Fonseca 1995), the Maya of Yucatan (Hanks 1990), the Warlpiri of Central Australia (Jackson 1995), and the Kaluli of Papua New Guinea (Feld 1982), life is a road, and in traveling it we both follow the tracks of those who have gone before and leave traces of ourselves which become, as Herodotus divined in his notion of *istorias*—trackings and tracings—our individual stories. As Michel de Certeau notes (1984), stories possess a "spatial syntax," partly because they encode the correct itineraries and protocols governing movement within a social environment, partly because they provide "delinquent" and tactical clues as to how boundaries may be infringed, gulfs crossed, and movement varied.

We glimpse here an explanation of the place of narrative in human life. Prioritizing neither the cultural uses to which storytelling may be put nor the social meanings it may convey, this explanation locates the source of narrative form in the elementary structures of movement in the human lifeworld. According to this view, the reciprocal gestures, expressions, and vocalizations that inform the interactive play between infant and caregiver presage the to and fro movements that define the mundane patternings of all social life.[9] Thus, in every human society people fare forth at the beginning of each day from some hearth or homeplace and, at the close of day, return to some such place to rest, recover, and, most importantly, recount their experiences, both commonplace and curious, solitary and shared, of what has befallen them (Jackson 1994, 1). Metaphors of journeying and of storying simply convert this habitual sense of moving to and fro in the world into spatial and temporal terms. But the intelligibility of any story or journey will depend on this unconscious bodily rhythm of going out from some place of certainty or familiarity into a space of contingency and strangeness, then returning to take stock.

A sense of existential peril always attaches to such migrations. Whether it is the seasonal movement of West African farmers from village to the bush to clear their farms, or the daily commute of suburbanites to a city center, journeys throw one open to the unknown, and, when related as stories, involve, first, losing one's way, then trial, tribulation, and lucky breaks—such as an alliance with some supernatural helper—and, finally, a denouement or moment of closure when justice is meted out, social bonds are reaffirmed, and moral meanings are revealed. In this way, stories and journeys conform to the cycle of intimate and quotidian life, the closure achieved at the end of day when, within a circle of family or friends, the traveler, migrant, pilgrim, or commuter recounts his or her day's experiences in the form of a story.

Broken Journeys

If stories, lives, and journeys are so entwined, what happens to our capacity to tell stories when our lives are torn apart? When we are forced from the place we call our own, when the public spaces in which we have lived and worked with others become spaces of terror and of death, when we lose touch with the people who know our names and speak our language, when life is no longer a journey or narrative the meaning of which is consummated in return, or even, indeed, in time, and when suddenly we have no settled place from which to venture forth each day, nor haven at the end where we can recover our lives in the stories we share, what becomes of our stories and our lives?

Many of the chapters in this book focus on precisely these questions, for while the need for stories is linked to the human need to be a part of some kindred community, this need is most deeply felt when the bonds of such belonging are violently sundered. We are all familiar with the stories of human distress that appear in lonelyhearts and bereavement columns, that are recounted in psychotherapy, that emerge from secret griefs, resentments, and anger, or take shape in whispered prayers and petitions to God. But in a mediatized age, dominated by stories of political violence and natural disaster, suffering has become so conspicuously social and global (Kleinman, Das, and Lock 1997, ix–xxvii) that our attention inevitably turns to the place of stories in the lives of dispersed communities that often number hundreds of thousands of sorrowing souls, and we are led to ask what power storytelling has, after people's needs for food, shelter, medicine, and asylum are met, to help mend broken lives.

Both natural disasters and social upheavals destroy the balance of power between a person's immediate lifeworld and the wider world. At such times, not only do questions of choice and freedom become desperately acute, but the very possibility of storytelling is thrown into radical doubt. In totalitarian regimes, where state-sponsored terror and violence destroy the individual citizen's capacity to speak and act openly in the public domain, or affirm any kind of common value, people are often driven back into privacy and isolation. Under such conditions, a kind of cultural agoraphobia prevails, in which storytelling becomes involuted or fugitive, a fitful approximation to public action (Arendt 1973). Something similar occurs among refugees and pariahs in democratic states; their stories from the outer edge have little currency and validity within the polis. A comparable situation is also brought about by globalization, when boundaries between local moral worlds and the wider world are effaced by electronic communications, mass migrations, new epidemic diseases like AIDS, and the spread of new commodities. Though those who control and profit from globalization often glibly speak of the world as getting smaller, millions of people experience it as becoming bigger and more alien. The last decades of the twentieth century saw a dramatic widening of the economic divide between haves and have-nots, both globally and within the affluent societies of the West, but the true meaning of this statistic lies in the *existential* crises it signifies, for not-having tends to be also experienced as a form of not-being, and marginality to both the global polis and agora finds expression in a sense of increasing insignificance, isolation, and powerlessness. Under such disorienting conditions, which, as George Devereux has shown, simply extend the monstrous dimensions and structural complexities of modernity to an even more psychologically-intolerable degree, storytelling may cease to mediate between private and public spheres and go underground—the disempowered seeking refuge in magical thinking to retrieve some sense of control and comprehensibility in their lives (1980, 198–99). The range of these modes of symbolic reempowerment is infinite—from "imagined communities" that provide a quasi-familial, fantasized sense of collective belonging, through forms of madness in which one imagines that external reality is susceptible to the processes of one's own thinking, to "techniques of the self" in which consciousness and the body are subject to all manner of symbolic manipulations.

All such stratagems are scripted in some way. They depend on some form of narrative warrant or accompaniment. This is why stories and storytelling may, more than any other form of art or artifice, provide crucial insights into the human struggle to overcome the felt opposition between two counterpointed realms of symbolic determinacy and power, the first focused on the self and the lifeworld with which it most intimately and immediately identifies, the second focused on the not-self, and on all that is considered foreign, inimical, and unfamiliar to oneself. Existentialists often refer to these antithetical poles as being and nothingness, autonomy and anonymity, for the simple reason that the domain in which we are recognized and our actions matter tends to be close to home, while the domain in which we experience least choice and control tends to be removed in space-time from us. This is not, however, invariably the case. Human beings can be as tyrannized by their immediate situations and inner preoccupations as much as by external structures of the state, and there is, in any case, always such two-way traffic between local and extralocal worlds that any attempt to identify the subjective with freedom and the social with alienation is romantic and absurd. Rather than seek to define the essential difference between such domains, I propose to focus on the ways in which storytelling mediates between them, providing strategies and generating experiences that help people redress imbalances and correct perceived injustices in the distribution of being, so that in telling a story with others one reclaims some sense of agency, recovers some sense of purpose, and comes to feel that the events that overwhelmed one from without may be brought within one's grasp.

PART I

DISPLACEMENTS

THE STORIES THAT SHADOW US

No more fiendish punishment could be devised ... than that one should be turned loose in society and remain absolutely unnoticed by all the members thereof. If no one turned round when we entered, answered when we spoke, or minded what we did, but if every person we met "cut us dead," and acted as if we were non-existing things, a kind of rage and impotent despair would ere long well up in us, from which the cruellest bodily tortures would be a relief; for these would make us feel that, however bad might be our plight, we had not sunk to such a depth as to be unworthy of attention at all.

—WILLIAM JAMES, *Principles of Psychology*

M y aim in this chapter is to explore the relationship between violence and storytelling, and to examine the ways in which stories help people cope with the consequences of violence.

Because violence, like storytelling, occurs in the contested space of intersubjectivity, its most devastating effects are not on individuals per se but on the fields of interrelationship that constitute their lifeworlds. This is why violent threats against those one loves, or the loss of family and homeland, can be more damaging than any assault against oneself, and why a person's powerlessness to speak or act against such events is so terrible; for in violence one can act only under the threat of pain, of degradation, or of death—and speak only to debase or incriminate oneself, or assent to the other's will. In such situations, recovering one's freedom to speak and act becomes a matter of life and death, for, as Hannah Arendt puts it, a "life without speech and without action ... is literally dead to the world; it has ceased to be a human life because it is no longer lived among men" (1958, 176).

To argue that storytelling is crucial to this process of reempowerment does not mean, however, that stories themselves have power; rather, it implies that by enabling dialogues that encompass different points of view, the act of sharing stories helps us create a world that is more than the sum of its individual parts. While it is true that stories may sanction inequality and division, my interest here is in the ways in which storytelling involves not the assertion of power *over* others, but the vital capacity of people to work together to create, share, affirm, and celebrate something that is held in common. In this sense, storytelling is like any other speech act in which the force of language derives not from its own internal essence or logic, but from the social and institutional context in which it is deployed and authorized (Bourdieu 1991, 107–16). For example, when C Company of the 28 Maori Battalion in Aotearoa/New Zealand set up a trust (*Nga Taongao Nga Tama Toa*) in 1998 to create an archive of soldiers' oral stories, photographs, and memorabilia, this event depended on the discovery of a letter written around the time of the Second World War by the famous Ngati Porou leader, Sir Apirana Ngata, in which Ngata suggested that such an archive would be an important postwar project. In other words it was Ngata's blessing and authorization that allowed these unvoiced stories to be told, and gave legitimacy to the conversion of private memories into a public (tribal) record. This process may be likened to confession, or to the "talking cure" in psychoanalysis: there is no automatic or magical efficacy in speaking one's mind unless the institutional framework of a community, a profession, or religion, contextualizes and recognizes the act. But in all such cases of confession, we are dealing not simply with the human need for recognition, but with a deeper need for some integration and balance between one's personal world and the wider world of others, such that one's voice carries weight and one's actions have repercussions in the state, nation, or community with which one identifies. When, as is the case with the stories of suffering I discuss in this chapter, state or institutional recognition is withheld, stories are not only not told; they are salted away in subjectivity and silence, often becoming marks of insignificance and of shame. That is to say, when storytelling loses its dialogical dimensions it becomes not only self-referential and solipsistic, but pathological. As Hannah Arendt puts it, when stories fail to effect a transposition of the self-centered (*idion*) to the shared (*koinon*), they "greatly intensify and enrich the whole scale of subjective emotions and private feelings" but at the expense of our social existence, for it is "the presence of others who see and hear what we hear" that "assures us of the reality of the world and ourselves" (1958, 50).

Violence as Reciprocity

When Marcel Mauss invoked the Maori spirit (*hau*) of the gift to elucidate the threefold character of reciprocity (1954, 8–12), he glossed over the fact that the Maori word for reciprocity—appropriately a palindrome, *utu*—refers *both* to the gift-giving that sustains social solidarity *and* to the violent acts of seizure, revenge, and repossession that are provoked when one party denies or diminishes the integrity (*mana*) of another.

Analytically speaking, violence is not an expression of animal or pathological forces that lie "outside" our humanity; it is an aspect of our humanity itself. Rather than dismiss it as antisocial behavior, as the bourgeois imagination tends to do, we must approach it as a social phenomenon whose conditions of possibility inhere in the "three obligations of reciprocity—giving, receiving, repaying" (Mauss 1954, 37).

The logic of reciprocity governs relations with those one loves as well as those one hates, and provides a rationale for both the giving and taking of life. Thus, while gift-giving is an interminable process, compelled by the felt inequality of the social capital given and received in any single exchange, "violence" is similarly cyclical,[10] sustained by the impossibility[11] of both parties ever deciding unambiguously when a score has been settled, when wrongs have been righted, when debts have been paid, and losses made good.

Although reciprocity frequently invokes notions of quantity ("I owe you one," "I am in your debt," "Now we are even"), it also rests on qualitative notions that cannot be easily substantivized ("You have saved my life; how can I ever repay you?" "Nothing you do will ever make up for the suffering you have caused me"). Because, as Mauss put it, "things have values which are emotional as well as material" (1954, 63), two incommensurable notions of value are always at play in any exchange—the first involving the strict calculation of determinate values, the second involving elusive moral values (Mauss's "spiritual matter") such as rightness, fair play, and justice. Another way of making this point is to say that all exchange involves a continual struggle to give, claim, or redistribute some scarce and elusive *existential* good—such as recognition,[12] love, humanity, happiness, voice, power, presence, honor, or dignity—*whose value is incalculable.*

The two frames of reference are often symbolically coalesced, to be sure, which is why a verbal apology or an expression of sympathy may be given and received as a gift, but such metaphorical fusions mask the perennial difficulty of bridging the gap between the way we measure the world and the way we experience it. It is this ambiguity that makes fairness, justice, and equity so difficult to attain. One man's gift is always another man's poison, and one person's gain is inevitably construed by another as a loss.

From an existential point of view, "balanced reciprocity" (Sahlins 1968) implies any interplay of intentions and actions in which a sense of justice as fairness is at work redressing the imbalance of the "goods" that each party deems necessary for its very being. On either side of this median, however, lie two extreme positions that I will characterize as all-giving (Sahlins's "generalized reciprocity")—wherein that which is given may not necessarily be returned—and all-taking (Sahlins's "negative reciprocity")—though we should note that it is rare that a violator sees himself as simply taking; rather *he* is the aggrieved party, he is righting a wrong, he is only taking back what is owed.[13] In the case of generalized reciprocity, the line between self and other is so blurred by empathy, codependency, and physical intimacy that one could not conceive of life without the other. The trust between mother and child exemplifies this modality, as may the bond between a patriot and the motherland or fatherland. At the other extreme, self and other are so sundered and polarized that the very condition of the being of one is the annihilation of the other. The absolute antipathy, paranoid fantasies, and ethnic divisions that underwrite genocidal violence provide an obvious example.

These modalities of intersubjectivity imply modalities of power, but power not reduced to the possession of a position or of things, but understood existentially—as the possession of being. While metaphors of unimpeded movement and free speech characterize situations of balanced reciprocity, the ontological metaphors that surface in situations of radical victimage tend to express loss or limitation in one's freedom of movement (being bound, cornered, trapped, cut off, imprisoned, petrified, paralyzed, exposed, alone, stuck, crushed, oppressed, undermined, thrown) or severe restrictions on one's freedom of speech (being gagged, silenced, stifled, speechless, dumbstruck, unheeded).[14] These are the recurring metaphors in stories of rape, refugee flight, child abuse, separation trauma, political persecution, and warfare, in which one finds oneself powerless in the face of some external force or Other that is deaf and indifferent to one's very existence. But victimage and violation are never simple functions of *physical* subjugation or speechlessness; they encompass the deeply-engrained, disguised, and habitual forms of "structural violence" that systematically negate the will and deny agency to vast numbers of people in modern societies simply because they are poor, "colored," infirm, elderly, vagrant, or migrant. Bourdieu uses the term "symbolic violence" to describe such "disguised" and "euphemized" patterns of domination that produce the malaise that he calls *la misère du monde* (1977, 190–97), while Kleinman has coined the phrase "social violence" to describe the pervasive indifference, endemic oppression, and sense of abjection that can make a person feel as though he or she is a mere object, nameless, of no account, ground down, in a world where agency seems to be entirely in the hands of others (Kleinman 2000). Among Arthur Kleinman's many examples is the totalitarian state, where regulations on movement, suppression of free speech, and the contradiction between state propaganda and lived reality lead to a "deep reservoir of rancor, bitter resentment, fantasies of revenge" that the Chinese refer to as "eating bitterness." "You are 'deaf and dumb', you 'can't speak out', you 'eat the seeds of the bitter melon'" (Kleinman 2000, 234). One may also cite stories of military personnel seeking compensation for irreparable damage to their health, suffered in the course of state-sponsored wars of dubious political value, or stories of hemophilia patients in France and North America routinely exposed to infected blood products in the early years of the AIDS epidemic, or stories of men and women whose lives have been compromised after having being used unwittingly as guinea pigs in the testing of nuclear devices. All such circumstances have entailed social death—a disempowering descent into passivity and privacy, solitude and silence—circumstances in which, as W. H. Auden notes in *The Shield of Achilles*, men die as men before their bodies die.

These instances of social violence confirm that violence arises not in aberrant *subjective* impulses or desires but in intersubjectivity. Thus, those who are prone to violence have generally been themselves victims of violence. Harangued, demeaned, degraded, scorned, oppressed, they harbor fantasies and plan strategies for turning the tables, getting even, and reclaiming the being that has been "taken" or "stolen" from them. Underlying this pattern of extreme reversals are the conceptual distortions that stem from splitting, distancing, and lack of dialogue, each person tending to reduce the other to the status of a thing, cipher, nonentity, or species,[15] while arrogating will, voice, and truth entirely to himself or herself. Though violence may or may not entail physical harm, we may conclude that a person's humanity is violated whenever his or her status as a subject is reduced *against his or her will* to mere objectivity, for this implies that he or she no longer exists in any active social relationship to others, but solely in a passive relationship to himself or herself (Sartre's *en-soi*), on the margins of the public realm. For this reason, it may not matter whether a person is made an object of compassion, of abuse, of attack, or of care and concern; all such modalities of relationship imply the nullification of the being of the other as one whose words and actions have no place in the life of the collectivity.

Silent Casualties

The deeply disabling and disempowering experience of soldiers during wartime, that has been variously labeled "reactionary psychosis," "shell shock," "battle fatigue," "war neurosis," and most recently "post-traumatic stress disorder" has been the subject of extensive study. But my focus here is the "silent casualties" among New Zealand's veterans of the Second World War; my goal is neither to document a clinical condition nor to explore a literary trope (e.g. Greenberg 1998), but to describe a modality of extreme experience that will help elucidate the conditions under which sociality and storytelling become possible or impossible. My analysis is informed by the existential assumption that the difference between traumatic and non-traumatic experience consists in the degree to which individuals are able to "manage" and "master" experiences that have suddenly and overwhelmingly taken them out of their depth—beyond the limits of any previous experience and understanding. Trauma may thus be likened to extreme physical pain, at once the most private and unsharable of all experiences (Arendt 1958, 50–51; Scarry 1985). In pain, trauma, and such clinical conditions as depression and schizophrenia, subjectivity may be said to collapse in upon itself. Language becomes involuted or fantastic, and memory distorted—victims often imagining that they are responsible for their own pain. In such situations of social death, storytelling all but ceases.

I became interested in the invisible wounds of war in the course of my 1998 research on refugee trauma, and was fortunate in having Alison Parr's documentation of soldier's stories (1995) to work with, as well as being able to interview and discuss my work with Les Cleveland, a close personal friend, who served as an infantryman with the Second New Zealand Expeditionary Force in World War 2 and whose book *Dark Laughter*, published in 1994, elucidates the role of song in war and popular culture. As with many Vietnam vets, the New Zealand soldiers interviewed by Alison Parr confessed that since the end of the war in 1945, they had suffered in silence and isolation, prey to recurring nightmares, debilitating depression, hyper-irritability and anger, while generally overwhelmed by an appalling sense of failure and helplessness. In every case, Parr notes, fear and the fear of fear were at the heart of their suffering (1995, 18–19). But the word fear is too abstract, and needs to be deconstructed into the raw, vernacular metaphors that veterans themselves use when recounting their experience of battle.

John Watson was among allied soldiers driven from Greece, then Crete, by the rapid German advance. They "just completely routed us. We just did not have the equipment to defend ourselves with. It was terrible. We were running away all the time. We were on the run, and that's awful. From the very first day, we were defeated … Completely and utterly beaten" (43). Another soldier, Jim Cusack, taken prisoner in North Africa, described watching a fellow-prisoner being beaten. "We saw it happening, yeah. And you daren't do anything about it, well you couldn't do anything about it because there was all barbed wire between us … [It] was terrible when you knew you couldn't do anything. We did yell out, you know. 'Oi, hey', and all this sort of stuff, but they never took any notice" (58). Pat Sheehan was a despatch rider and mine-lifter with the Engineers. "What I disliked about being in the Engineers, I used to get everything thrown at me. The shells thrown at me, the mortars thrown at me, the bloody machineguns firing at you, everything going on at you. It was frustrating and we were vulnerable … With Engineers you can't drop everything and fire a gun. You can't hit back … That's the thing, if you can't retaliate you get all this tension built up inside and that gets you upset … If you were in the Infantry, the more you got thrown at you, the more wild you became and you'd charge in and get you own back. It's a bit like if someone hits you, it helps if you can hit back, even if you don't win" (102). Tom May was a tank driver. Here is how he describes the powerlessness he felt in battle. "You're a sitting duck … especially in daylight when you were going into an attack and you knew the German 88-mm gun was there. I don't mind admitting I was very frightened, till the guns, our guns, started firing and then you felt a bit better, for some unknown reason. I suppose you felt you were doing something" (65). Rear-gunner Jack Marshall echoes this view. "It was the sitting there that was the worst part … Naked is the way to describe it … Just waiting for the end, waiting for it" (109, 110, 111).

In every one of these stories, terror consists not only in a crushing sense of being powerless to act or make the slightest impact on one's external situation;[16] it arises out of one's immediate subjective inability to control one's body (paralyzed or shaking with fear) and one's inner emotions.

For many soldiers, the imbalance of power on the battlefield could be redressed off the battlefield in fantasy, in language, and in symbolic action. Many soldiers dreamed of escape—of extricating themselves from engulfing mud or darkness, of breaking out, of getting to some safe haven. Many recorded their thoughts and fears in private diaries, or wrote letters home, often daily, as they struggled to reclaim ties to a sustaining homeland. In a taped interview in March 1999, Les Cleveland told me: "the enormous amount of letter writing that went on is perhaps an attempt to see yourself as still part of a family, part of a village, or connected to the homeland in some way that means you can see yourself as a kind of tourist, or temporary traveler, but always reaching out and touching the homeland and the people there." At the same time, many soldiers recovered a sense of social solidarity in subversive stories, ribald songs, wild escapades, and drinking bouts that ritualistically resisted for a moment the soul-destroying effects of mechanical routine and violent battle (Cleveland 1994). "Military folklore," Les Cleveland observes, is "an expression of resistance to the idea of powerlessness." It provides strategies for trying to get one's "experiences into some manageable framework, something that will make sense of it. Otherwise, I think you'd have to admit that it was chaos and you were being blown about in it like a leaf in a storm."

For the traumatized soldier, this image is definitive, and his total inability to bring himself or his situation under control is subsequently converted into a sense of personal impotence, inadequacy, and failure—a flaw that war has revealed in his character, a stigma that he must thenceforth bear. This is why, after the war, many wished that they had been physically annihilated rather than that they should survive to endure the nightmares and shame of neither being able to control their inner thoughts and feelings, nor confidently return to public life.

For traumatized New Zealand veterans, the inhibition against recounting their experiences came from without and within. A psychology of denial had its counterpart in a social conspiracy of silence. "I'm a private person," declared one veteran. "I don't talk to people about private things." The comment reflects a characteristic Anglo-New Zealand ethos of reticence and self-control, but, more pointedly, reveals a reluctance to burden loved ones with stories of humiliation and of extreme experience. As Les Cleveland put it, "How the hell can you explain to them what's bugging you? They are in a state of innocence. It's quite difficult, I think, to expound terror and one's admission of fear to people who have not experienced any of those aspects of the world. It seems monstrous to attempt such a thing … so you shut up about it." Though old anxieties—of being too afraid to fight, of being a POW unable to find enough food—"burst out in dreams and in odd behaviour," the code of the warrior keeps one's lips sealed. "It's a deficiency to be showing a weakness. A warrior doesn't behave unheroically, he grits his teeth and puts up with various dangerous and murderous activities like Germans trying to kill him all the time. He somehow manages to control himself and keep a stern face on things."

At the same time that one's family is too innocent to hear one's story, the nation is intolerant of any narrative that calls its charter myths—focused in New Zealand and Australia on the Anzac debacle at Gallipoli in 1915—into question. Consequently, the chronicles of war were, for many years, confined to official histories (commissioned by the New Zealand government) that were so bereft of personal experience that it was as though a censor had edited them. Gradually, however, these "paradigmatic narratives" (Bruner 1990) were displaced by stories recounted by individual soldiers, in which fear is admitted and what Les Cleveland calls the "curious mixture of boredom, hazard and chaos that typifies 20th century warfare" made public for the first time.

The disemia evident here between official and unofficial stories is a function of a set of incompatibilities: the gulf between the experiences of individual soldiers and loved ones who have had no direct knowledge of war; the gulf between state-sponsored and individually authored stories;[17] the gulf between codes of military conduct and actual patterns of human behavior under fire; and the gulf between the face one turns toward the world and the face reflected within. To close these gaps between private and public domains requires, on the one hand, that the state recognize and validate soldiers' stories, and, on the other hand, that soldiers themselves make their stories public. In fact, very few soldiers had enough education to be able to write and publish accounts of their war experiences. As for the state, it usually requires a generation, and another war, for the truth about the old war to be admitted to the public record—and then only if it does not seriously contradict current official and military myths of national identity and belonging. But even when a nation declares that it is open to the truth, and soldiers are willing and able to tell it, there may be no one alive who is both knowledgeable and neutral enough to bear witness to that truth. Such, writes Dori Laub, was the case with the Holocaust, which destroyed all those that would have understood the survivors' stories, who would have recognized them as subjects, and confirmed what they had to say. The reality of the Holocaust "extinguished philosophically the very possibility of address, the possibility of appealing, or of turning to another" (1995, 66).

Stolen Children

For comparative purposes, I turn now to another body of violent stories that chronicle the fallout from the erstwhile assimiliationist policies of Australia that saw more than 100,000 part-Aboriginal children taken from their parents under federal and state laws during the post-World War II period,[18] and placed in state institutions, or adopted and fostered in white families. In practice, these policies and laws spelled social death for Aboriginal children of mixed descent, whose names, parentage, histories, and homeplaces ceased to have legitimacy in the eyes of the state, and thereby became, for a while, for these children, marks of shame.

Hannah Arendt observed that the worst thing about being a pariah is not the maltreatment one suffers at the hands of the state. The "greatest injury which society can and does inflict is to make [the pariah] doubt the reality and validity of his own existence, to reduce him in his own eyes to the status of a nonentity" (Arendt 1944, 114).[19] In stories told by Aboriginal people in the course of their submissions to the *National Inquiry into the Separation of Aboriginal and Torres Strait Islander Children from Their Families* in 1997, incidents of physical and sexual abuse, forced labor, rape, and public humiliation are commonplace. But such torments did not in themselves destroy a person's humanity, as the stories make very clear. As with soldiers, violence consisted in being reduced to the status of an isolated and insignificant object. Trapped in impersonal, institutional milieux, bound by physical constraints and enforced rules, yet all the while desperately fantasizing and needing to belong to an intimate, interpersonal world, many children ran away from home.

At fifteen, Sherry Atkinson left a note for her foster parents: "Thank you for everything you've done, I'm sorry I'm not the perfect daughter that you want me to be but I have to find out who my mother is and my family is and where I come from. Don't come looking for me because it won't change anything" (Edwards and Read 1989, 34). Rick McLeod describes how running away from home at fifteen gave him a temporary sense of independence. "It was good. I was on my own, doing my own thing" (Edwards and Read 1989, 63–64). But despite these desperate bids for freedom, you felt illegitimate and anomalous in a rule-governed world where no one affirmed you, no one would listen to your story, no one would tell you the truth. What these children would remember were the continual invalidations of their being. John remembers entering the Kinchela Boys' Home when he was ten. Up until this time he had been told he was white. "This is where we learned that we weren't white. First of all they took you in through these iron gates and took our little ports off us. Stick it in the fire with your little bible inside. They took us around to a room and shaved our hair off ... They gave you your clothes and stamped a number on them ... They never called you by your name; they called you by your number. That number was stamped on everything" (Bird 1998, 57). Paul recalls the same traumatic experience of being reduced to a cipher: "For eighteen years the State of Victoria referred to me as State Ward No 54321" (HREOC 1997, 68). He then goes on to describe how, growing up in a white foster family, his color was alternatively denied and derided. "I had no identity. I always knew I was different. During my schooling years, I was forever asked what nationality I was, and I'd reply, 'I don't know.' I used to be laughed at, and was the object of jokes. I would constantly withdraw; my shadow was my best friend" (Bird 1998, 22). Millicent's story is similar, and typical. In the home where she lived, Aboriginality was disparaged as a sign of primitiveness, degeneracy, and ignorance. "They told me that my family didn't care or want me and I had to forget them. They said it was very degrading to belong to an Aboriginal family and that I should be ashamed of myself, I was inferior to white fellas. They tried to make us act like white kids but at the same time we had to give up our seat for a white fella because an Aboriginal never sits down when a white person is present" (29).

Not only was it impossible to establish one's true identity, but *any* attachment, interaction, or continuity with one's Aboriginal past was denied. Siblings were systematically separated and dispersed, and contact with mothers cut off. As Peggy observed, you passed from the control of your mother into the "care and control of the Government" (HREOC 82), and your whole life became regimented, restricted, rostered, reformed, and routinized according to state protocols. Children were also frequently moved from one foster home or institution to another. Consider William's comments: "Then we were all taken away again to a new home, to another place. We were shunted from place to place, still trying to catch up with schooling, trying to find friends. I had no-one. I just couldn't find anybody. And when I did have a friend I was shunted off somewhere else, to some other place. Wanting my mother, crying for my mother every night, day after day, knowing that she'd never come home or come and get me. Nobody told me my mother died. Nobody " (371).

As with soldiers who incriminate themselves for their failure to be invincible, many of these Aboriginal children grew up feeling that *they* were responsible for their own misfortunes. And this self-stigmatizing, self-denigrating tendency to experience the violence against yourself as a sign of your own failings—a punitive response to your own intrinsic moral inadequacy—was abetted by mission doctrines that made Aboriginality a metaphor for fallenness. Pauline McLeod puts this powerfully in her poem "Never More" (cited in Edwards and Read 1989, 22).

Separated
Fretting, sad.
Given into other hands.

Parents, sister, brothers gone.
Wondering what did
I do wrong!?!

Institution big and cold
All this happen
when one year old

Confused and lost
I didn't know
That the Government decreed it so.

Different places
till five year old
Then to a family
as I was told.

(Going once ... Going twice!
Sold!
To that lovely couple
Who's not too old ...)

The sense of shame that condemns one to remain silent about experiences that cry out to be told is a function of the impossibility of converting what is felt to be private into a story that has public legitimacy or social currency. Shame, in other words, is an affective measure of the socially constructed and uncrossable line between private and public space. This sense of shame that accompanies traumatic memory explains why many of the Aboriginal people who told their stories to the National Inquiry could not bring themselves to use their real names or give their consent to publication of their photos.

As with any "recovered" memory of trauma, the stories of the stolen generation broach, for many, questions of authenticity and objectivity. But it is important to remind ourselves that authenticity does not necessarily consist in an exact and objective recollection of a moment in the past that is frozen, as in a photograph, for all time. Rather, the "truth" of any remembered trauma is both selective and practiced—a product of a succession of intersubjective relationships between the "victim" and the situations and interlocutors with which he or she has had to contend. As such, every story told blends a desire to do justice to experience and a calculated interest in producing effects that will improve the storyteller's lot.

What is most crucially important about the stories told to the Human Rights and Equal Opportunities Commission is not their "truth to the past" but their "truth to power"[20]—the ways in which the stories of the stolen generation challenge the core assumptions of the "cosmologies of the powerful" (Das 1995, 139–40) that displace the root causes of suffering from the state onto the victim, the same process that in wartime leads to the diagnosis of traumatized soldiers as neurasthenic (Skultans 1997, 763), that, after the Bhopal disaster in India, saw the medical and judicial establishment blame the victims' poor health and panicked reactions for their suffering (Das 1995, 155–56), that, in totalitarian states, punishes dissidents as criminals or lunatics (Kleinman 1982), and that, in the poverty-stricken regions of northeast Brazil, sees medical workers treat hunger as a nervous condition treatable by drugs rather than a result of entrenched structures of political inequality (Scheper-Hughes 1992).

Though it will always be debatable whether or not Australia's assimiliationist policies amounted to genocide, one may readily understand the symbolic truth of the term for Aboriginal people who now use it to describe the sense that they were at the mercy of a concerted attempt by the Australian state to erase and nullify them as individuals, and to separate them forever from their history and their roots.

"Why me; why was I taken? It's like a hole in your heart that can never heal." "Actually what you see in a lot of us is a shell …." (HREOC, 177). "I just feel like I've really been cheated, cheated bad of my life" (Edwards and Read 177).

Recovering Narrative

In the wards of Salpêtrière hospital, Paris, a hundred years ago, the pioneering psychiatrist Pierre Janet observed that the inability of a person to consciously recollect or manage traumatic memories is to some extent a function of his or her inability to recount disturbing experiences *in narrative form*. While ordinary or narrative memory implies an ability to integrate new experiences with already engrained understandings, either idiosyncratic or shared, traumatic memory resembles Proust's *mémoire involontaire*; it is entirely private, and allows little or no two-way traffic between the mind of the individual rememberer and the social world in which he or she lives (van der Kolk and van der Hart 1995, 160–63; cf. Benjamin 1968, 202). In his clinical accounts of his patient Irène, a 23-year-old woman traumatized by her mother's death from tuberculosis, Janet noted that Irène's accounts of her mother's demise were not addressed to anyone in particular, took no one else's experience into account, and required no social context to be told. As with most amnesiac reenactments, the "story" was essentially a solitary, asocial activity (van der Kolk and van der Hart 1995, 161)—compulsive, long-winded, and incomprehensible. For the patient to be cured, a change from passivity to activity would have to occur. For Janet, this transformation would involve the patient actively taking charge of his or her own memories, a process entailing the recovery of narrative memory—"the action of telling a story" (175).

If we consider specific cases of this "action of telling a story," we can see how critical it is that the story receive recognition from outside the immediate world of the individual—ideally, even if symbolically, from the very social field—often the state—that is held accountable for having "stolen" or "cheated" the victim out of her humanity in the first place.[21] However, if the modern bureaucratic state is, in Arendt's words, ruled, like Kafka's Castle, by Nobody—with "nobody left with whom one can argue" or "to whom one could present one's grievances" (1969), how is it possible for the state to listen and apologize to those it has harmed, let alone compensate them for what it has taken from them? And given the fact that the bureaucratic state, as Weber noted, "does not establish a relationship with a person ... but rather is devoted to impersonal and functional purposes" (Weber 1968, 959), how can its utterances be anything but the rhetoric of bad faith?

That the state *is* addressed under these circumstances may, I suggest, have less to do with the hope of material compensation than with the need to be recognized by some ultimate authority. In an age in which many individuals feel that they are drawn into, diminished, and damaged by global forcefields that they cannot completely control or comprehend, recognition of their plight, their experiences, and their needs becomes increasingly desperate. Oprah Winfrey-style shows and truth and reconciliation commissions alike indicate the force with which this search for a national stage on which to share one's stories with others and be recognized is now felt. And in this search, some symbolic closing of the gap between one's own small world and the inscrutable worlds of the bureaucratic state or multinational corporations is critical. For if the individual is to regain some sense of power, the state or corporation must symbolically forfeit some of *its* power. Hence the need for a public apology in which the powerful acknowledge *the truth of the experience* of the powerless.

However, recounting one's story to a sympathetic listener or powerful authority figure does not necessarily heal the harm that has been done. As increasing numbers of Aboriginal people relate hitherto untold stories, voice longstanding grievances, and recount communal histories *on the national stage* during the course of land claim hearings and various national inquiries—notably the *National Inquiry into Aboriginal Deaths in Custody* and the *National Inquiry into the Separation of Aboriginal and Torres Strait Islander Children from their Families*—some admit to finding "the act" of telling their stories personally therapeutic (Bird 1998, 9), while others feel as though salt has been rubbed into their wounds. William was repeatedly raped in the orphanage where he was placed. Today he says, "I still suffer. I can't go to sleep at night. It's been on for years. I just feel that pain ... I've had my secret all my life. I tried to tell but I couldn't. I can't even talk to my own brothers. I can't even talk to my sister. I fear people. I fear 'em all the time. I don't go out. I stay at home. It's rarely I've got friends" (HREOC, 372).

Similarly mixed results have followed the Truth and Reconciliation Commission hearings in South Africa in 1996–1997. Speaking specifically of Mozambique, Alcinda Honwana makes the point that many people believe that giving voice to the evils of the past risks visiting those evils upon oneself again (1997, 6). On another note, referring to Alexandra township, Belinda Bozzoli notes that many testimonies remained private and unforgiving,[22] while several witnesses did not accept the point of recounting their stories without the guarantee of reparation (1998, 189–92), though in other cases, storytelling had real effects. In one particularly compelling case, a man called Lucas Baba Sikwepere recounted how he had been shot in the face by police after questioning their right to disperse a small community meeting near the township of Crossroads. The shooting left him permanently blinded. When Baba Sikwepere had finished telling his story, one of the commissioners asked him how he felt now that he had had an opportunity to tell the commission what had happened the day he had been shot. Baba replied, "I feel what—what has brought my sight back, my eyesight back is to come back here and tell the story. But I feel what has been making me sick all the time is the fact that I couldn't tell my story. But now I—it feels like I got my sight back by coming here and telling you the story" (cited in Krog 1998, 31).

Comparable stories are told by war veterans. When Pat Sheehan was granted a War Disablement Pension on account of his war-related agoraphobia, he felt he had reclaimed his dignity. "Being recognised by the authorities, that was very important. Recognition that the military authorities, indirectly or directly, have been taking notice, that this is just as much an illness as a loss of a limb. That was very important. See, when you go to a doctor, and you say, 'look I've got a sore leg,' it's you that has got to say which leg it is, he can't tell by looking at it, because that's aching inside. Same as agoraphobia. It's aching inside. You just can't say where it is. But you go through all the symptoms. It's an incredible thing" (Parr 1995, 172).

Speaking of atrocity and trauma, Lawrence Langer argues that the release or consolation provided by relating the story of one's suffering may all too often mean that terrible events get swept under the rug of history and forgotten (1997, 55). But should those who suffer bear, together with their pain, the burden of our collective memory? And isn't it imperative that we acknowledge that in sharing stories, we affirm life in the face of death, rejoining the dead to the living, and ourselves to one another? To say that storytelling may have the power to heal is not, therefore, to say that stories repress memory or deny history, but to point out that in bridging the gap between private and public realms, storytelling enables the regeneration and celebration of social existence, without which we are nothing. Re-presenting traumatic events as a story is a kind of redemption, for one both subverts the power of the original events to determine one's experience of them, and one moves beyond the self into what Buber calls an essential-we relationship, so opening oneself up to the stories of others and thereby seeing that one is not alone in one's pain. In comparing notes, exchanging views, and sharing stories, the sufferer is no longer condemned to singularity and silence, and the burden of shame or guilt that was the intrapsychic price paid for one's isolation, is lifted.

Consider, for example, Coleridge's Ancient Mariner, whose mindless act of shooting an albatross brings about immediate ostracism. Not only does this condemn him to absolute aloneness; it effectively brings time to a standstill—a ship stuck in an endless ocean, hallucinating silence, unbroken drought, and the nightmarish reliving of the original sin.

> Alone, alone, all, all alone
> Alone on a wide wide sea!
> And never a saint took pity on
> My soul in agony.

For life to be brought back to this frozen world, the mariner must tell his story—but not as a repetition of the events as they occurred (for this will only perpetuate the terrible stasis) but as a story that breaks free of the past into a new understanding. This new understanding must, however, take the mariner beyond himself, and involve a common bond with others—"To walk together to the kirk / With a goodly company." The shrieving of the mariner entails, therefore, crossing the gulf that divided his world from the world of others, a conjoining of that which has been put asunder—hence the force of the metaphor of marriage—the background against which the Ancient Mariner unburdens himself of his "ghastly tale."

The Ancient Mariner

In the West, when we explain the liberation that follows the telling of a long-suppressed story of guilt and suffering, we all too often have recourse to notions of catharsis and confession. People need to get things "off their chests" or "out of their systems," we say, in order "to move on," to be forgiven or absolved. Coleridge's *The Rime of the Ancient Mariner* is a paradigmatic case.

> Forthwith this frame of mine was wrenched
> With a woeful agony,

Which forced me to begin my tale;
And then it left me free.

Since then, at an uncertain hour,
That agony returns:
And till my ghastly tale is told,
This heart within me burns.

It is interesting to compare Coleridge with another great English poet, Ted Hughes. In 1999 Ted Hughes was posthumously awarded the Whitbread Book of the Year prize for *Birthday Letters*, a volume of poems about his relationship with his first wife, the poet Sylvia Plath. In a letter to a friend shortly after the book was published in 1998, Ted Hughes wrote:

> I think those letters release the story that everything I have written since the early 1960s has been evading. It was a kind of desperation that I finally did publish them—I had always thought them unpublishably raw and unguarded, simply too vulnerable. But then I just could not endure being blocked any longer. How strange that we have to make these public declarations of our secrets. But we do. If only I had done the equivalent 30 years ago, I might have had a more fruitful career—certainly a freer psychological life. Even now, the sensation is of inner liberation—a huge, sudden possibility of new inner experience (cited by Glaister 1999, 29).

In her book on Sylvia Plath and Ted Hughes, however, Janet Malcolm comments on Ted Hughes's sustained and exasperating silence over his marriage to Sylvia Plath and her suicide in 1963. "Hughes has never been able to drive the stake through Plath's heart and free himself from her hold" (Malcolm 1994, 140–41). But the emphasis here on unburdening or expressing some painful experience that has been "bottled up" too long within the individual's psyche (festering, poisoning, consuming him), reflects a very Eurocentric, ego-centered way of understanding the motives that lie behind the telling of life stories. If confession were all that was needed to be released of a burden of shame or guilt, to be absolved and able to begin anew, one would feel no compulsion to repeat one's story over and over again to whoever will listen or pretend to listen to it, as in the case of Coleridge's Ancient Mariner. To be efficacious, confession must involve a symbolic return to the person or place or sphere of life that is felt to be the source of one's misfortune. In the soldiers' stories and the stories of the stolen generation that I considered above, this involves closing the gap between one's own subjective life and the life of the state, since it is the state—imagined as an alienating "system" or a monstrously anonymous, minatory, and oppressive collectivity—that is held accountable for one's suffering, and that is believed to have "stolen" or "cheated" one out of one's life. Given the tendency of human beings to conflate their experience with their identity, the act of getting public recognition for one's story implies recognition of oneself, a symbolic acceptance back into the body politic of a soul that has been ostracized from it. But transformations effected in art do not always imply rebirth for the artist. Ironically, while Coleridge's Ancient Mariner is at last shrived of his sin, and awakened to a vision of a metaphysical bond and universal love that unites "all things both great and small," Coleridge himself never overcame the guilt that oppressed him as a result of unassuaged feelings of grief and complicity in his father's death and his brother Frank's suicide. Though *The Rime of the Ancient Mariner* was "an unconscious attempt at repairing his haunting loss by bringing Frank back from the dead" (Weissman 1989, 122), Coleridge never fully addressed the Cain and Abel complex of which he was half-aware, and survivor guilt condemned him throughout his life to aloneness in a wide sargasso sea of solitude, to compulsive replayings of primal events, to self-lacerating guilt, and to opium-induced escapes into the imagination.

There is, of course, never any guarantee that telling one's story will bridge the gap between solitariness and sociality, the singular and the shared, and this may be particularly true of cultures that exalt and privilege selfhood as *the* authentic mode of being. In the South African Truth and Reconciliation Commission hearings, Archbishop Desmond Tutu invoked the "African" concept of *ubuntu* to argue that reconciliation required a movement from "I" to "we," and the psychologist Nomfundo Walaza made a similar point, excoriating the self-indulgent privatizing of feelings (include feelings of guilt) that he associated with capitalism, and exhorting people to act together as members of one family, one community, and one nation (Krog 1998, 160–61). It is not that individual praxis counts for nothing, for all social activity, including storytelling, is initially individual action; rather that the focus of agency is on each person's relationship to others rather than on his relationship with himself or his personal salvation. Though stories emanate from personal experience, it is not the imprimatur of individual identity that gives a story value, but the imprimatur of a community. The ghastly stories of the Apartheid era have value, therefore, not in absolving individual guilt but in healing a damaged nation through a "piacular ritual," that, as Belinda Bozzoli notes, replaces "individual representations" with "collective beliefs," and recasts personal stories in ways that make them "emblematic" of all who suffered (1998, 169). In helping stories and lives "carry meanings beyond the personal" the TRC worked to reconcile different people to one another as members of a single commonwealth of humanity. Although the question remains to be answered whether any modern state—at once so complex, impersonal, and gigantic—can recapture and copy the responsive intimacy of traditional communities, this "African" emphasis on the "we-group" has some analytical value in taking us from a concern with the possible correspondance or concordance between stories and personal truth to a pragmatic interest in the compatibility of stories with collective goals. Such a view implies that social viability rests on effective strategies for bridging the gap between subjective dispositions and social structures. Storytelling is one such strategy. By relating our stories to others in ways and in contexts that enable them to play a part in determining the narrative and ethical shape that will be given to our particular experience, we avoid fetishizing this experience as something inward and unique. Though most experience—but especially extreme experience—often seems to us singularly our own, storytelling discloses that which is held in common.

There is, however, a paradox here, of which Hannah Arendt was acutely aware, for in the translation of experience from privacy to publicity vital elements are inevitably lost or betrayed. Indeed, what Norman Finkelstein has recently called "the Holocaust industry" is a compelling example of how lived experience may become fetishized, made grist for an ideological mill, converted into schlock for mass consumption, made into public spectacle, and exploited for political and economic gain (Finkelstein 2000).

Fortunately, though, the transformation of the personal into the social is never completely consummated, experientially or practically. In the cases of traumatic experience that I have explored in this chapter, no narrative does more than create a necessary illusion of fusion or balance between personal lifeworlds and the transpersonal world we define by such abstractions as society or the state. This is partly because such collectivities, though imagined to possess the will and agency of persons, communities and families, are in fact virtual and "blob-like"[23] subjectivities that can, at most, only symbolically "hear" the cries of those who plead to be given back the lives stolen from them. At the same time the real groups that lurk, ghost-like, behind such imaginary collectivities as society and the state, often no longer exist to answer the individual's cries for justice and restitution. Every person's story remains, therefore, irreducibly his or her own, imperfectly incorporated into the collective realm. And yet, it is precisely because personal experience remains on the margins of state discourse and ideology that it may become, in any society, a critical force that perennially unsettles received wisdom and challenges the status quo. Contrary to the naive view that stories and lives are isomorphic, it is this indeterminate, non-iconic relationship between stories and experience that makes it possible for storytelling to bring us back and bear witness to the reality of how we really live. Hannah Arendt often lamented the indifference, passivity and callousness that comes over us when reduced to a mass, obedient to the will and authority of others, mere faces in a crowd. Paradoxically, however, she seems never to have connected her view that our humanity is best preserved by individuals who remain apart from the crowd with her view that storytelling redeems us, not only through its power to convert private experience into general knowledge but through its power to confront, confound, and critique all received opinions by referring them back to lived experience and personal testimony. Thus, soldiers' tales perennially undermine the politically cavalier view that warfare can resolve international differences. Refugee stories challenge the complacency of a culture that assumes that victims of violence in other lands should gratefully and unobtrusively assimilate themselves to the cultural norms of the society of asylum. And the stories of the stolen generation are chilling testimony to the concealed complicity between the project of nation-building and the logic of extermination (cf. Hage 1996).

"YOU NEVER SAW YOUR OWN FACES": REFLECTIONS ON PRIVACY AND PUBLICITY IN THE LIVES OF REFUGEES

> We lost our home, which means the familiarity of daily life. We lost our occupation, which means the confidence that we are of some use in this world. We lost our language, which means the naturalness of reactions, the simplicity of gestures, the unaffected expression of feelings. We left our relatives in the Polish ghettos and our best friends have been killed in concentration camps, and that means the rupture of our private lives.
>
> —HANNAH ARENDT, *We Refugees*

In 1944 Hannah Arendt observed that though the Jews in the history of Europe had always been what Weber called a "pariah people," their outcast status had been subject to "alternative portrayals" and *lived* in ways that were not *entirely* reducible to the determinations of history (Arendt 1944). Thus, Heinrich Heine's depiction of the *Schlemihl*, who escapes the difficulties of the human world by steeping himself in the "true realities" of nature; Bernard Lazare's politicization of the Jew as a "conscious pariah" who fights for freedom on behalf of the oppressed; Charlie Chaplin, who poignantly evokes "the time-honoured Jewish truth that, other things being equal, the human ingenuity of a David can sometimes outmatch the brute strength of a Goliath" (111); and Franz Kafka's "man of goodwill" who, oppressed by a powerful and anonymous regime that rules from above, comes to realize that he is not only unable to "determine his own existence"; his existence may in fact *have* no reality or validity (118–19; 114).

It is this Kafkaesque image of being reduced in one's own eyes "to the status of a nonentity" (114) that comes to mind when one thinks of refugees—people whose *circumstances both in their homelands and in countries of asylum* seem to allow little freedom, unless it is to renounce all that they have been, and assimilate to a world predetermined by others (Arendt

1978, 55–66). In this chapter I look at how this tension between being and nothingnesss finds expression in the refugee's lived experience of private and public realms.

Intersubjectivity and Violence

When one considers the relational character of human existence cross-culturally, two things quickly become apparent. First, singular selves are usually thought of as parts of a commonalty, sole but also several, not only islands but part of the main (Jackson 1998a, 6). Second, just as ego and alter are implicated in any conception or sense of who one is, so there are seldom fixed or impermeable boundaries between the worlds of persons, words, ideas, animals, and things. Accordingly, ancestral homelands, family graves, family dwellings, spoken words, personal names, material possessions, spirit entities, and significant others may figure severally, equally, and actively in the field of the intersubjective. Experientially, all these elements merge with and become indispensable parts of one's own being; one cannot live without them. As such, subjectivity is not really a fixed attribute of persons, but the product of any purposeful and committed activity we enter into with those we love and the things we value. This view is poignantly captured in the words of a Greek Cypriot refugee, pining for home. "You ask me, what is the essence of the village, if it's the fields and the houses, which we've lost, or the people, our fellow villagers? My answer is that it's the people and the houses and fields—all together" (cited in Loizos 1981, 131).

Neither are intersubjective relationships ever entirely passive or static. Indeed, whether between persons or between persons and ideas, objects or words, they tend to be unstable and continually contested. As I have argued earlier in this book, this volatility of intersubjective life may be understood existentially. Any human life may be seen as an ongoing struggle to strike a balance between an immediate and intimate world we call our own—in which we expect to have some say, be recognized, and make a difference—and alien worlds that we accept as being only contingently within our comprehension and control—such as the worlds of gods, spirits, and ancestors, of cosmic and natural forces, of fate and history. This balance between being an autonomous subject for-oneself and an anonymous object for-others is seldom satisfactorily struck or successfully sustained. It is threatened continually by the vagaries of climate and disease, by accidents and natural disasters, and by the contingencies of history. We speak of tragedy when there is an absolute and irredeemable loss of this balance between microcosm and macrocosm—when one's own familiar world is overwhelmed and eclipsed by external forces that one is powerless to understand or withstand.

Consider for example Maja Povrzanović's harrowing accounts of the lived experience of war in Croatia 1991–1992. In these accounts, two sets of images stand out. First are images of homes—places of intimacy, privacy, and security—suddenly "defamiliarized" into places of "anxiety and deprivation" (Povrzanović 1997, 157). Second are images of *public* places—streets, cafés, neighborhoods, and town halls—just as abruptly transformed into places of danger and death. But most arresting in Povrzanović's ethnography are anecdotes about how ordinary people resist these brutally imposed transformations by clinging to "minimal normality" in "the space they used to inhabit" (158)—remaining in their homes despite shelling, helping neighbors repair bomb damage, keeping up routines of communal life such as the morning excursion to buy bread, the evening promenade, visits to a café, attendance at funerals and protest meetings, *even at risk to their lives.* Clearly, these modes of resistance exhibit both an existential and political character. In the former sense, they are stratagems for escaping the humiliation of being passive in the face of danger, ways of working to master one's fear and reclaim some active purchase on the world (57). In the latter sense, they are self-conscious acts of political defiance that deny one's public space to the enemy.

Stigmata and Status

In destroying homes and cities, war destroys the *intersubjective* routines, relationships, and movements that sustain a vital relationship between private and public realms. Once this field of relationships is shattered, people's lives tend to be radically polarized—either cast onto the street or the open road (places marked by panicked activity and the complete absence of privacy) or driven, in transit camps and countries of asylum, into privacy and passivity. Both extremes are forms of social death, and are commonly experienced as shame.

Such shame isn't necessarily connected to guilt or wrong-doing; it arises, as Sartre observed—and as Arendt also notes in her comments on Kafka—when the recognition of who one is ceases to be mirrored by those one loves, and comes to be determined by one's appearance in the eyes of others, filled with indifference or hate. Thus there is an uncanny echo of Kafka's castle, towering darkly over the village below, and the hidden gun emplacements and snipers *overlooking* defenceless towns like Dubrovnik and Sarajevo. But the aggressive gaze of the anonymous other that stares through gunsights from some point of absolute advantage is also felt when one is stripped of one's possessions, one's home, one's clothing, and transformed into a mere object of the other's will. Under such circumstances, any inner reflections on *who* one is are eclipsed by the external definition of *what* one is in the eyes of others. No longer a subject for oneself, one is reduced to being an object—isolated, exposed, fixed, categorized, and judged by the Other (Sartre 1956, 221–22, 288–91). As one refugee put it, "You never saw your own faces" (Jansen 1990, 112).

Whether as an object of curiosity, contempt, or compassion, the refugee stands out and stands apart. "If we are saved we feel humiliated," wrote Hannah Arendt in her 1943 essay, "and if we are helped we feel degraded" (1978, 60). One effect of this isolation is that the refugee feels that he or she has no place in the polis, no confidence or right to enter the public sphere—neither the communal space he or she is forced out of, nor the communal space into which he or she is obliged to seek refuge.

All refugees know this acute self-consciousness, focused on the clothes they wear, the language they speak, the food they eat, the icons they worship, the gestures they make. And equally familiar are the voices of those who take it upon themselves, in the name of racial purity or national pride, to defend "their" cultural space against refugees and asylum-seekers, telling them to "go home to where they belong." A sense of cultural agoraphobia is therefore common among refugees—a sense of being conspicuous, exposed, ostracized, and stigmatized. This is sometimes expressed as a sense of being intimated or disoriented by the plethora of rules that governs life in transit camps and countries of asylum (cf. Ex 1966, 20, 29). This is not because there were fewer ground rules or bylaws in the homeland; rather that the notion of rule conveys the force of non-negotiable facticity, the sense of being overwhelmed or impinged upon by something that is not only outside one's own understanding and governance but seemingly indifferent to one's individual humanity. To complain about being rule-governed is thus to register one's sense of being crushed, diminished, engulfed, and depersonalized by a public sphere in which one no longer has rights or powers. Observed one Vietnamese refugee in Australia: "Even though I was so happy to arrive here, I felt as if at every moment the government controlled how and where I could live. I can move about freely but always within the housing determined by government regulations and always following the council rules" (cited in Thomas 1996, 108). For this reason, refugees often feel that there is no authority to whom they can turn to make good their loss, no court of appeal (cf. Berger and Mohr 1976, 134). This was a recurring theme among the Somali refugees I met in New Zealand: mindful of what they had suffered through the political machinations of the state, many regarded governments and bureaucracies as not merely indifferent but as actively machiavellian: organized against rather than for them, suspicious rather than supportive, hostile rather than helpful. As Abdi Bihi explained to me (personal communication 1998), powerless individuals often feel that the open expression of their thoughts and feelings risks rejection or invites persecution, which is why they so often have recourse to social withdrawal, camouflage, and dissimulation to allay the suspicions of outsiders, to appease authorities, to protect themselves against encroachments upon their autonomy, or to gain some small advantage in a hostile environment. For the desperate, "honesty" is often a psychological privilege they cannot afford.

One result of feeling exiled from the polis is that the refugee often feels that the sole domain in which he or she now exercises any freedom is the domain of private emotions, the personal body, and the domus—though even here the national gaze penetrates, exposes, and shames the outsider, as in the national fetishization of female genital operations as signs of barbarism and superstition in such countries of asylum as France, Australia, Britain, and the US (Povinelli 1998, 577–78). Because the outside world, the world of others, is seen as inimical, one tends to withdraw, to remain indoors, within the mind, within the past, even though this can be a trap. "I got very depressed," said an Indian woman from Kenya. "I was feeling terrible. When you're under a depression, you just close the walls in yourself. I couldn't face going out, because people mightn't like me, or mightn't talk to me" (cited in Jansen 1990, 17). A Vietnamese woman spoke in a similar vein about the way she took refuge in herself. "When I don't want to tell someone about things and they keep questioning me I go silent. They think I am just being a timid Vietnamese woman, but it's not that. I just don't want them to know. They are strangers" (cited in Thomas 1996, 213). In a study of Bosnian refugees resettled in New Zealand, Vladimir Madjar found that three quarters of the people he interviewed "expressed a sense of social isolation and lack of integration into the wider New Zealand community." Projecting both a subjective sense of loneliness *and* commenting on an objective condition, most Bosnians confessed "that their neighbours were either aloof or that they had nothing to do with them" (1998, 183). Typically refugees feel that their experiences open up an unbridgeable gap between themselves and others. "Those who aren't refugees do not understand the pain of those who are—it cannot be shared," observed a Greek Cypriot woman. "But the refugee can talk about his suffering to another refugee, and between the two of them, the suffering is controlled. The one understands the other, but the non-refugees don't feel things, they aren't affected in the least" (cited in Loizos 1981, 127). This sense of being isolated by and trapped within one's own experience exacerbates the feeling of being isolated in the world. To find oneself alone in an unfamiliar neighborhood is to be overwhelmed by the dread of speechlessness and the panic of flight. Moreover, because one's own face, one's own language, and one's own gestures are not mirrored in the world around one, one becomes invisible. People stare at you or look right through you. You feel exposed and alone. Even opening the door to a stranger may make one feel threatened. "I was frightened sometimes," said a Laotian woman. "A lot of religious people knocked at our door, wanting to sell a book or something, and I didn't know how to answer them. I asked a friend what to do. She said, 'Just say no, and shut the door.' It's awful when someone knocks at the door and you open it, and there are these big tall people outside who you can't understand" (cited in Jansen 1990, 113). Some of the relentlessly emphatic gratitude that refugees express when newly arrived in the country of asylum may be seen as a self-protective gesture of appeasement—a performative act to keep the outside world at bay while rebuilding their own inner lives.

The Fall into Inwardness

A basic principle of phenomenology is that consciousness is not passive to the world but conditioned by the constantly changing projects, intentions and actions that define a person's relationship *with* the world. By implication, any radical erosion of these modalities of interaction between the world of self and the world of others threatens the very basis of a person's being. In trauma, this is precisely what occurs, and consciousness may seem to take on a life of its own, indeed, to become a foreign force outside one's governance, something one suffers, that holds one hostage and in thrall. To use the metaphor of the stream, we might say that for a person in deep shock, consciousness becomes a flood, drowning the island of the self, collapsing its banks into it. The surrounding world engulfs the inner world. That world of alterity, with which one had worked out a modus vivendi, suddenly becomes a threat, an enemy, a contagion. One is petrified and powerless before it. *It* now seems to possess consciousness, not *I*. Reempowerment consists in redressing the lost balance between self and not-self, between the stream of consciousness and the social landscape that shapes its course and through which it flows. Initially, however, consciousness wavers between seeking refuge in itself, hiding its shame, and confronting the external world—or at least symbolic images of it. Some kind of balance is sought between regression and aggression. "It's painful for me every time I think about everything that has happened," says a Laotian woman. "It reminds me of so much, and then it keeps going around in my head, and I can't get away from it for a few days. Sometimes it makes me dream about Laos, and about our house there. But even though remembering is difficult, we don't want to forget. We also want our children to know what we've been through, and where we've come from" (cited in Jansen 1990, 120). Gaining control of the unrelenting reel of images that runs through the mind, oscillating wildly between scenes from the past and the present, may be accomplished by manipulating familiar words and things—making them, in effect, objective correlatives of the inward states. But though the homes of migrants and refugees often resemble "memory museums" (Boym 1998, 516), they are museums characterized by interaction rather than static display. Mementos or photos that symbolize the past, salvaged or sent from the homeland, are carefully organized on mantlepieces or shelves, enshrining an order and balance that is sought within the mind. Or food is prepared and served with ceremonial care. In this domain of what Michael Herzfeld (1997) has called "cultural intimacy," domestic space becomes fused with the space of the body. Openings of the body and doors and windows of the house are all made foci of anxiety and activity. And in this struggle for control over one's own interiority, over one's own space, sexuality and commensality become crucial terms. Being able to prepare and consume one's own food is often a critical issue for refugees in transit (Liev 1995, 107; Ex 1966, 71), and the significance of control over sexuality has been dramatically focused in the struggle in France and the United States over so-called "genital mutilations." Though clitoridectomy has been outlawed in both countries as "shameful" and "barbaric," those who lay claim to the practice as vital to their social identity remind us—whatever our own views on the matter—that refugee autonomy is always under seige (cf. Povinelli 1998, 575–79).

Though refugees struggle to rebuild their lives within the confines of domestic and ethnic enclaves, and the state has no such limitations, an analogy may be drawn between the bureaucratic and governmental acts of containment and control that increasingly characterize refugee adjudication in countries of asylum and the cultural emphasis on containment and control that exist within refugee communities themselves. As Mary Douglas has observed (1966), order is universally conceived as a modality of cleanliness or purity. Purity, therefore, should not be interpreted solely in terms of pathogenic hygiene; it connotes an order of things in which every item is symbolically in its proper place, correctly ordered, classified, and culturally contained. Matter out of place is thus dirty and polluting. Perhaps nowhere is the connection between propriety and refugeeness more marked than among European Gypsies, who, with the Jews, may be called the oldest refugees in Europe. "Cleanliness, especially symbolic cleanliness," reports Isabel Fonseca, is focused on taboos which guard against contamination—of the group, the person, the reputation.

> They constitute Romipen—"Gypsyhood"—and they are the key to the unusual ability of Gypsies everywhere to endure persecution and drastic change of many kinds and remain Rom. Relations between gadje and Gypsies are highly regulated and restricted, as are relations between Gypsy men and women—and the burden for keeping such customs falls

mainly on the women. The parts of the body are symbolically cordoned off from each other; washing and language have a rich symbolic language that goes far beyond getting out the dirt and getting the salt passed, and these codes exist among Gypsies from Tirana to Tyneside to Tulsa (Fonseca 1995, 48–49).

To wear the clothes or eat the food of *gadje*—outsiders—is to defile oneself, to lose control of the boundary between one's own world and theirs, and to risk being cast out into the wilderness of the road. If outsiders distrust Gypsies and consider them dirty, Gypsies distrust outsiders even more: they are seen as threats to Rom integrity, invasive and unclean. And not only is the outsider avoided, lied to, and kept at a distance; within the mind, one's history and memory of traumatic contact with the *gadje* world is systematically erased. In Holocaust literature, references to the tragedy of Europe's Gypsies are few and far between. This is not entirely because of the bias of historians; it reflects the emphasis of the survivors themselves, for whom the "devouring" (*porraimos*, i.e. the holocaust) is less significant than the vitality that enabled them to conquer death (Fonseca 1995, 253).

Among Roma, writes Isabel Fonseca, "'forgetting' does not imply complacency: its tenor is one of—sometimes buoyant—defiance" (275). "The Jews have responded to persecution and dispersal with a monumental industry of remembrance. The Gypsies—with their peculiar mixture of fatalism and the spirit, or wit, to seize the day—have made an art of forgetting" (276).

Inevitably, however, the question arises: at what point do these all-too-human coping strategies work against the refugee's adjustment to life in the country of asylum. To what extent do the magical and imaginary elements that confine adaptive strategies to the mind and to the domus prevent the refugee from engaging effectively with the polis. The refugee may regain inner strength through such "techniques of the self," but does he or she gain power, for power, as Hannah Arendt notes "arises only where people act together" (1973, 30).

Consider the following anecdote (Ghassan Hage, personal communication 1998; also see Hage 2000):

There was this mad man in Sydney who had migrated from Lebanon and he used to be seen in the suburb of Campsie crossing the road on a marked crossing for hours on end, crossing from one side to another and just crossing back, and then back to the other side again. When he was asked what he was doing he pointed to a coming car while crossing and said: "See, they stop for you." In his madness this guy did not fail to discover in migration a process which gave him a sense of his value as a human being (the cars stopped for "him") in a way that his lost homeland didn't (if you attempt to cross the road in Beirut you will be ignored, if not abused, hit, shouted at, etc…). The point is that we often see migrants and refugees from the perspective of what they have lost and how they are trying to regain it. This is clearly the most important aspect of their lives. But, it is also important to remember that they have their eyes open and for all their losses they know when they are on to a good thing as they say.

Clearly, the sense of existential control that is conjured through stopping cars on a crosswalk, managing a household, or fetishizing the body, can work to isolate a person from others rather than mediate relationships with them. The boundaries one creates to safeguard one's sanity and integrity may become barriers. For one Hindu woman in Britain, her house was such a safe haven that the outside world became a terrifying place. "When I come to this country, six months, I not go outside. My children help me." Outside, she said, she felt her eyes swiveling, the sounds of traffic assaulted her ears, strange smells filled her nostrils, her mouth felt dry, her legs buckled, and she felt dizzy (Gubbay 1989, 296). In a sense, home had become a prison. Noted one Cambodian refugee: "My elderly relatives feel they are being held under house arrest. They only go out and see other fellow country people if I can take them." Another observed, "During the Pol Pot regime, we lived in a prison without a wall, but we were not able to go anywhere. Now here we are in a free country, I found myself almost all of the time confined to my home although I have the keys" (Liev 1995, 120). This strict separation of self and not-self, inside and outside, that enables one to recover a sense of control over the unregulated traffic of the mind leads to a schizmogenic situation in which the polarized entities are drawn into an exaggerated dialectic of mutual negation. While citizens of the country of asylum may disparage refugees for clinging to exotic customs and remaining radically Other, so refugees themselves sometimes make sweeping generalizations about their new neighbors as "inhospitable," "reserved," "cold," and "racist." The homeland, by contrast, is seen nostalgically as a place of viable community, of warmth, laughter, and abundance, where rules and elders were respected. "The days of paradise," as Palestinian refugees say (Peteet 1995, 180). At the same time, the refugee is double-bound by impossible contradictions: the country so romantically celebrated as home also conjures images of terror and of death, while optimism about one's children's future is accompanied by a deep pessimism about one's own.

Publicizing the Lives of Refugees

If refugee lives involve a traumatic sundering of the relationship between privacy and publicity—a falling back into inward feelings of loss, nostalgia, guilt, and regret, or a sense of having no place, no future, and no recognition in the public sphere—the same sundering often characterizes the way we speak about refugees. Accordingly, any essay that pretends to understand refugee experience is bound to reflect upon the fact that its own premises lie outside that experience and may, as a consequence, be part of the very political problem that creates refugees in the first place.

In addressing this question, I want to move from a critique of Western discourse about refugees to a critique of the moral and legal assumptions that underpin not only this discourse but, by implication, contemporary social science.

Before embarking on research among refugees, my views were heavily influenced by media imagery. I was struck by the drastic and tragic scale reduction of refugee lives. Reduced to a handful of possessions, a makeshift shelter, a patch of dirt on a treeless hillside or plain, refugees seemed not only bereft of the basics of living; they appeared to embody the very essence of abjection and loss. In stripping them of almost everything that had comprised their intersubjective world—persons as well as possessions—violence had diminished, limited, and effaced them. At the same time, violence seemed to have robbed them of any place where their actions mattered, their gestures were recognized, their words were heard, and their plight was understood.

These are the assumptions that make us think of refugees as victims. Refugees appear to have no choice but to be as they are. Their freedom seems to consist solely in how they endure their lot, for the things they count as theirs and the power they feel they have in relation to these things have been nullified. Violence sunders things that belong together, makes passive that which has the power to act, renders inert that which moves, muffles and silences that which speaks, and reduces being to nothingness. This is how W. H. Auden describes this process in *The Shield of Achilles*:

> Barbed wire enclosed an arbitrary spot
>   Where bored officials lounged (one cracked a joke)
> And sentries sweated for the day was hot:
> A crowd of ordinary decent folk
>   Watched from without and neither moved nor spoke
> As three pale figures were led forth and bound
> To three posts driven upright in the ground.
>
> The mass and majesty of this world, all
>   That carries weight and always weighs the same
> Lay in the hands of others; they were small
>   And could not hope for help and no help came:
>   What their foes liked to do was done, their shame
> Was all the worst could wish; they lost their pride
> And died as men before their bodies died.

A great deal of violence in our lives is contingent and transitory, which is to say criminal.[24] And—as in cases of rape and murder—its victims tend to be individuals. But we live in a world in which an increasing amount of violence is institutional and structural. Though torture, abuse, rape, enslavement, theft, and murder remain the stock and trade of such violence, it is initiated, advocated, and enforced systematically by laws and institutions of the state or corporate organizations. Such organized violence has two aspects. First, its target is constructed socially not as an individual but as a category. State violence effectively extinguishes the person as an individual subject through a process of iconic essentializing that transforms him or her into a mere instance of a more general case: a species, a specimen, a pathology, a class. Second, the category so defined is then subject to categorical obliteration through programs of incarceration, torture, exile, and extermination. Refugees suffer, exemplify, and symbolize the worst excesses of this twofold dehumanizing process. Not only do they—like rape victims or abused children—endure trauma and torture. Not only do they lose the intimate lifeworlds where they possessed the right and power to act—places they called their own. Not only do they endure years of social isolation in transit camps, under regimes that provide little hope or preparation for new lives. But the fortunate who find asylum often remain marginal and powerless in their new "homes." In part this is because many refugees enter countries of asylum as cultural strangers without work skills or knowledge of the local language, while grappling inwardly with loneliness, depression, anxiety and ill-health. But all too often it is because the new country remains for refugees an oppressive place where state decrees, bureaucratic protocols, assimilationist assumptions, and social resistance to foreigners effectively deny them opportunities to recreate their own lives and regain control over their own destinies, at least in the public sphere. This process may be likened to internal colonization, in which the "stigmata of refugeeness" (Malkki 1995a, 160; cf. Arendt 1978, 55)—the shame of being different, dumb, and dependent, *and of being labeled "refugee"*—undermines refugees' attempts to re-empower themselves in the new land.

The problem for anyone writing about refugees is one of avoiding the discursive conventions that conspire to reinforce these colonizing and stigmatizing processes. Of not writing off the refugee. This means, first, radically critiquing our conventional usage of the word loss. As Oliver Sacks notes, disease is never simply a loss or impairment of function; there is "always a reaction, on the part of the affected organism or individual, to restore, to replace, to compensate for and to preserve its identity" (1986, 4). The same principle of recruitment—whereby lesions are repaired and losses made good by new growth—obtains in social life. As long as we think of refugees solely as victims, we do a grave injustice to the facts of refugee experience, for loss is always countermandered by actions— albeit imaginative, magical, and illusory—to regain some sense of balance between the world within and the world without.

Doing justice to refugee experience also demands that we reflect critically on the tacit links between the ways in which refugees are conventionally constructed in academic and bureaucratic discourse, and the ways in which they are stereotyped in vernacular discourse and the media (Malkki

1996, 386; Kleinman 1997a). Many anthropologists have been troubled by the inordinate amount of quantification, objectification, and technicism in the field of refugee studies—the apparatus of statistics, graphs, tables, category terms, and authoritative generalization that are brought to bear, in the name of both humanitarianism and the public good, on the so-called "refugee problem" (cf. Malkki 1996, 378–79). This style of discourse likens refugees to primitives, peasants, children, or the elderly—categories of persons who are marginal to centers of power. Defined in terms of their emotionality, appetites, instincts, and dependency, "they" form an undifferentiated and anonymous mass, a crowd, a pathology (Kleinman 1997a). In this discourse, there is an uncanny parallelism between media cliches and expert commentaries. The photo images are of huddled masses, lost souls with hands outstretched for help, or of people on the move like migrating herds (cf. Malkki 1996, 387–90). Ranajit Guha's ground-breaking work on subaltern consciousness is directly relevant here. In colonial India, Guha notes, "a sense of identity" was imposed on the peasant "by those who had power over him by virtue of their class, caste, and official standing. It was they who made him aware of his place in society as a measure of his distance from themselves—a distance expressed in differentials of wealth, status, and culture. In other words, he learnt to recognize himself not by the properties and attributes of his own social being but by diminution, if not negation, of those of his superiors" (1983a, 18). This "negative consciousness" was allegedly mindless. The peasant was supposed to possess neither will nor agency or rationality. If he rebelled, the phenomenon was naturalized, and likened to the outbreak of a thunder storm, or an earthquake, or the spread of wildfire, or an epidemic (Guha 1983b, 2). The ruler was subject; the peasant was object—capable of spontaneous activity but not of reason. This is often how those who control the destinies of refugees—both inside and outside their countries of origin—tend to construct refugeeness. As the antithesis of ourselves, defined not according to who they are, but in terms of what they lack.

Given the plethora of academic essays, white papers, and compendious monographs devoted to refugee issues, why are there so few studies that give voice to and work from the lived experience of refugees themselves?[25] To what extent do we, in the countries of immigration, unwittingly reduce refugees to objects, ciphers, and categories in the way we talk and write about them, in roughly the same way that indifferent bureaucracies and institutional forces strip away the rights of refugees to speak and act in worlds of their own making? I contend that this question—focused dramatically in the case of refugees—implies even more imperative questions concerning relations between what Veena Das calls "cosmologies of the powerful" and "cosmologies of the powerless" (1995, 139–40). But there is an even more fundamental issue at stake here; namely whether it is warranted to speak of "refugeeness" at all (Malkki 1995b, 496; Ranger 1996, 319–20). On what grounds can we claim that "refugeeness" is a sui generis phenomenon that covers a well-defined class of persons, a discrete cluster of ostensive traits, or a specific field of human experience—as is assumed in almost every essay or monograph on the subject that begins by citing the number of refugees in the world today, both external and internal, and invoking the 1951 Geneva Convention Relating to the Status of Refugees. Arguably, the trauma suffered by refugees is no different than the trauma suffered by anyone who has been bereaved, raped, persecuted, tortured, imprisoned, exiled, or traumatized by a natural disaster; all that singles out the refugee is the fact that he or she has suffered more deeply and perhaps irreversibly than most. But the real problem in pursuing questions of definition and identity is not one of reducing ambiguity or refining terms. Nor is it a question of the way definition betrays the irreducible complexity of lived experience. The problem lies in the homelessness of our times. When Adorno writes aphoristically in *Minima Moralia* that "dwelling, in the proper sense, is now impossible," that "the house is past," that it is no longer possible "to be at home in one's home" (1978b, 38–39), he means both that the devastation of Europe in 1940–1945 presaged an epoch of unprecedented emigration and statelessness *and that the long-standing goal of philosophy to establish and arbitrate truth has been lost.* After Auschwitz (one could as readily say "after Srebrenica," or "after Rwanda"), "our feelings balk at squeezing any kind of sense, however bleached, out of the victims' fate." "We cannot say any more that the immutable is truth, and that the mobile, transitory is appearance" (Adorno 1973, 361). This view, which I share, only sharpens one's sense of the ways in which the tragic circumstances and unsettled states of mind that we conventionally encapsulate in the concept "refugee" overflow and confound the category term, and permeate and overlap our own lifeworlds. This is why I prefer to treat "the refugee" as a discursive figure rather than as an individual subject—making the word define a site of intersubjectivity rather than biography, a modality of consciousness rather than a category term, "a logic," as Veena Das puts it, that renders "the self radically fugitive and the world radically fragmented" (1991, 65).

Judgment, Redemption, and Recognition

There is nothing new in asserting that academic discourse disguises political agendas and ideological interests. Less often noted, perhaps, is the manner in which it conceals a theodicy. By this I mean that the project of the academy—commonly defined as the pursuit of knowledge and truth—secularizes but never quite transcends a quasi-theological, quasi-legalistic search for deciding between what is right and wrong. In Michel Serres's terms, Enlightenment science simply translates theodicy (who's to blame?) into epistemodicy (what's the cause?) (1995, 23).

I want to contest these moral and legal undertones in academic discourse by calling into question the assumption that the most significant fact about human existence is that it has meaning, and that human lives are redeemed by the discovery of this meaning, even if it is made after the fact.

Generally speaking, both academic and bureaucratic representations of the refugee are driven by what one might call salvationist assumptions (cf. Mimica 1993), the "triste trope," as Sahlins describes it, "that what life is all about is the search for … the melioration of our pains" (1996, 395). I speak here against our impulse to exoticize trauma, making it the latest object of the ethnographic gaze, and, by extension, our habit of constructing the refugee as victim and seeing oneself as rescuer or savior. In both cases, an unequal power relation is implied and perpetuated between "them"—the objects of our concern—and "us"—the source of their deliverance. At the same time, the refugee is likened to a martyr, someone whose suffering and pain have moral value, whose survival is providential and even implies some saving grace. But as Lawrence Langer observes, speaking of the Holocaust:

> Such situations mock the good intentions of utopian hopes. They introduce us to a reversal of expectation that lies at the heart of any attempt to appreciate modern suffering. The Holocaust and subsequent large-scale

atrocities exist in an orbit void of the usual consoling vocabulary: martyrdom, the dignity of the dying, guilty conscience, moral rigor, remorse, even villainy, which in literary tragedy so clearly distinguishes the victim from his or her persecutor. None of these verbal categories illuminate the devastation of the Holocaust, or for that matter the killing of millions by Stalin in the 1930s by enforced famine, the ravages of Cambodia, or the merciless destruction of civilian populations in Yugoslavia today (1997, 54).

Yet we persist in seeing the refugee, albeit in secular terms, as a deserving cause, worthy of sympathy, assistance, and a new life. We, in the countries of asylum, will redeem his suffering, make good his loss. In this discourse, the injustices suffered by refugees are played up while the human failings of individual refugees are played down, as if trauma transcended or purged all ordinary imperfections. Thus, the endurance of hardship is made a prelude to salvation in the same way that hard labor is said to merit a well-earned rest. At the same time, the tone of this discourse is of righteous indignation. Littered with oughts and shoulds, it often winds up with recommendations to governments, exhortations to action, and gestures of censure directed at indifferent bureaucrats and fellow-citizens who "are not doing enough to help." I am not advocating that we cease caring for those who suffer; I am simply calling into question our discursive habit of understanding meaning as a matter of deciding between right and wrong worldviews or theoretical positions, and then translating this decision into a distinction between the virtuous and the culpable. There may be no more value in sanctifying suffering than in demonizing the sufferer as somehow responsible for his or her own misfortunes. I take this view, partly because no clear-cut, comfortable demarcations exist in the real world between victims and persecutors (Levi 1989, 36–69), partly because this discursive habit has its origin in a logocentric and Judeo-Christian worldview that effectively invalidates non-Western theodicies, and imposes "our" meanings on "them" (see Kleinman 1997b, 318–19). Like Primo Levi, I can find no ethnographic or experiential evidence that pain and suffering necessarily bestow virtue. Misery no more improves a person than religious ecstasy. And the meek do not inherit the earth. In short, I want to say that showing how the refugee problem can be solved is analogous to showing how the refugee can be saved. Both agendas visit "our" goals on "them"; "their" suffering is made to take on "our" meaning. But this renders the refugee as invisible to us as colonized people are to the colonizer. The refugee no more wants to be saved than the colonized want to be civilized; what both demand, on the contrary, is that they be recognized as who they are for themselves. And this means that they be given the right to participate in the decision-making processes of the polis, to be drawn from the margins of the state toward its center, integrated as equals rather than subject, as rank outsiders and victim of loss, to degrading rituals of assimilation.

This takes us from questions of social justice to the question of how we can do justice to experience? Odo Marquard makes the following point about theodicy:

> Experience of life seems to me to show that when one is up against suffering, under its immediate pressure, the problem is never theodicy; for what is important then is simply the ability to hold up through one's suffering or one's sympathy. It is stamina in enduring, in helping, and in comforting. How can I reach the next year, the next day, the next hour? In the face of this question, theodicy is not an issue, because a mouthful of bread, a breathing space, a slight alleviation, a moment of sleep are all more important in these circumstances than the accusation and the defense of God. Only when the direct pressure of suffering and compassion relents, under conditions of distance, do we arrive at theodicy (1991, 11–12).

I share Marquard's pragmatist view. For any writer, this implies that in an unjust world, one should not have to wait upon social justice for all before one commits one's energies to describing in depth the ways in which people actually experience and cope with life. In my view, we are justified, as anthropologists, in exploring and documenting human lifeworlds without necessarily allying our endeavors to social policies that promise to improve the objective conditions of those who inhabit those lifeworlds. In working among people who have suffered deeply and unjustly, I do not seek, as a prior justification for my work, solutions for problems, either epistemological or social, nor bear witness to the truths of humanism. It may be true that human problems can be solved, causes discovered, blame apportioned, pain alleviated, and broken lives can heal. But this is not my concern. My concern is to understand better how people deal with the vicissitudes of their existence, what resources they call upon, what changes they wreak, without positing "a meaningful world or a just god or a comprehensive scientific discourse within which suffering can be made comprehensible" (Das 1995, 140). To this end, I find myself returning to the Stoic dictum that "endurance is fundamentally far more important than happiness" (Berger and Mohr 1976, 134), and invoking the Gypsy way of meeting adversity in a spirit of defiant acceptance. "Every person is part Judas, part Christ … only luck decides him" (cited in Fonseca 1995, 241). Behind this kind of acceptance lies recognition: the deep and possibly tragic realization that there, as the saying, secularized, goes, but for an accident of fate or history, go I.

But such a recognition of oneself in the other may lead all too readily into resignation and narcissism. Just as Hannah Arendt noted the estranging effects of the archimedean viewpoint—in which the project of human understanding is compromised by being put at the service of policies of administrative control—so empathy may all too readily become a folie-à-deux, fostered by regressive dreams or utopian visions.

How is it possible, then, for the project of understanding to carry us beyond the conditions that govern us, and into a more fruitful engagement with the world?

Like K—who is neither "of the castle" nor "of the village"—the refugee is, for our century, an iconic figure. Forced from the intimate, local, and familial lifeworlds in which their words and actions had some value, and bewildered by the global world in which they are expected to find their future, refugees find themselves in limbo. But is "exhaustion" the only possible fate for them, as Arendt suggests, in her pessimistic review of Kafka's work (1944, 122), or can their very marginality offer us new insights into how we become more at home in the world?

In going along with Arendt in answering this question in the affirmative, I am, however, mindful of how few examples there are of people whose marginality has not exhausted or destroyed them, and how difficult it is to draw from these examples any *general* understanding of how the world might be changed, let alone understood. This is why we now live in negative capability, knowing that, though some human beings are able to salvage and create viable lives under even the worst circumstances, there is probably no way in which we can avail ourselves of any insights they may offer to *collectively* create the conditions under which this possibility may become the norm.

IN EXTREMIS:
REFUGEE STORIES/REFUGEE LIVES

We want to describe the indescribable: nature's text come to a standstill.
But we have lost the art of describing the one reality whose structure allows
poetic representations: impulses, intentions, oscillations.

—OSIP E. MANDELSTAM, *Conversations about Dante*[26]

Because stories carry us vicariously from place to place, and through
time, it is easy to sympathize with Salman Rushdie's observation in
Shame "that the resentments we *mohajirs* engender have something to do
with our conquest of the force of gravity. We have performed the act of
which all men anciently dream, the thing for which they envy birds; that is
to say, we have flown" (1995, 84). But flight is an ambivalent image, a two-
edged metaphor. Associated with freedom, it is also synonymous with
fear. In German, *Flüchtling* refers not to someone who is free but someone
who is seeking asylum, struggling to be free, fleeing totalitarianism (Peck
1995, 116). And for refugees, the experience of floating "upwards from history, from memory, from Time" of which Rushdie speaks, is far from liberating. For refugees, flight is, to use Wendy James's compelling phrase,
one of the names of fear (1997).

A casualty of transition, the refugee embodies the transitive. As a tran-
sient, or as someone in flight, he or she belongs nowhere—constituting at
once a problem for administrative order and for the discourse of social science, grounded as it is in the discursive habits of a sedentary culture that
favors substantive, intransitive, bounded notions of identity and meaning
(Harrell-Bond and Voutira 1992; Malkki 1992; Gupta and Ferguson 1992;
Krulfeld 1993; Olwig and Hastrup 1997).[27] Indeed, what makes it difficult to empathically describe refugee experience is the fact that it is often
characterized by fleetingness, uncertainty, and flux—by what has slipped
through one's hands rather than what is firmly held.

A Phenomenology of Flight

In his radical empiricism, William James emphasized that consciousness is a succession of movements between transitive and intransitive extremes—like a bird, James says, that is sometimes in flight, sometimes perched or nesting in a tree (1950, vol. 1, 243). A theory of consciousness that singled out the intransitive and downplayed the transitive (or vice versa) would be as absurd as a theory of birds that emphasized perching or nesting and failed to mention flight. To use another metaphor, one might say that the stream of consciousness sometimes flows steadily and without interruption, is sometimes broken by a submerged snag, sometimes whirls or eddies because of countercurrents, and is sometimes driven faster by narrowing banks. Just as the being of a bird consists in both its flight and its perching, or the being of a stream consists in both its flowing and not flowing, so consciousness must be understood dialectically. Both intransitive states and transitive moments are implicated, as when, for example, a person observes that the time is exactly 12.30 p.m., then notes how time flies, or drags, depending on the context. Most of the time we are not troubled by these fluctuations, switchings and oscillations of consciousness—indeed, we are scarcely aware of them. We declare that we are in two minds, or in a quandary over a certain issue, without any sense that our life hangs on how we resolve it. But there are times when these vacillations imply unbearable conflict and become freighted with a sense of existential peril. Deciding between alternatives, or bringing the confusion of the mind under control, is felt to be a matter of life and death. Indeed this schizoid condition (Laing 1965) of not knowing which way to turn, of not being able to settle to anything, this split between opposing images, these moods, memories and imperatives that seem to belong to incompatible worlds, may so torment a person that he will imagine extinguishing his consciousness altogether, taking his own life, in order to ease the pain. Cambodian refugees describe this pathology as one of *gkuet cj'roun*—"thinking too much." Typically, it is a condition of disequilibrium and uncontrolled thinking brought on by isolation, anxiety, and grief (North 1995, 201–5). Though John Keats argued that we should make a virtue out of negative capability—"being in uncertainties, Mysteries, doubts"—the fact is that most human beings can only celebrate the transitive moments of consciousness when they are secure in the intransitive.

But the refugee *is* in flight. A flight Liisa Malkki describes as filled with "apocalyptic confusion and fear," compounded of blind panic, of being buffeted and propelled over unfamiliar terrain, of being pursued, tripping, falling, hiding, of fetid bodies and fatigue, of never knowing whether one has reached the border to safety or not (Malkki 1995a, 109–10). But this unintelligible landscape across which the refugee flees, with its attendant "apocalyptic physicalization of the body" (110), has as its corollary a confusion within consciousness itself that continues long after the frontier has been crossed. Words such as displaced, dislocated, fugitive, uprooted, and stateless describe the refugee's objective situation, but they describe with equal metaphorical force his or her state of mind. In a 1997 report on a violent incident in a refugee transit camp in southwestern Ethiopia, Wendy James touches on this dialectic relation between movement in the world and mode of consciousness. Her focus is the correlation of flight (event) and fear (experience). For the Uduk, "apprehension-fear" is simultaneously embodied (in the liver) and located (in the external social and material environment). In flight, as in bereavement, a person's intersubjective world is shattered. While we might speak of a person "going to pieces" or "falling apart," the Uduk speak of the liver being under uncontrolled "attack" from without. But in either case, images of death press in on the mind, conveying an experience of moving through a totally destabilized and devastated lifeworld. As one refugee put it, "Fear has struck us because of that road from home, and these ideas about it hurt us all the time. I think that maybe some of us will die from thinking about it all, and the attacks of fear. This comes from thinking about our homeland, the earth of our country and the road we've come. We try to figure it out, and worry about how to get back. But we don't know any way to get back home, ever" (in James 1997, 125). Flight and fleetingness define, therefore, not only external attributes of refugeeness; they disclose a panicked mode of consciousness in which a person is at the mercy of wild oscillations between polar extremes—here and there, past and present, present and future, living and dead, immediate and imagined. One cannot control this pandemonium of contradictory images. But while it goes on, every intention or impulse is at once countered or invalidated by its opposite, which is why one cannot act. In a compelling essay on Sri Lankan

Tamil refugees, E. Valentine Daniel and Yuvaraj Thangaraj describe a man in his forties—a onetime teacher of Tamil literature, and a witness to an "atrocity" in northern Sri Lanka—now living in a South Indian refugee camp. Most of the time this man sits in silence, seldom moving, showing no interest in food, indifferent to danger. But during an interview with the anthropologist, the man points to his nephew walking toward him on the beach, and says: "Now that child is walking and I know he is walking. Then [i.e., when in his "vegetative state"]: That which walks doesn't walk, that which doesn't walk walks, that which doesn't walk doesn't walk, that which walks walks." Val Daniel points out that the Tamil word for "walk" (*natai*) also means "happen," so the quatrain could be read: "What happens won't happen, what won't will, what will will, and what won't won't." The nihilism is reminiscent of Beckett's *Watt* or the narrator of *The Expelled*—people immobilized by contemplating what is entailed by putting one foot forward after the other in order to walk. Comment Daniel and Thangaraj of the Tamil refugee: "By covering all possibilities, he has chosen none. The reign of caprice is total. To the extent that he talks about this ineffable state, we may say that he (we) are caught in a contradiction." Though—as Daniel and Thangaraj argue—the man's knowledge is not exactly about nothing, it remains "self-negating"; it occurs in an "eddy of absolute mistrust" (Daniel and Thangaraj 1995, 230–31).

Flight and Narrativity

Many writers have noted that one of the most arresting things about refugee stories—and, more generally, the stories of people in crisis, in torture, and in flight—is that life all but ceases to be narratable (Das 1990, 346; Feldman 1991, 14; Frank 1995, 98; Malkki 1995a, 107; Povrzanović 1993, 1997; Skultans 1997, 765–66). "I cannot describe that situation," Croatian refugees confessed to Maja Povrzanović; "it can't be told" (1997, 156); "I don't know, I don't have any words" (Povrzanović 1993, 146). Not only is there a loss of the social context in which stories are told; the very unities of space, time, and character on which narrative coherence depends are broken. For refugees, life is no longer a journey or narrative the meaning of which is consummated in return, or even, indeed, in time. Writing in her great memoir about those who survived Stalin's Gulag, Nadezhda

Mandelstam observes: "It was a feature of almost all the former camp inmates I met immediately after their release—they had no memory for dates or the passage of time and it was difficult for them to distinguish between things they had actually experienced themselves and stories they had heard from others. Places, names, events and their sequence were all jumbled up in the minds of these broken people, and it was never possible to disentangle them" (1975, 455). In his work on the testimonies of Holocaust survivors, Lawrence Langer speaks of this as a movement from chronology to duration. One's life is reduced to a series of events that have no connection to the life one lived before the Holocaust or to any life one may hope to live thereafter. "Testimony may *sound* chronological to an auditor or audience," Langer writes, "but the narrator, a mental witness rather than a temporal one, is 'out of time' as he or she tells the story" (1997, 55). This sense of being out of time is, of course, a corollary of the sense of being no*where*. The sense of chronology that imparts meaning to both a life story and to the history of a people is normally concretized in the image of journeying, of going somewhere. But arbitrary and untimely death can neither be construed as the consummation of a journey nor the conclusion of a story. The event simply occurs, a fact without significance, or, in Hannah Arendt's memorable phrase "an unbearable sequence of sheer happenings" (Arendt 1973, 106). Such facts, unlike stories, are disconnected, and cannot convey meaning, for meaning, as the word suggests, implies some kind of striving and strife, some kind of intentionality or purposeful unfolding in which the significance or import of one moment becomes revealed in the next. In death or disaster, succession and seriality give way to simultaneity. The present is stuck like a gramophone needle in the groove of one fateful moment in the past (cf. Das 1990, 359). One's sense of time unfolding is so disturbed that the future is continually referred back to this moment in the past and cannot break free of it. This is why refugee stories typically juxtapose nightmarish recollections of flight and nostalgic images of Paradise lost. Accounts are sometimes rendered by traumatized people, to be sure, but they are not like the stories we ordinarily tell. They do not carry us forward to any consoling denouement. They do not require others to listen to them or respond. There is no prospect of closure. There are victims, but few free agents. They may bear witness to an event, describe a journey, or recount a tragedy, but they suspend all consideration of salvation or justice. As Lawrence Langer notes of atrocities such as the Holocaust, the enforced famines in Stalin's Russia, the killing fields of Cambodia, and the genocide in Rwanda and Bosnia, such events "exist in an orbit void of the usual consoling vocabulary: martyrdom, the dignity of the dying, guilty conscience, moral rigor, remorse, even villainy, which in literary tragedy so clearly distinguishes the victim from his or her persecutor" (1997, 54).

Consider this fragment of a story told by a Vietnamese boat-refugee now living in New Zealand. "Three days passed again. Nobody came to help us. Oil contaminated all the food and we were hungry. The people tried to collect oranges which were scattered in the sea. The children cried at first, but after that they had no energy to cry or wail. They all closed their eyes to avoid the heat of the sun and the coldness of the wind. Death was very near. All fell into silence" (in St. Cartmail 1983, 122). Here is another account of flight from a very different time and place: the village of Lloqan in Kosovo, June 1998. "It started at about 9 am. We suddenly heard shooting from a small hill nearby, not just bullets, but terrible big guns. I heard the cows trying to get back to the compound and I ran out to open the doors to let them in. Then I felt something hit my shoulder and when I turned round another bullet grazed my back. My husband went into the woods with another man. They were both shot" (Have Kusumaj, a woman in her 40s, cited in Steele 1998, 1).

Refugee stories are driven by existential need rather than emotion, epistemology, eschatology, or ethics. By this I mean that they do not tell us what we may know, what we may believe, how we may judge, or how we may feel; they attest to the fact that telling stories is, like our need to breathe or defecate—as necessary as it is pedestrian.[28] This is why refugees find it cruel and ironic when the administrators of refugee camps and resettlement programs demand precise dates and places in order to authenticate stories and approve asylum, for in trauma, these are the very details refugees are incapable of recollecting (Abdi Bihi, personal communication, 1998).

Sheer Happening

I turn now to some accounts of "sheer happening" in order to explore a little further this experiential field in which narrative falters and fails. My first example is the Partition of India on August 15, 1947.

In the Punjab, there are rumors and threats, but most people believe that life will soon return to normal. "We heard about partition through the papers but we thought that this division would not disturb us," said one survivor. But then all hell breaks loose. People are dumbstruck, dazed, stunned. In pandemonium and flight no one can think. Finally, in a place of comparative safety, thinking back, people are incapable of much more than a spare and strangely detached listing of a chain of events. "We were attacked again," one woman reported. "When they started using spears we ducked under a moving cart. Only three of six in our party did this. I don't know what happened to the other three. We walked or crawled about 150 yards under the moving cart when we saw fifty young men of our caravan engaged in hand to hand combat with the Muslims. But we didn't go to their aid. We passed them (still under the carts) and never learned their fate" (cited in Keller 1975, 57). Veena Das, who recorded similar stories from Hindu women almost fifty years after the event, speaks of the "fractured quality" of these narratives of loss (Das 1990, 347), of a third-person tone of voice, of a "resort to the formal" (Das 1991, 66). "I had just put a *chapati* on the girdle when we heard such a roaring noise—we fled—I did not even take the girdle off from the fire," one woman said. "I ran," said another, "with *nange pair* (naked feet)"—a conventional expression denoting sudden flight (71). In one sense "anti-narratives" (Frank 1995, 98), the fragmented character of these Partition stories recalls refugee stories from elsewhere and other times. In his account of Vietnamese boat refugees, John Knudsen speaks of "still-life images refusing to yield" (1995, 19). In his work among Tamil refugees and torture victims, E. Valentine Daniel speaks of the bored parsimony of Tamil stories, of "flat-toned recitations devoid of conviction, the speaker pausing now and then as if to wonder how these details could interest anyone" (Daniel 1996, 143). This sketchy, listless, unemotional manner, comments Daniel, reflects an "overwhelming sense of the sheer worthlessness of all attempts to communicate something that was so radically individuated and rendered unshareable" (143). Liisa Malkki, in her work among Hutu refugees in Tanzania, refers to the "messy" and "unmanageable" character of Hutu stories of flight, which administrators of the camps could do nothing with and saw no point in recording. An example: "We heard the guns: bum! bum! bum! bum! And then there were helicopters, and when we saw a group of men on the ground, they killed them. We, we left home. We went into the forest and hid ourselves in the rocks. Others, they took flight immediately, all the way to Tanzania, but we stayed three months in the rocks—from April to June. We put the children under the rocks, and then we looked around" (Malkki 1995a, 107–8). Not only do refugees struggle with a sense that language cannot do justice to their experience; the suspicions and indifference of administrators in both camps and countries of asylum reinforce this tragic sense of not only having lost one's autonomy and homeland, but of having one's life story doubted or dismissed as a form of deceit.

We speak of trauma as something that "shatters" or "fragments" a life, "tearing it apart." This is understandable. The habitual patterns of inter-subjective connectedness and trust that link our lives to the lives of others, as well as to familiar objects, places, and stories, are broken. This loss is centered on the loss of language. In its resistance to and its shattering of speech, trauma creates a deep sense of unsharability (Scarry 1985). And as trauma reduces us to unbearable solitude, so our stories become reduced to contingent events. The loss of emotion, of narrative design, and of moral conclusion that one sees in stories of traumatic experience are signs that the refugee has momentarily lost his or her sense of being connected to a world that can be recognized, chosen, or known. As Lisa Capps and Elinor Ochs observe in their work on agoraphobia, traumatic experiences "do not easily fit, or may indeed contradict, the identities and worldviews we wish to maintain" (Capps and Ochs 1995, 175). The shamefulness of suffering consists in this sense of being singled out, of being the victim of some inscrutable cosmic joke, of standing alone.

Any accident has the same effect. Suddenly, time stands still, and the world is reduced in scale to the one small place where pain cries out for ease. Take, for instance, John Berger's account of a woodman who becomes pinned under a fallen tree. Berger accompanies a doctor to the accident site, guided by a friend of the woodman. When they reach the woodman, the friend says: "He's been screaming ever since. He's suffering something terrible doctor." Berger goes on: "The man would tell the story many times, and the first would be tonight in the village. But it was not yet a story. The advent of the doctor brought the conclusion much nearer, but the accident was not yet over: the wounded man was still screaming at the other two men who were hammering in wedges preparatory to lifting the tree" (Berger and Mohr 1976, 17–18).

What does John Berger mean when he says that this event was not yet a story? It is in the very nature of an accident to break the connections between before and after, between ourselves and others, between inward and outward realities, and between stories and lives. A fatal accident of course clinches this argument. Death takes away someone we love, but it momentarily also robs us of speech—our sole means of recovering any sense of continuity and connection. A death produces the most terrible silence. Then come the cries of protest, the sobbing torn from the heart, the semi-articulate form of lamentation and chant. But it is not for some time that speech is possible, let alone stories, though all mourning involves an attempt to recapture the power of stories. This is why Veena Das says that death "may be considered at one level as essentially marked by its non-narratability, by its rupture with language" (1990, 346).

There are several reasons, then, why tragedy and trauma preclude stories. One is the sense of inconclusiveness that I have spoken of. For refugees, their stories remain open, like wounds, for as long as it takes for dispersed families to be reunited, for lines of communication between them to be reestablished, for the suffering and uncertainty in the homeland to end, and for the shock of resettlement to pass. The lives of refugees are split, and until the two halves are rejoined—like the halves of the classical symbolon—healing is delayed and closure is impossible. Refugees also feel inhibited about telling their stories because they are powerless; in so far as their stories of maladaption and misery may be construed as criticisms of the country of asylum or complaints about their lot, they fear adverse repercussions such as delays in reunification, withholding of social services, and social prejudice. A third reason for the refugee's silence is the conviction that one's experience has been so terrible that no one will believe one's story. Writing about prisoners who survived Auschwitz, Primo Levi observes, "Orally or in their written memories, (all would) remember a dream which frequently recurred during the nights of imprisonment, varied in its detail but uniform in its substance: they had returned home and with passion and relief were describing their past sufferings, addressing themselves to a loved one, and were not believed, indeed were not even listened to. In the most typical (and cruelest) form, the interlocutor turned and left in silence" (1989, 12). A Greek Cypriot refugee told anthropologist Peter Loizos: "Those who aren't refugees do not understand the pain of those who are—it cannot be shared. But the refugee *can* talk about his suffering to another refugee, and between the two of them, the suffering is controlled. The one understands the suffering of the other, but the non-refugees don't feel things, they aren't affected in the least" (cited in Loizos 1981, 127). This is why refugees are the best qualified people to work with refugees. Even if others are prepared to listen, there is often such a manifest discrepancy between the world they inhabit and the world the refugee has survived, that the sharing is inhibited. Barbara Einhorn shared this story with me: A group of women were exchanging stories about claustrophobia. One said she panicked every time she went up in an airplane. Another was anxious about being trapped in an elevator, and the lights going out. A woman who had survived Auschwitz was in this group. If she spoke she felt she risked appearing to trump the others. Or would kill the conversation by taking it onto another plane. She remembered the cattle trucks, the railhead. She kept silent. Silence was the only way of honoring the truth of her experience. Another story: in the course of researching an oral history of the Frankton railway settlement in New Zealand, my mother-in-law met a veteran of the Second World War who told her his story. Taken prisoner by the Germans in Greece, he and others were force-marched to Poland where he was put to work making cement. At the end of the war he returned home. His parents had planted hollyhocks and delphiniums outside his bedroom window. His room was just as he had left it when he went off to war. During the next four days he suffered more terribly than he had suffered during his four tormented years in Poland—the trivial talk about the weather, about his childhood, about where he might find work, and the realization that nothing, absolutely nothing of his wartime suffering, could be shared. He took work on a trawler and spent the next four years in silence and solitude.

Under these conditions, it is easy to understand how a survivor's sense of isolation may become a sense of being cursed, marked out, and stigmatized. One's suffering is felt to be shameful. Sometimes this is because of survivor guilt—the sense that one has no right to be alive when so many friends and family perished. Sometimes it is because of specific cultural values, such as the silence of Indochinese women about experiences of rape or forced marriage—experiences so profoundly incompatible with womanly integrity and cultural identity that they are too shameful to be spoken of (Muecke 1995, 41–44),[29] or in the case of traumatized Hindu women, torn between silence or disgrace (Das 1990, 1991). But reticence and repression may arise because one's experience has no *social* currency in the world in which one finds oneself: the country of asylum for the refugee, or the homeplace to which survivors return. As John Knudsen observes, many refugees come to feel that their lives change ineluctably "from being shared ... to becoming private" (1995, 26) in part because close contact with kin is difficult and because their positions and identities in a familiar community are lost, in part because the culturally anomalous character of traumatic experience enforces isolation and depersonalization. Though one's story may concern events that have befallen thousands or millions like oneself, in the place where one finds refuge it takes on the status of private experience because so few share it or have endured experiences that remotely compare with it.[30] Reticence, evasiveness, equivocation, and withdrawal into private worlds that provide a sense of safety and security are characteristic of survivors, not necessarily because of any stoic attitude, nor because others will not listen to what they have to say; these traits mark the limits to which an outsider may cross into the world of the insider, and the limits to which biography can be made compatible with history, or life stories reconciled with conventional narratives.

Sociality and Emotionality

Part of the difficulty in recounting stories of great suffering is that such stories are emotionally overdetermined. Without falling into the Eurocentric trap of dichotomizing emotionality and sociality—the former made synonymous with spontaneous, intrapsychic, irrational, and subjective life; the latter with cognitive and cultural reality (Lutz 1988)—it is important to recognize that, in all human societies, speech is sometimes so flooded by affect and fragmented by flashbacks that it resists lineal ordering and cannot be integrated with any body of stories that is conventionally told. In such cases, emotion is an embarrassment. It marks an individual off from others; it signifies a failure of the social to encompass the subjective; and affect is seen as inimical to the social order because it appears to be ungoverned by social constraints. That is why emotionality in many societies connotes loss of control, a shameful form of incontinence.

One solution to the dilemma of how to reconcile affect and sociality is to cultivate, as a social virtue, a neutral tone and affectless persona in the face of suffering. This kind of self-control, taught during the ordeals of initiation, is not uncommon in Africa (Riesman 1977, 146–47). Or one can simply suppress emotion—as Aboriginal people do by putting the memory and name of the dead out of circulation for a generation, sweeping the ground clear of that person's tracks, destroying his or her personal posesssions, and moving away from the place where one shared a life with him or her. Another strategy is to switch one's emphasis from emotion to action. This involves playing up the shared nature of suffering, not through the expression of personal emotion but by the expression of solidarity and the offering of token sympathy when others are in distress. Thus, among the Kuranko of Sierra Leone, one might say to someone in pain, "You suffer," or at a funeral give a "sympathy gift" to the bereaved, in acknowledgement of the fact that death touches everyone. Yet another strategy is to replace all spontaneous outpouring of individual emotion with performative or theatrical displays of feeling. Thus, in Aboriginal Australia, when grieving men lacerate their thighs and mourning women gash open their scalps with sharp stones, this is not necessarily because they are moved to do so; they do so because these conventionalized displays of grief demonstrate publicly that one wished the deceased no harm and is mortified that he or she has passed away. Another solution is to have surrogates display emotions on behalf of those who have been overwhelmed by them. Among the Kuranko, as in many other societies in the world, the bereaved are banished from the public space of grieving, and their emotions acted out by persons less intimately related to the deceased (Jackson 1989, 78–85). Thus, subjectivity is not so much suppressed but transferred from the intrapsychic to the intersubjective, and accorded a *social* function. This does not preclude what we would call "authentic" grief finding expression in mortuary rituals (or romantic love finding expression in arranged marriages); it simply means that personal disposition and individual emotion are not made the basis of social organization. This is the emotional obviation that Veena Das records in the narratives of Hindu women: the articulation of the idiosyncratic as something common to everyone.

Stories participate in this sleight of hand, as I show in my study of Kuranko narratives (1982) which, like folktales everywhere, permit the expression of personal quandaries precisely because they are shorn of all references to the personal, much as masks, by presenting a fixed and conventional image to the world, allow the expression of highly charged personal feelings beneath them. As forms of theatricality, then, stories seldom represent experience as straightforwardly as a mirror reflects an object. Rather, stories create a semblance of truth, creating effects and contriving solutions to recurrent human quandaries. It is this ubiquitous conflation of narrative and magicality that creates, in all societies, a problematic tension between stories considered sacrosanct or true and another corpus of tales that is admittedly makebelieve and imaginary. In many ways this distinction corresponds to the distinction I have made between an extrapersonal domain of It-ness—symbolizing all that one cannot oneself comprehend or control—and a personal world of I-ness that encompasses the domain in which one can exercise, or at least experience, some degree of choice (Jackson 1995, 122–24, 1998, 19–20). In Africa, the antinomy is between true ancestral charter myths and antinomian folktales; in urban-industrial societies it is between scientific facts and science fictions. But in every case, reason and administrative order get associated with the first, while emotionality and license get linked to the latter. The arts are critical of the sciences, folktales are satires on the myths of rulers, and both are barely tolerated, and—in our society—underfunded. Factuality is friendly to administrative control while fiction threatens it. Storytelling is thus marginalized. Assigned to the private domain, a modality of leisure, a discourse of the uneducated, an artefact of childhood, it loses even the moral authority that not so long ago attached to the folktale. As Walter Benjamin noted, the demise of storytelling goes with the disparagement of experience, which is set up in opposition to knowledge as a refractory or raw material that only becomes intelligible and meaningful when subject to rational reprocessing.

Rather than perpetuate this kind of unhappy antinomy between science and art, fact and fiction, I think we should try to see that each is necessary to the other—ironically counterpointed rather than mutually contradictory. In traditional societies, the line between unquestioned truth and pure fantasy is very subtly drawn. This may be because a pragmatist conception of truth holds sway: the truth lies less in the essence of a thing than in the consummate use one makes of that thing in some context of social action. Accordingly, both charter myths and folktales, facts and fictions, have their uses, and there is no point in arguing which is more essential to human well-being. Applying this principle to our distinction between fact and fiction we would refuse to decide between the truth of the administrator and the truth of the refugee on epistemological grounds, but study the social consequences of the two orders of discourse. The sort of stories that refugees tell are different at different times. Needs change. But without these stories, nothing would change. In particular, these stories enable refugees to move from private grief to shared experience, from the solitude of I to the commonalty of we.

What Happens to Who We Are

There are always two spheres of governance in our lives. On the one hand there is the immediate sphere of family and friends, of our local community, the world of which we have a complete and intimate knowledge, where our words carry weight and our presence makes a difference. Then there is the wider world of which we know little, in which we count for nothing, where our voices are not heard and our actions have next to no effect. Every human life is a struggle to strike some kind of balance between these two spheres, to feel that there are things one decides, chooses, governs, and controls that offset the things over which one has no power. Stories help us negotiate this balance. And the succession of stories that refugees tell offer us, far more than so-called facts, glimpses into the process whereby control over one's destiny is recovered and the imbalance between contingency and necessity redressed. "The reward of storytelling is to let go," writes Hannah Arendt (1973, 99). But this is only to comment on the expressive and therapeutic power of stories. Though stories may concern events that seem to have singled a person out, isolated and privatized his or her experience, storytelling is, in the final analysis, a social act. Stories are composed and recounted, their meanings negotiated and renegotiated, within circles of kinsmen and friends. Like religions, they not only allow people to unburden themselves of private griefs in a context of concerted activity; they bind people together in terms of meanings that are collectively hammered out. It is this sharing in the reliving of a tragedy, this sense of communing in a common loss, that gives stories their power, not to forgive or redeem the past but to unite the living in the simple affirmation that they exist, that they have survived. One of the most moving anthropological accounts of this phenomenon is Richard

Werbner's *Tears of the Dead*, a social biography of a family from western Zimbabwe and of the bloody war for independence and its aftermath in the region between 1964 and 1988. Toward the end of his book, Werbner recounts a conversation with two widows, Baka Sala and Baka Lufu, concerning the brutalities they and their families had witnessed and suffered during the war. By contrast with the kinds of stories people had related before the war—stories about political intrigues and life crises within families—the war stories were all about people's relations with a world that had violently invaded and shattered their lives, and how they had survived such suffering (1991, 157, 1995, 108). "And we are surviving," Baka Sala told Richard Werbner. "We are truly alive because we are able to see you once again. But we were not very much alive before when we had no way of knowing whether we would ever see anyone like you again. The [most recent] war was so overwhelming. We lay down, but not to sleep. We had nothing to eat. We fled our homes. We were beaten [with poles]. What could we do? They [soldiers of Zimbabwe's national army] drove lorries into the field over there, took all our maize, filling their lorries, and ate it by themselves. We ourselves had to climb trees to escape. We thought our people were going to be killed in our homes. And we who had climbed the trees begged them to let us alone. We went along like this, shivering and trembling. Yet God is here, and we lived. But others among us did not survive. We who survived are now really alive, seeing again our child with whom we lived so well" (1991, 166).

Survival is clearly not just physical survival; it is the ability to survive socially, as a family, its meaning consummated in a moment of reunion with someone one has known before tragedy overwhelmed one's life. And it is existential—being able to make plans again, to choose, to outlive that time when one was reduced to nothingness, beaten like an animal, ordered to do the most shameful and terrible things in order to be allowed to live, defeated by one's abject powerlessness. To tell the story of the times through which one lived is to rehearse the contrast, slight as it may seem, between then and now, to clarify and bear witness to what one has salvaged and retrieved. "Did we really live?" Baka Lufu asked Richard Werbner. "We can never forget that life that captured us. No, we can never forget. How can we ever forget?" But then, as Werbner suggests, Baka Lufu's terrible questions *were* answered, not by anything anyone might say to her, but by the social fact that she was "speaking to me at home, sur-

rounded by some of her favourite kin, children, grandchildren, and immediate neighbours. She addressed herself to them as well as to me, asking,
even urging, their agreement as witnesses who knew and understood
from their own experience the self-evident truth" (1991, 172). The rhetorical questions that punctuated Baka Lufu's story were thus ways in which
her story was opened up to others—*including the dead*—drawing them all
into a dialogical process of reconstruction and moral redefinition (173).
Veena Das has made a very similar observation in her essay about survivors of the riots that followed the assassination of Indira Ghandi in Delhi
in 1984. Though the subject who narrates the story is always an individual
woman or child, the personal voice is always "interwoven in a polyphony
of other voices … the voices of women as they sat huddled in camps or
parks, mourning the loss of loved ones, of homes, of things they had built
together" (1990, 346). But without stories, *without listening to one another's
stories*, there can be no recovery of the social, no overcoming of our separateness, no discovery of common ground or common cause. Nor can the
subjective be made social. There can only remain a residue of tragic events,
as disconnected from each other as the individuals who have experienced
their social lives engulfed and fractured by them.

There is a subtle form of discrimination that allows some stories to
be told but not others. Perhaps it is easier for us to deal with stories of
nation-building and cultural identity than stories in which nationality,
culture, and identity are obliterated by the sheer complexity and critical mass of lived experience—as in the stories refugees have to tell. Perhaps such stories are too harrowing, too anachronistic. Not built around
familiar concepts, and leading to no salvationist conclusions, they challenge our cultural ways of framing meaning. Sometimes such stories call
our social mores into question, first, because refugee stories require for
their completion not only our willingness to listen but our active involvement in refugee affairs, second because they imply a criticism of the language games of academe. But accommodating such radically different
views, ourselves seen from elsewhere, is one of the ways we can escape
the intellectualism and Eurocentricism that has always dogged our discipline, and foster a pluralism in which otherness is not reduced to cultural
identity or knowledge, but is seen in terms of lived experiences that, with
imagination, anyone anywhere may find a way of understanding from
within his or her own humanity.

Trauma stuns, diminishes, and petrifies. The shocking suddenness of refugee flight transforms a person almost instantly from subject to object. "Who" he or she was is eclipsed by the question of "what" he or she has become: mere physicality, a category term, an objective label—a refugee. For these reasons, the critical question for the refugee, and for anyone writing about refugee experience, is an existential one: how can this immobilization, reduction, and nullification of the person be resisted and transfigured, so that self-determination and power is regained. My thesis is that constructing, relating, and sharing stories is basic to this reclamation of a person's humanity—of turning object into subject, givenness into choice, what into who. As Hannah Arendt observes: "*Who* somebody is or was we can know only by knowing the story of which he is himself the hero—his biography, in other words; everything else we know of him, including the work he may have produced and left behind, tells us only *what* he is or was" (1958, 186).

DISPLACEMENT, SUFFERING, AND THE CRITIQUE OF CULTURAL FUNDAMENTALISM

> When the state or quasi-state ... and the self-contained subject ... become coeval models of each other, xenophobic nationalism—which is but human subjectivity totalized—is the result.
>
> —E. VALENTINE DANIEL, *Charred Lullabies*

Perhaps at no other time in recent history have the concepts of culture and nationality been so fervently fetishized. Though Benedict Anderson notes that "nation-ness is the most universally legitimate value in the political life of our time" (1983, 12), the same could be said of culture, just as, not so long ago, the same was true of race—a word that "culture" now euphemizes (Kahn 1989; Appadurai 1996a, 12; Wikan 1999, 58). In emphasizing bounded belonging and safety in numbers, such concepts are, of course, linked to widespread anxieties among marginalized peoples about their ability to grasp and influence the global forces overwhelming their lifeworlds. While globalization has become an empowering myth of the affluent West—where the celebration of market rationalism, information superhighways, and the retributive justice of smart weaponry now complements imperialist myths of manifest destiny and white supremacy—cultural and ethnic identity have become the catchwords for many of those disadvantaged by colonial and postcolonial inequalities in the distribution of power. In emergent notions of cultural identity and national sovereignty, powerless, dispersed, and disparaged peoples imagine that they recapture something of the integrity and authenticity they feel that they have *personally* lost. "There is no salvation without culture," observed Maina Karanja, a former Mau Mau fighter and now spiritual leader of the Kikuyu Nine Clans (Kenda Muiyuru) sect in Kenya. "If we truly want to be saved we must … go back to our traditional ways" (cited in Gough 1999, 3).

This point is crucial. Although concepts of culture, race, and nation denote abstract, imagined, and collective subjectivities, their meaning is inextricably connected to the experiences of individual subjects. This does not mean that nationality is "essentially a belief—a deep sense of conviction concerning one's personal identity (Davies 1981, 9), but rather that the national imaginary operates with *both* "we" and "I" forms (Hage 1996, 478). Thus, notions of nationhood draw on images of intimate homelife and parental protection (Hage 1996), or hold out the promise of personal salvation, significance, and continuity (Anderson 1983, 18–19), while simultaneously evoking ideas of belonging that transcend individual subjectivities. This fetishization of the nation may be understood as a totalization of human subjectivity (Daniel 1997, 352) that, by fusing the personal and the social, the biographical and the historical, provides alienated individuals with an empowering sense of solidarity with others.

Underlying such quests for solidarity and belonging lies a universal human assumption that each person's individual being not only *is* but *must be* embedded in collective fields of being that outrun it in both space and time, such that the actions, words, and energies of everyone are consummated in his or her relations with the many. This need to embed one's own being within some general, transcendent field of being helps us understand the functional necessity of such category terms as cosmos, culture, society, world, and genealogy in human thought, as well as the need to know one's origins and one's fate. The search for roots or ancestry, and for ends and afterlives, is less a search for determinate moments when the ego emerges from nothingness or disappears into the void—moments that have no before or after—than for extensions or beginnings in a time and place *before one's own*, and for continuity in a time and place that *outlives and outlasts one's own singular existence*. Stories that link microcosm and macrocosm provide these crossings between the singular and the trans-subjective.

In what follows I focus on the way that storytelling works out a rough synthesis of individual and iconic subjectivities, such that self comes to be identified with and experienced as coterminous with one's culture, history, race, or nation. My critical aim is, however, twofold. First I examine the conditions under which storytelling becomes polemical. My focus here is on reification—the ways in which general knowledge claims are made on the basis of narrated events, and the *process* of storytelling becomes eclipsed by the *product* that the story is pressured into yielding—a moral point, an irrefutable argument, a doctrinal conclusion. Bruce Kapferer's observation is pertinent: "Nationalism makes culture into an object and a thing of worship. Culture is made the servant of power" (1988, 209). My second aim is to examine the opposite tendency, whereby storytelling remains a particular and private matter, unable to bridge the gap between the I and the we, or negotiate general understandings on the basis of individual experience.

Culture in the Discourse of the Other

Much has been written about the ways in which the culture concept has been substantialized and territorialized within anthropology (Appadurai 1996a, 1996b; Dresch 1995; Gupta and Ferguson 1992; Herzfeld 1997; Stolcke 1995). My concern here is with the ways in which iconic terms such as culture, race, and nation are deployed among the people with whom anthropologists have customarily worked. Though culture may be said in both cases to sanctify sweeping generalizations based on spurious notions of primordiality, homogeneity, coherence, and timelessness (Abu-Lughod 1993, 6–15), these modes of identifying and othering tend to differ subtly in academic and indigenous discourse.

At its inception as a science in the late nineteeth century, anthropology borrowed the bourgeois concept of culture from German romanticism (Jackson 1989, 120–21), and the history of our discipline during the twentieth century may be seen as a succession of critical revisions in which empirical findings and polemical repositionings have led us to purge our discourse of the idealist connotations of the culture concept. Nowadays, we accept without question that culture is invented as well as inherited, contested as well as received, textual as well as contextual, territorialized as well as deterritorialized, material as well as mental, practical as well as discursive, embodied as well as ideal, high as well as low, local as well as global, and that the difference between tribal societies and modern societies cannot be reduced to a distinction between superstition and science or irrationality and reason, and that knowledge is always tied to historical, ethical, political, and practical imperatives.

It is ironic, however, that as these deconstructions of the culture concept have taken place within anthropology, there has been a substantive conceptual shift among political conservatives toward a xenophobic rhetoric of cultural fundamentalism that excludes immigrants and foreigners from the European nation state (Stolcke 1995, 4), while, ironically, at the same time, many of the people among whom anthropologists traditionally worked have embraced the idea of culture and begun using it, also in an essentialistic, exclusionary sense, for their own counter-hegemonic ends. As anthropologists repudiate place-based notions of culture and explore "post-culturalist" positions (Rapport 2001), many indigenous peoples have become "deeply involved in constructing cultural contexts which bear many resemblances to such cultural entities" (Olwig and Hastrup 1997, 11; cf. Sahlins 1999; Wikan 1999).

In Australia, Aboriginal activists have adopted the culture concept to denote a venerable and unique "spiritual" heritage, tied to land, language, and collective identity, i.e. Aboriginality. In Aotearoa New Zealand, many Maori speak of their culture in a similar vein as *taonga* (treasure)—a sacred heritage that has survived the brutality of conquest and colonial rule. And throughout Melanesia and Micronesia, culture—in the symbolic form of *kastom*—has become central to the counter-colonial discourse of identity (Keesing 1982). In all these cases, we are dealing with abstract and ambiguous terms—Aboriginality, *Maoritanga*, *kastom*—whose appeal lies less in their correspondence to any objective reality than in their strategic value for mediating private and public realms. The culture concept thus functions like a ceremonial mask, bringing together idiosyncratic and abstract features in a single gestalt.

One sees this clearly in many of the stories submitted to the *National Inquiry into the Separation of Aboriginal and Torres Strait Islander Children from their Familes*. In some cases the story of losing one's mother and one's birthright is experienced as a "wound that will not heal" or a hole that cannot be filled—"something missing" that makes a person "an empty shell" (HREOC, 177, 178, 210). As one witness noted: "I wish I was blacker. I wish I had a language. I wish I had a culture" (Bird 1998, 109). In other stories, however, reunion with one's lost birth mother presages the recovery of a general sense of *cultural* belonging.[31] As one person put it, "For the first time I actually felt like I had roots that went down into the ground. But not only into the ground—that went through generations" (HREOC, 242). Another observed, "I started taking interest in Koori stuff. I decided at least to learn the culture" (Bird 1998, 77). And after meeting her mother and family for the first time, Jeanette Sinclair said she found it easier to identify as an Aboriginal:

> I had somewhere I belonged. That was really great and it was like that hole you walked around with had been totally filled. The first time I went back, that's what it was like although I realise now it can never be really filled in. Ninety per cent of the hole can be filled in but I think you are always missing that ten per cent. That's just my personal opinion. You can never get the ten per cent back because you missed out on the bonding, the fondling and the cuddling. Also you've missed out on building relationships over a period of time; you can't create a relationship out of thin air (cited in Edwards and Read 1989, 191–92).

Still other stories document the ways in which childhood flight from the culture of one's adoption—expressed in unassuageable longings to be with one's original family, in fantasies of family reunion and of rescue, and in running away from home—become transformed into a *political* repudiation of the dominant *culture*. Indeed, it may be that because the *National Inquiry* was nationally publicized that stories of personal grief occasionally took on this kind of ethnic and political edge, the logic being that in negating the culture that negated you, you magically affirmed your true birthright, your original being.

What is interesting about this mode of affirmation is its subtle shift of emphasis from a specific biographical situation to the situation of Aboriginal people in general:

> I think compensation for me would be something like a good land acquisition where I could call my own and start the cycle of building good strong foundations for Aboriginal families (cited in HREOC, 298).

> I've learned skills in my life but I have never lost sight of the fact that I'm an Aborigine first and foremost. That is why I am working in the Aboriginal Medical Service. I've finished my training, I'm very proud of that. I've

achieved something. I wanted my poor old mother to be so proud of me … I wanted her to know and to understand why I'm working with my people" (Nancy de Vries, cited in Edwards and Read 1989, 193–94).

It is in this generalizing of subjectivity from self to society, this shift from personal story to shared history, that a political discourse begins to emerge—a progression that Ghassan Hage speaks of as one from "homely" to "sovereign" belonging (1996). Indeed, when one compares the stolen children stories published by Edwards and Read in 1989 with the testimonies and stories told before the *National Inquiry* in 1997 there is a noticeable increase in the degree to which Aboriginal people frame "personal" experiences in "political" terms—a reflection both of the way in which the issue of the stolen generation has entered public and national consciousness in the intervening years and of the extent to which many of the "stolen generation" have moved from addressing their own separation and loss to helping others deal with theirs (Edwards and Read 1989, 193). But generally speaking, the stories told to the *National Inquiry* are stories that remain collapsed in privacy—a function, partly, of the Inquiry itself, which "needed" tragic stories to make its case for social justice, and partly of the marginality of Aboriginal people in Australia, where land rights, recognition, and "sovereign belonging" are still to be achieved. As one witness put it, "all we've got is sort of ourselves" (HREOC, 239).

Us and Them

In order to explore the culture concept in its most iconic and essentialized form, let us consider the following story from Aotearoa/New Zealand. Drawn from a popular magazine, the story concerns a young Maori couple who, like many other young Maori, have revived traditional Maori facial tattoo (*moko*) as a way of affirming their cultural identity.

Most married couples show their commitment to each other by wearing wedding bands but Bay of Plenty husband and wife Chris and Taukiri Natana have more obvious symbols of their love. The pair, from Ruatoki, have moko on their faces. They say that, as well as empowering them in their fight for Maori sovereignty and strengthening their link with family and ancestors, the moko signifies their unity as a couple.

"To me, the moko is showing who you are; what culture you are; what you believe in," says Chris. "Just as other cultures wear a ring around their finger to represent their unity, this represents our unity, our oneness, on our faces. It's been drilled there to stay" (*NZ Women's Weekly*, May 26, 1997, 39).

Chris Natana's comments help us understand that as a cultural icon, *moko* implies a nesting set of identifications, encompassing personal and transpersonal frames of reference. At one extreme *moko* symbolizes a set of unities—of the couple, of the family, of the *iwi*, and of Maori; at the other extreme it symbolizes a distinction between Anglo-Celtic and Maori culture. In fact, it was this implication that most concerned the parents of the young Maori couple, who argued that it would be seen as "confrontational and threatening."

However, the question I want to broach is less concerned with these symbolic strategies for achieving unity despite difference (the exchange of rings and *moko* that weld, as with the classical symbolon, two halves or hearts into one), than with the potentially divisive and reified polarities that these strategies make use of. While the aim of invoking "cultural identity" may be to transform old hierarchies of dominance and subordination into new egalitarian alignments, this is seldom all that occurs. Just as European bourgeois notions of culture tend to imply what Roy Wagner (1975, 21) calls an "opera-house" conception of civilized sensibilities that stand in contrast with and bring into relief a notion of plebian taste or "popular" culture, so current uses of the term culture in Australia, Melanesia, and the Pacific tend to iconicize tradition as superior to modernity. The result of invoking culture is not therefore an ironing out of difference in the name of some notion of common humanity, but the radical inversion of existing inequalities. As Frantz Fanon pointed out, decolonization inevitably entails a "complete and absolute substitution"—a radical reordering of the world in which the last become the first and the first become the last (1968, 29–30). Thus, in Australia, many Aboriginal activists use quantitative European chronology rather than indigenous mythology to emphasize the length of time that Aboriginal people have inhabited the continent. The image of 40,000 years of continuous settlement then underwrites ideologies about the depth of people's spiritual relationship with country, the antiquity of art and ritual, and the primordial power of Aboriginal values. In Aotearoa, New Zealand, many Maori also use firstness as a powerful rhetorical figure—an expression of what Liisa Malkki calls "romantic autochthonization" (1995, 52–63): Maori are *tangata whenua*, people of the land, having settled the country one thousand years before pakeha arrived. The primordial, venerable character of indigenous culture then gives force to the argument that Maori people are wiser than pakeha, more eco-sensitive, more caring in their family lives, more attuned to community. As Maori activist, Kathie Irwin, puts it: "Pakeha culture, derived as it is from Western civilization, is primarily concerned with the rights of the individual. Maori society is primarily concerned with the rights of the group, which provide the context within which the rights of the individual are considered" (Irwin 1993, 299).

Hearing such polarizing generalizations, liberal pakeha sometimes accuse Maori of "reversed racism," which it is not, at least as long as the discourse is not at the service of power elites but remains a rhetoric of the powerless struggling to regain some sense of *turangawaewae*, some sense of autonomy and self-determination in a country where, historically, they have been second-class citizens. The word racism, like the term rape, refers to violently asymmetrical situations in which the strong dominate the weak; the terms simply do not apply in reverse. Still, I want to ask whether this kind of iconic othering and cultural fundamentalism—"strategic essentialism" as Schor and Weed call it (1994)—is in fact compatible with reconciliation and pluralism.

My feeling is that any kind of identity thinking (Adorno 1973) is insidious, because like all reification, it elides the line that separates words and worlds, language and life. By reducing the world to simplistic, generalized category oppositions such as Us versus Them, such thinking tends to become self-perpetuating, and admits neither synthesis nor resolution. Always defensive and idealistic—as is all magical thought—it resists empirical test, fearing that direct experience will weaken, complicate, or confound its premises. This is why I want to propose that when popular thought promulgates naturalized and localized definitions of identity anthropologists must place this essentializing strategy in historical perspective and social context and guard against adopting it themselves.

Before elaborating further on anthropology's role in "denaturalizing identity" (Daniel 1997, 351), let me critically review a second case of identity thinking in contemporary Aotearoa/New Zealand.

In an article on immigration policies in New Zealand, published in 1995, Ranginui Walker observes that according to the second clause of the Treaty of Waitangi, the Crown guaranteed the "sovereign rights" of chiefs over "their lands, homes and treasured possessions" (1995, 282).[32] On this basis, the High Court of New Zealand found, in October 1987, that the government's Fisheries Management System breached customary Maori fishing rights under the Treaty. Subsequent negotiations between the treaty partners—Maori and the Crown—ended in settlement. Ignoring the division and dissent that actually plagued this case, Walker argues that this kind of negotiation between equal partners should be seen in "all fields of human endeavour" in Aotearoa (284). But it has conspicuously not been applied in the field of immigration policy, where the Crown has decided unilaterally to admit 25,000 immigrants a year from ninety-seven countries around the world. Although under article one of the Treaty, immigrant intakes are a Crown responsibility and do not require consultation with Maori in every case, Walker argues that the "original charter for immigration into New Zealand is in the Preamble of the Treaty" (284) and limits immigration to the countries of Europe, Australia, and the United Kingdom. Any deviation from this agreement requires consultation with Maori—a stricture reinforced by the Human Rights Commission. It is biculturalism, not multiculturalism, that New Zealand needs (286). However, Walker says, there appears to be collusion between corporate business interests and the Crown to use immigration to counter "the Maori claim to first-nation status as *tangata whenua* (people of the land)" (286). As *tangata whenua*, Walker argues, Maori have "prior right of discovery and millennial occupation of the land" and are not therefore immigrants in the same sense that non-Maori are, and should not be compared (as they are, incidentally, in recent books by two pakeha academics—Anne Salmond and James Bellich) with the Europeans who colonized the country under force of arms in the mid-nineteenth century or the Pacific rim immigrants of the postwar period. Moreover, as *tangata whenua*, Maori have the right to reject migrants from any culture or nation that is not specified in the Treaty they signed with the British Crown in 1840. Specifically, this means Asian migrants, who form about half the 21,927 migrants who entered New Zealand in 1990. Particularly abhorrent to Walker is the way in which New Zealand citizenship has been commoditized and Asians welcomed to New Zealand simply because they bring capital into the country. The effect of this policy will be to marginalize poor and unskilled Maoris, to increase Maori unemployment, and to produce a neo-colonial situation in which the country's assets, resources, and land are sold—like citizenship—to "foreigners" (302).

I concede that Walker's intention is not, like Pauline Hanson's in Australia, to demonize wealthy "Asians," though the designation itself is inaccurate and perjorative. Nonetheless, everything about Ranginui Walker's article conspires to reinforce non-negotiable distinctions based on culture, history, wealth, and ethnicity. While the distinctions purport to be ways of protecting Maori interests and *our* Treaty partnership, they leave little room for revising our views as to who and what are "foreign" and antithetical to New Zealand. Though Walker's avowed concern is with "wealthy Asians," his Treaty-based argument for deciding who can and cannot be admitted to New Zealand effectively excludes a vast proportion of global humanity, including poor Asians from Vietnam, Laos, and Cambodia, as well as recently-arrived refugees from such troubled countries as Iraq, Somalia, and Bosnia. Indeed, Walker uses the Treaty in bad faith—as a historically sacrosanct charter for deciding which potential migrants to New Zealand are compatible with Maori cultural interests, and which are inimical—since he admits (283) that the Treaty has *already* undergone "deconstruction" and hermeneutic renegotiation as a result of Waitangi Tribunal hearings, and has now clarified the meaning of Maori sovereignty *not as it was understood by the Crown in 1840* but as it is necessary for New Zealanders building a bicultural partnership in the late twentieth century.

Using culture ethnocentrically and essentialistically is always problematic; it always entails demarcation, denial, division, and exclusion, and, as such, visits the danger of inhumanity and intolerance upon us. Multiculturalism may redraw the line to include more people than were hitherto included—as Te Papa, the national museum of New Zealand, shows, with its displays that incorporate Pakeha, Pacific Island, Chinese, Maori, and European peoples as part and parcel of "our place"—but as long as culture is invoked as the discursive means of drawing and redrawing boundaries, vast areas of human experience and reality are going to be suppressed, abolished, and ostracized. And always one will be haunted, for good historical reasons, by the possibility that culture will extend itself logically, through a "horripilation," as E. Valentine Daniel calls it, born of its perennial insecurity and fright, into an ideology of nationhood built around notions of true belonging and true believing that demand as a condition of these truths that those who do not belong, those who do not believe, those who are outside the truth, be exterminated as threats to the nation's integrity (Hage 1996).

Thinking Ourselves beyond the Nation[33]

Let me now pursue this pragmatist critique of culture by exploring some recent anthropological research on social suffering in which the language of cultural essence and national identity is annulled.

As Elaine Scarry observes, people who have endured extreme pain speak of its particularity, its unsharability, and its resistance to language (Scarry 1985). Pain reduces a person to his or her visceral bodiliness. One's whole being is subtracted from one's ordinary personality, identity, and routines, even from the family and friends that defined one's intersubjective world. One becomes merely a vulnerable bodyself that either functions or malfunctions, that either lives or dies, depending on forces outside one's control, and despite one's worth, wealth, or cultural identity. Pain makes questions of identity trivial. As Maja Povrzanović notes of the Yugoslavian war, while the "grammar" of nationalism figured significantly in the discourse of international commentators and national leaders, the "forgotten majority" of civilians were struggling "to defend not primarily their 'national territory' but the right to continue their lives in terms of gender, occupation, class, or place of residence *and not be reduced to their national identities*" (2000, 154, emphasis added). One is reminded of E. Valentine Daniel's observation about torture victims: "At this level of experiencing pain it appears that one is unlikely to find any significant effect of culture" (1996, 142).

Ranginui Walker privileges the politics of cultural identity over all other ways of thinking about human imperatives, experiences, and rights. This is not because he is hard-hearted, or mindless of the personal plight of immigrants and refugees; it is because he shares the conservative view—

albeit for non-rightwing reasons—that a discourse built around solidary, centralizing notions such as culture, nationhood and identity better serves political ends than an experience-near discourse centered on pain, confusion, and rootlessness. While the former promotes collective transcendence, the latter lapses into subjectivity, and too easily individuates and psychologizes the phenomenon of loss. But there is evidence that diaspora and social suffering may indeed provide the critical environment in which new and vital forms of pluralism emerge. Thus, it is interesting that many urban Maori—children of the urban migrations of the 1950s and '60s: "people of the four winds" (*nga hau e wha*)—have repudiated *iwi* centered notions of identity, solely constructed around the icons of land, genealogy, and language (see Kernot 1972, 64–65). Dispowerered and disaffected though they may be, many young Maori refuse to see Maoritanga as their salvation; indeed, they regard such "cultural" trappings as abstract, artificial, antiquated, and irrelevant (Meijl 1996; Poata-Smith 1996). What they seek is not an identity but a life.

Some of the most compelling evidence for the *dépassement* of nation and culture comes from studies of refugees. Consider the case of recent Tamil refugees in the UK. Before the civil war in Sri Lanka, Tamil immigrants and expatriots in Britain set great store by their cultural heritage, their national history, and their language. For the last wave of migrants, however—mainly refugees and asylum seekers—quite the contrary is true. These people are "nation-averse"; they have "opted out of the project of the nation" (Daniel 1997, 311). While previous generations of Tamil immigrants emphasized a "land-bound" notion of nationhood, the last wave have given up on solid boundaries and claims to territory, either at home or in the UK; the future, for them, is fluid—a matter of strategic opportunism and constant movement (328–29). "You ask me about Tamil nationalism," one refugee said to E. Valentine Daniel. "There is only Tamil internationalism"—by which he meant moving about the globe, seizing whatever opportunities arose, taking whatever initiatives one could, to survive. There is no going back. "The only past they knew or cared about—and did not want to be caught in—was the recent past of war, rape, torture, and death that they had just escaped" (343–44). Valentine Daniel speaks of a "disaggregation of identity," a "diaspora of the spirit," an indifference to the very idea of the nation state, reflective of the way Tamils now participate in a world of shared suffering rather than cultivate a belief in a common homeland or history. Daniel's findings may be compared to those of Ann-Belinda Steen Preis, who has made an intensive study of the videotapes in circulation among Sri Lankan Tamil refugees in the West. Struck by the fact that these videos do not project any unified, standard image of Tamil culture, Steen Preis makes use of Daniel Sibony's argument that "in the current malaise of identity, both subjective and collective, where boundaries vacillate and identity sometimes collapses, sometimes condenses, the idea of difference is no longer satisfactory to account for this stir; it is too simple and too congealed" (1997, 88). Empirically, one confronts "globally unfolding 'mutations' of identity" or a "myriad of bolting identities" in which territorialized notions of culture, having become untenable, are replaced by open-ended *questions* of belonging, broached through seemingly contradictory images of dispersal *and* reunion, continuity *and* discontinuity, attachment *and* loss (96–98). These studies suggest that the marginalization of "culture" in migration literature as "irrelevent or ideological," which Gillian Bottomley has noted (1992, 71; cf. Malkki 1992), may thus reflect a marginalization of the concept in migrant experience itself.

> "There's no such thing as 'England' any more," declared a young white reggae fan in "the ethnically chaotic neighbourhood of Balsall Heath in Birmingham." 'This is the Caribbean! ... Nigeria! ... There is no England, man. This is what is coming. Balsall Heath is the center of the melting pot, 'cos all I ever see when I go out is half-Arab, half-Pakistani, half-Jamaican, half-Scottish, half-Irish. I know 'cos I am [half Scottish/half Irish] ... who am I? ... Tell me who I belong to? They criticise me, the good old England. Alright, where do I belong? You know, I was brought up with blacks, Pakistanis, Africans, Asians, everything, you name it ... who do I belong to? ... I'm just a broad person. The earth is mine ..."(from Hebdige 1987, 158–59, cited in Gupta and Ferguson 1992, 10).

I now turn to two Central African examples of what Barbara Myerhoff has called "accidental communitas" (Myerhoff 1975; cf. Malkki 1997, 91). In her research among Hutu refugees in rural western Tanzania, Liisa Malkki draws a contrast between refugees in the camps and those who dispersed and settled in and around the township of Kigoma on Lake Tanganyika. While the camp refugees define themselves as a nation in exile, recollecting "traces and afterlives" (Malkki 1997, 93) in order to nurture their dream of returning to a homeland where they truly belonged, the "town refugees" have sought ways "of assimilating and manipulating multiple identities—identities derived or 'borrowed' from the social context of the township" (Malkki 1992, 36). This has engendered a cosmopolitan, creolized sense of self that celebrates its adaptiveness and "impurity" (37). Concludes Malkki, "deterritorialization and identity are intimately linked" (38). But equally critical to this link is social suffering and the struggle to survive.

Consider the multiplex and opportunistic world of the modern African city. Academic or ideological antinomies of tradition and modernity, or of synthesis or syncretism, fail to cover the empirical complexity of such life-worlds. In Kinshasa, for example, strategies of adaptation and the ethos of community reflect the quotidian struggle against poverty and crime (Devisch 1995), and cannot be understood in terms of external concepts such as Europeanization, Zairianization (through the state-sponsored *Recours à l'authenticité* (Recourse to Authenticity)), Traditionalism, *or even a combination of these terms.* If there is any symbol that unites the disparate domains of household, market, street, church, and politics, it is maternal (1995, 625–27)—an icon that immediately recalls the symbolic centrality of the Madonna among poor Italian migrants to the New World. As Robert Orsi notes in his seminal work on the everyday religious life of Italian migrants in East Harlem, domus and neighborhood were "the source of meaning and morals" (1985, 75). Indeed, "These people could not understand the proud italianità of Italian Harlem's middle-class immigrant professionals who had managed to find some identification with the Italian nation. *The immigrants did not know an Italian nation—they only knew the domus of their paesi*" (78, emphasis added).

What is at play in these multi-ethnic contexts are the exigencies of survival, not ideology.[34] Quotidian life involves a kind of perpetual bricolage in which whatever is at hand is taken up, tried out, rejected or put to use in order to cope, in order to endure. As with people in crisis anywhere, life is ad hoc, addressed anew each day, pieced together painfully, with few consoling illusions. To get through the day, or through the night until morning, little or no thought is given to what is true, meaningful, or correct in any logical or ideological sense; one's focus is on what works, on what is of use, on what helps one survive. Under such circumstances, cultural and national identity, imagined or imminent, are, as Orsi notes above, luxuries the poor cannot afford.

I do not want to make a case for internationalism over nationalism; both may be effective, if magical, strategies for coping with powerlessness. Neither do I want to argue that a people's degree of suffering or dispersal may always explain why they abandon territorialized notions of identity. But though we cannot confidently pin down the *determinants* of alternative refugee responses to loss we can evaluate their *consequences*.

I have argued that cultural fundamentalism, whether nostalgic or utopian, risks setting groups off one from the other on the basis of differential rights that reflect different origins, essences, and aspirations. The result may be that refugees—the last-arrived, the least-powerful, and most lost—are made victims of secondary colonialism. In Aotearoa, New Zealand, for example, so absorbed have Maori and the Crown become in creating the apparatus and protocols of a bicultural state, that habits of radical othering, disempowerment, disparagement, and prejudice—once directed toward indigenous people—are fast becoming projected onto new migrants, whose voices of protest and claims for cultural recognition and respect often go unheeded and unheard.[35] "Why do you wear your national costume in public places?" an Anglo neighbor recently asked a Somali migrant. "For the same reason you do," the Somali replied. "But we don't," retorted the neighbor. But of course we do, and it is only our blindness to the way in which cultural symbols are caught up in discriminatory power relations that permits such a question to be asked. Like clothes, cuisine, speech, and belief, skin-color frequently focuses this unspoken sense of refractory difference. Radhika Mohanram, a Tamil-New Zealander, states it powerfully: "The black immigrant disturbs the biracial Maori-Pakeha body by revealing the hierarchy of bodies. In this hierarchy, Pakeha come first, Maori second, and the black immigrant a distant third" (1998, 27). In secondary colonialism, the denigrated third becomes the dumping ground for both the erstwhile subaltern (the Maori) and the erstwhile elite (Pakeha).

However, it is the experience of the least powerful—people like refugees—and of the most marginal—who may define the very grounds on which a pluralistic (rather than a multicultural) society can be created, and provide our most trenchant criticism of the language of cultural and national difference. Let me consider several examples in which categorical identity gives way to the kind of experience-based "diasporic pluralism" (Appadurai 1996a, 173) I am talking about here.

In contemporary Britain, people of "mixed race" (the very term is a pleonasm) are fast becoming the rule rather than the exception. Sebastian Naidoo, whose father is South African Indian and whose mother is white and British is not untypical of this exasperated generation. Presented with questionnaires that require one to specify one's ethnic identity, Sebastian sometimes checks "Indian," sometimes "Other," but once "I just scrawled 'human' over the whole lot. I wanted to make fun of their questions and show them how arbitrary their racial categories were" (Younge 1997, 23). The same problem of identity thinking arises in cross-cultural marriages. Of one such marriage—between a Romanian-born Jew and a Hindu—the Indian wife commented, "I don't see cultural differences; I can only see him." Another British-born woman married to an Australian-born Chinese husband spoke in a similar vein: "In day-to-day life we tend to think that 'my perspective is my perspective', it has nothing to do with race or culture. I hope our children will be interested in both cultures and get the best of both worlds" (Freeman 1997, 11).

Another way of getting beyond identity thinking is suggested by the novelist Edmund White. In a perceptive essay in which he contrasts his experience of living in the US and in France, White observes that while Americans emphasize a "politics of identity," foregrounding and focusing their particular affiliations, local communities, and special interests, the French extol the virtues of centrism. "In France there is no Jewish novel, no black novel, no gay novel; Jews, blacks and gays, of course, write about their lives, but they would be offended if they were discussed with regard to their religion, ethnicity or gender" (White 1993, 127). White's observations remind me of James Baldwin's account of why he left the US for France. "I wanted to prevent myself from becoming *merely* a Negro; or, even merely a Negro writer. I wanted to find out in what way the *specialness* of my experience could be made to connect me with other people instead of dividing me from them (Baldwin 1961, 17).

The problem with identity terms and collective nouns such as culture, nation, race, or tribe is the same problem that inheres in any discursive strategy that seeks to convert subjects of experience into objects of knowledge.[36] Such strategies are inevitably reductive. In transmuting the open-endedness and ambiguity of lived experiences into hermetic and

determinate items of knowledge, persons tend to become epiphenom-
enal instances, examples, or expressions of reified categories. The truth is,
however, that it is the phenomenal interplay between persons and such
categories—between the confusion and flux of immediate experience on
the one hand, and finite forms and fixed ideas on the other—that constitutes the empirical reality of human life, and should constitute the object
of scientific understanding. This is why I insist that culture be seen as
an idiom or vehicle of intersubjective life, but not its foundation or final
cause. Though this view echoes the conclusions of writers like Appadurai,
who see the task of contemporary ethnography as the "unraveling of a
conundrum: what is the nature of locality as a lived experience in a glo-
balized, deterritorialized world?" (1996a, 52), I do not think the resolution of this conundrum can come from simply demonstrating the ways in
which the cultural imaginary is conditioned by global forms of electronic
media and mass migration *unless these phenomena are existentialized*—that
is, unless they are seen, like culture itself, as specific instances of an intersubjective dialectic that has, from time immemorial and in countless societies, reflected the human struggle to strike a balance between autonomy
and anonymity, so that no one person or class ever arrogates agency so
completely to itself that others are reduced to the status of mere things,
or creatures of circumstance. Every person demands, as a condition of
being human, that he or she have some say over his or her own existence, some place in the world where his or her actions count. Despite the
impinging or competing demands of others, and the overwhelming force
of that which simply happens *to* us without our cognizance or choice, each
of us expects to call some of the shots, to resist being merely a piano key
moved by the will of others or the inscrutable workings of fate, and move
as an equal among equals, in a world that is felt to be as much one's own
as it is beyond oneself.

PART II

RETURNS

PREAMBLE

Year in and year out, the Western media seize upon some third world country at war with itself, and regale us with images of savagery and chaos. So Rwanda succeeds Cambodia, Bosnia succeeds Rwanda, and then, full circle, we are returned to the original heart of darkness—the Congo. Momentarily, in January 1999, that "heart of darkness" became Sierra Leone. "Freetown is burning," wrote *Time* correspondent Edward Barnes. "The sky is barely visible through the gray clouds of smoke curling up from the eastern side of the city. The occasional finger of white African sunlight that pokes through the haze falls on piles of dead bodies. The soft sands of Lumley beach, which sits on the north edge of town, are blanketed with dead soldiers, and the tranquil bay that lies between downtown and the airport is an oily, grisly mess, teeming with floating bodies and body parts (Barnes 1999, 32).

For ten years I had watched from a distance as Sierra Leone descended into civil war, all the while hoping that the remoteness of the north would protect the people with whom I had lived and worked from the violence engulfing the south. In January 1999, my wishful thinking was shattered by an article in the *Guardian Weekly* concerning events in the Kuranko village of Kondembaia:

> Fina Kamara, a slim, quiet 28-year-old, occasionally caressed the stump of her left arm as she told of the attack in April [1998] at her village of Kondembaia. She had come home from planting peanuts when "suddenly we heard gunfire," she said.
>
> Armed men appeared, seizing Kamara, her daughter N'Damba, 6, and seven other villagers. They gathered the villagers at a large tree, and "one man told us that 'since you want a civilian government, we're going to cut off your hands or kill you,'" Kamara said. Another man announced that they would start with N'Damba, and called, "Little girl, come here." But N'Damba cried and refused, Kamara said, speaking in the national language known as Krio. So "men grabbed her out of my lap and stretched

her out on the ground," Kamara recited slowly. They held her arm down on a big root of the tree and a machete swept down, severing the arm below the elbow. Amid a scene of screaming, blood and confusion, Kamara remembers being seized next, and then the blow that severed her arm. Thrust aside as the men wrestled down their next victims, Kamara ran to her daughter and fled the village, holding the bleeding stumps of their arms. N'Damba "started to faint and asked for water," but when Kamara approached a house to seek help, an alarmed resident threatened to kill her if she entered.

Kamara said she strapped her daughter to her back, alongside her unin-jured infant son, "and I carried them out into the bush. I found a place to hide them, and then went out to the road" to find help. She was lucky. She met her husband and an uncle, who carried her and her daughter, getting them to a nearby town for treatment within two days. Refugees told of seeing rebels chop off villagers' ears or buttocks. Many victims have given coinciding accounts of rebels forcing residents into buildings or wrapping them in mosquito nets before setting them on fire (Rupert 1999, 12).

I had friends in Kondembaia, including Keti Ferenke Koroma and Kinya Fina Marah, whose stories I had published in *Allegories of the Wilderness* (1982). My first thought was that I should go to Sierra Leone—as if my being there would make a difference. But this salvationist impulse seldom amounts to anything more than a magical manipulation of one's own emotions, an attempt to screen out the suffering of others through a self-serving empathic identification with them. No one is helped by this, nothing is changed. My thoughts then turned to friends in Freetown, particularly S. B. Marah, who had been Leader of the House since the Nigerian-led ECOMOG force ousted the military junta in March 1998 and restored Ahman Tejan Kabbah's civilian government to power. Despite maintaining its hold on the capital after the "battle of Freetown" in March 1998 and "Operation Burn Freetown" in January 1999, the government was powerless to prevent rebel control of the interior. Given the close identification in national consciousness of S. B. Marah, his party (SLPP), and the Kuranko area, it was inevitable that erstwhile junta soldiers and their Revolutionary United Front allies would avenge their ouster from power by turning against Kuranko villagers. The atrocities in Kondembaia occurred only a few weeks after the return of Tejan Kabbah from exile. In the political imaginary of the rebels, the bodies of Kuranko individuals became surrogates for the political body that had displaced and defeated them. Severing the hands of defenceless villagers like Fina Kamara and her 6-year-old daughter was a "symbolic" way of destroying the power of those who had, by association, cut off their own access to wealth and power.[37]

What can one do in the face of such events? How can one admit them to one's understanding? How can one act upon them, rather than seek refuge in the blind alleys of one's own subjectivity, one's dismay, outrage, and fear? Wrestling with these questions I remembered the lessons of Kuranko initiation—that life is hard, and hardship is to be endured, if not to avoid the shame of showing weakness to one's peers, then for the sake of one's children—an ethos so deeply different from ours, in which relief from pain and adversity are demanded as a right, and death denied.

Once, in Firawa, when I was suffering from malaria, Chief Sewa paid me a brief visit. He stood at the door of my hut with a group of elders and said simply, *In toro*, you suffer. It was this *recognition* of my suffering that made a difference to me, not the prospect of medical intervention. To suffer in life is not, however, to endure it woefully, self-pityingly, or even stoically. It is to meet adversity head on, to carry it like a headload—as Kuranko say—bearing up under it rather than letting oneself be borne down by it, so that it ceases to be a deadweight, and will is returned from the load carried to the carrier. I can only guess how Fina Kamara and her child will fare. But it seems to me important that her story has been told, that someone from outside Sierra Leone has recorded her voice and relayed it to the world. Whether her story will ever be recounted in her own village, transposed from the status of a personal tragedy into the form of a folk narrative that speaks to the sufferings of others, I do not know. After the terror of the post-Independence civil wars in Zimbabwe, Richard Werbner returned to Matabeleland in 1989 to find a people stunned into silence by the unspeakable experiences they had endured and, in some cases, participated in. The "traditional" and familial stories that people used to tell before the war, with all their heroic emphases, had been displaced by stories of ordeals, victimage, stoicism, and survival (1991, 157–58). Doreen Klassen (personal communication) observed similar changes among elderly Shona women, who were reluctant to tell the stories of their childhood unless these stories could be told as veiled accounts of the historical present—the 1992 drought, the toll of AIDS, the civil war. Perhaps such changes will occur in Kuranko too. One hundred years ago, the Kuranko were decimated in the course of the Maninka warlord Samori Ture's invasion of their homelands, and it is tempting to see in the violent leitmotifs of many traditional folktales traces of this other brutal epoch. History, as Foucault reminds us, is never a matter of writing about the past in terms of the present; it "means writing the history of the present" (1979, 31).

Every place of violence and social suffering becomes, for a time, a place of silence. Deserted villages. Unmarked graves. Stunned survivors, whom words fail. Words are a travesty, for words cannot bring back what has been lost. At such times, traumatic experiences tend to be salted away in subjectivity, too painful and personal to be told. Gradually, however, the passivity and silence in which the trauma endlessly recapitulates itself give way to an impulse to rework one's experience and reclaim control over it. Events that seemed to occur adventitiously are subtly transformed into a story. Storytelling is an empowering act that helps move one from being the world's mere "matter" to an artificer of the world (Hobbes 1978, 19), of experiencing oneself not as a creature of circumstance but as someone who has some claim, some creative say, over how those circumstances may be grasped, borne, and even forgiven. For subsistence farmers in Sierra Leone, the loss of a hand or limb can mean the difference between life and death. But terrible though such losses are, it is rare that human beings fatalistically succumb to loss and *never* get beyond it. It is in this reclamation of being—of the power to speak and act in relation to others and to the world—that we may locate the key to what it means to be human.

This empowering aspect of storytelling is inextricably linked to the sharing and integration of one's experiences with that of others. In recounting one's own story, one salvages and reaffirms, in the face of dispersal, defeat, and death, the *social* bonds that bind one to a community of kindred souls. The politics of storytelling concerns the ways in which this passage from privacy to publicity is effected (Arendt 1958, 33). Two aspects of the political are implicated here. While the first involves a crossing between private and public spheres, the second involves relations between competing forms of discourse—the question of *whose* story will be told, and *which* story will be recognized as true and given legitimacy. Although Hannah Arendt speaks of storytelling as enlarging our understanding and helping to create plural communities, she tends to overlook the fact that all social polities are riven by competing interests, and the truth of stories violently contested. Let us return to media accounts of the civil war in Sierra Leone to dramatize this point. As with much reportage, "stories" about events in Sierra Leone exemplify the fallacy of naive objectivism—the notion that by describing the outward appearance of things, one successfully describes the way those things are *experienced*. Despite its detail—ranging from the "fact" that Sierra Leone is the least-developed nation on earth with an average life expectancy of 34 years, to gruesome reports of rape, mutilation, amputation, and murder—nothing in the *Time* story helps us understand the social and historical background to the war. Rather than point out that the rebellion is a response to decades of corruption and misrule by a succession of state governments and military juntas, the collapse of patrimonialism (Richards 1996, 34–36), and a struggle by marginalized Sierra Leonean youth for a stake in their nation's immense natural wealth, *Time* has recourse to time-honored Western stereotypes of African primitivism. In a scenario that contrasts instinctual rage with rational control, the Nigerian military and the Kabbah government are placed on the side of order (as were, incidentally, the South African mercenaries employed by Executive Outcomes in 1996), while the rebels are made to exemplify a negative consciousness, bereft of rationality, and likened to natural phenomenon (cf. Guha 1983b, 2; Kleinman 1997a). "ECOMOG forces patrolling Freetown's main streets were continually harassed by Kalashnikov wielding teenagers who slipped from dark alleys, machine-gunned them for 15 or 30 seconds and then slipped away again. After sunset the teenagers, many of them high on local hallucinogens, set houses on fire—night candles, they called them—to ward off the fearful dark" (Barnes 1999, 32). The *Time* article closes with a quote from a Nigerian major: "This is a battle between democracy and dementia" (33).

Other news reports of the Sierra Leone troubles during the 1990s recycle a vocabulary that has unfortunately become almost *de rigeur* when reporting on African affairs. Just as *Time* compares the rebels to a wildfire that cannot be extinguished (Barnes 1999, 32), the *Manchester Guardian* speaks of "mindless mutilation" and "savagery … dressed up as revolution by the rebels" (Huband 1996, 1), and *West Africa* magazine describes "gangs" of rebels "infesting" the countryside and imposing "mob rule" (Davies 1998, 566–69).

Constructing the other as alien, irrational, or evil does nothing to bring the other into the light of our understanding. Indeed, this kind of rhetoric of categorical difference disguises the violence that has accompanied the exploitation of Sierra Leone's mineral wealth by foreign corporations in direct collaboration with local elites over a period of thirty years, and overlooks the impoverishment, frustration, and disempowerment that are the very condition of the possibility of the emergence of "demented" and "drug-addled" mobs in a nation where, as one nonplussed emergency-relief specialist put it, "extreme violence is not characteristic" (Barnes 1999, 33). The facts are that for most Sierra Leoneans the price of the staple food, rice, became so inflated during the 1980s that few could afford it. At the same time, petrol and kerosene became either unavailable or unaffordable. State medical services were run down. Teachers and civil servants were paid a pittance if they were paid at all. People starved. It is this structural violence that we must address, a violence born of inequality—pervasive, constant, resentful, and quotidian—a violence that fails to make international news headlines, first, because it is so ubiquitous and banal, second, because it calls into question our discursive habit of exoticizing the third world as a place of tribalism, primitivism, and radical otherness.

Against the romantic and "Freudian" view of violence so common in the West, that sees violence as a sudden, uncontrolled eruption of normally repressed instincts, all the evidence points to violence being a more or less delayed reaction to previous violence, expressing an intersubjective logic of reciprocity and redress. Accordingly, acts of violence are usually nurtured, contemplated, and morally justified in the individual or collective imagination long before they find outward expression. This is why violence must be seen as a product of our humanity, not of some vestigial, instinctual, or repressed animality. The violence of Sierra Leone, Rwanda, Cambodia, Bosnia, and Kosovo may be understood as a kind of "symbolic labour" (Hage 1996, 465) that takes place against a backdrop of injustice, humiliation, and marginalization that, far from being some kind of primitive, local phenomenon, reflects global economic processes (Desjarlais et al 1995, 15–33) that from the 1980s have disadvantaged the poorest nations of the world.

RETALIATION AND RECONCILIATION

Declared to be a telling of deeds that are not of any time, that have not taken place anywhere, the *tali* concern nonetheless the fundamental experience of every Mandenka individual, an experience that breaks free from the trappings of age and primogeniture:

"At that moment
I carried my mother on my back;
My father trotted at my feet."

—Sory Camara (1972)

In the remote north of Sierra Leone, where I did my first fieldwork, Kuranko storytellers conventionally begin their stories with a stock phrase—*wo lai yan la* or *wule yan be la*—that sets the narrative "far off and long ago." As with our familiar "Once upon a time" or "There once lived," stories are thus situated outside the space-time in which they are actually told. At once a ruse that suggests that a line may be drawn between the imaginary and the real, a rhetorical trick that protects the storyteller from possible accusations of sedition, and a way of helping an audience identify with the tale's protagonists, such framing devices are characteristic of all forms of "play." Thus, when a traditional Arabian tale opens with the declaration "This happened and this did not happen," or an Ashanti narrative begins with the disclaimer "We don't really mean to say so, we don't really mean to say so" (Rattray 1930), or an Egyptian tale purports to have taken place in China, even though everything about it is manifestly Egyptian, listeners suspend their disbelief.

Where Stories Take Us

Stories transport us, we say. They take us out of ourselves. They make us forget, for a moment, the humdrum and the mundane. We like to think they carry us into distant and exotic places that are "purely imaginary." Such attitudes may explain why Kuranko storytelling is prohibited during the daytime (one risks a death in the family if one breaks the ban), and why stories belong to the night (when work is done, and one enters the antinomian world of dreams and darkness). Yet it would be a mistake for us to construe the imaginary as a negation of the real, for experiences that we disparage as "mere" fantasy or dream are as integral to our "real" lives as night is to day. This is why it is important to explore not only the ways in which stories take us beyond ourselves, but *transform our experience* and bring us back to ourselves, changed.

This reciprocal movement between the real and the imaginary is grounded in the intersubjective interplay of self and other. No one exists except in and through relationships, both empathic and antipathetic, with others. As a corollary, it is impossible to conceptualize one's experience except in and through a relation with otherness. The human imagination belongs to and is born of this process of othering. By articulating one's experiences with words and objects that are shared, yet whose existence is independent of the self, individuals can grasp their subjectivity, not as something singular and separate, but as something contingent upon what is held in common with others. T. S. Eliot referred to the words, objects, images, and ideas that we use as symbolic analogues of our own immediate experience as "objective correlatives." The stories that in any society are regarded as "traditional" thus provide a common resource and a set of raw materials with which each individual may work out and think through his or her relationship with others. Yet, as George Devereux observes, if stories are to be available for individual use they must first be freed of all traces of the idiosyncratic meanings, private fantasies, and subjective defenses that have become attached to them in the course of previous recountings (1948, 238). In exemplifying the way in which stories depict dramas of everyday life without the traumatic emotions they actually entail, folktales may easily fool us into thinking that they are simplistic. In truth, however, it is only when they acquire what Walter Benjamin calls their "chaste compactness" (1968, 91), their apparent neutrality, that stories can provide the "intrapsychic alibis" that help individuals see beyond their own particular circumstances and deal with their emotions in concert with others.

Every story told, then, shifts elusively and continually between idiosyncratic and collective levels of meaning. Like coins and leaves, stories are Janus-faced: the surface is a reverse image of the underside. Thus, while a story may unfold in a place allegedly far away, and involve imaginary beings, animal characters, disguised voices, and miraculous events, it remains tied to an immediate lifeworld—a parable or allegory of quandaries in the lives of those who tell and attend to the tale. Accordingly, a narrative about a nation's struggle for independence may simultaneously express the oedipal strivings of the storyteller; a writer whose parents died when he was a child may recount his sense of loss through the story of a migrant people's *collective* loss of homeland; a Kuranko storyteller's tales of conjugal distrust and infidelity may obliquely express the circumstances of his own unhappy marriages, while another's stories of a corrupt and autocratic ruler may allegorize his own unresolved relationship with an abusive father. The general is thus used analogically as a screen onto which are projected and reworked memories and emotions that are too close for comfort, too subjective to be focused, too painful to be told.

The reverse is also true, for while shared stories may conceal and merge specific biographies, their uses cannot be reduced to subjectivity. A dramatic example of this are the "mythico-histories" generated by Hutu refugees in the Mishamo resettlement camp in Tanzania during the period 1972–1986. As Liisa Malkki shows, these "charters" and "blueprints" that essentialized and polarized Hutu and Tutsi histories, are neither descriptions nor representations of events that occurred in the past, but radical, antagonistic, and subversive reworkings of the past, and an expression of a "collective voice" that anticipates an apocalyptic reversal of future fortunes (1995, 54–56). Malkki comments: "To be told and retold such similar, almost formulaic historical accounts, *and to see stories of people's own lives melt into the general themes of a collective narrative*, was a compelling experience" (56, emphasis added).

The art of Kuranko storytelling consists, then, in managing an interplay between general discursive subjects—such as the tension between junior and senior co-wives, the conflict between men and their elder sons, or the fate of *ferensola* (the "nation")—and particular existential subjects—Sira's unhappiness as a junior wife, Karifa's relationship with his overbearing father, Tamba's political ambitions. But this subtle movement to and fro between particular and totalized subjectivities depends upon an unobtrusive switching between present and past time frames, and between near and distant locations. In other words, the relation between the worlds of other and of self is assimilated to the relation between immediate and non-immediate domains of space and time. Consider, for example, the opening passage of a story told by Tina Kuyate in Kondembaia, on March 11, 1970:

> Long ago …. this is how ingratitude came into this world. It was on account of a certain man. It was this man who brought ingratitude into this world. He was a leper. He had no fingers or toes. He sat tormented in a far-off forest, under a great cotton tree that was as big as this cotton tree in front of the chief's compound here….

Though they shuttle back and forth between familiar and exotic locations, and between the mythical past and the here and now, Kuranko stories neither escape into fantastic elsewheres nor privilege the pressing subjective concerns of any one person. On the contrary, the very purpose of storytelling is to invoke and counterpoint *various* points of view. As exercises in what Hannah Arendt calls the "visiting imagination," stories cast doubt on the possibility of resolving ethical dilemmas according to any one principle, or on any *a priori* grounds. As we shall see, the actual performance of a story reinforces this relativity of perspectives, for in requiring the participation of both audience *and* storyteller in an interactive relationship of call and response, the storytelling event itself realizes both socially and dialogically an ideal of tolerant solidarity in difference. This interaction between storyteller and audience is particularly important at moments of hiatus and tension, when everyone joins his or her voice in song. Whatever private reveries, reactions, or memories have been induced during the telling of the story, the effect of the sung sections is to bring each person's awareness back to his or her immediate sense of being-with-others. Singing in unison thus affirms the very social bonds that have been brought into question by the unfolding events of the story itself.

The Faces of Janus

The ethical issue at the heart of this chapter concerns two quite different modes of resolving conflict in Kuranko life: retaliation and reconciliation.

While retaliation is predicated upon extremely particularistic identifications, based on rank, lineage, gender, estate, and ethnicity, reconciliation invokes more general notions of common humanity. As I shall show, the counterpoint between these two principles of hierarchy and humanity is basic to Kuranko ethics.

I begin with a story recorded in Kondembaia, Diang chiefdom, northeast Sierra Leone on March 8, 1970. Although thirty years may be a long time ago, and Sierra Leone's current plight seem a far cry from the way things were, Kondembaia is the village where, in April 1998, Fina Kamara and her six-year-old daughter Damba had their hands hacked off by RUF guerillas. The great cotton tree in whose shadow this event occurred—the same tree that figures in the opening of Tina Kuyate's story about the origins of ingratitude—is but a stone's throw from the house porch where Keti Ferenke Koroma recounted the story that follows. And this tree also recalls another past, for the immense cotton trees that today tower over many older Kuranko settlements grew from the defensive bush and pallisading that once encircled these hilltop sites. Indeed, many are living testimony to the catastrophic invasion of the Kuranko area one hundred years ago by mounted warriors (*sofas*) of the Mandinka warlord Samori Turé, in the course of which almost every Kuranko town was sacked and burned, thousands of villagers were killed, and thousands more fled into the bush. Kondembaia was built at the end of this period, on level ground—a place of refuge and rebirth (Trotter 1898, 34). As for the episode in the story in which Momori is blinded, this resonates uncannily with accounts from the mid-1990s by Médecins Sans Frontières surgeons—that ripping out tongues, gouging out eyes, and hacking off limbs had become deliberate strategies by the RUF rebels, intent on preventing refugees reaching help and reporting the murders and mutilations they had witnessed (Davies 1995–1996, 1994). For all these reasons it is difficult not to see the two Momoris in this story—one the incarnation of good, the other of evil—as icons of alternating epochs, some peaceable, some violent, and to read the story from a perspective which, while encompassing both the historical and the personal, repudiates any attempt to separate good from evil, or history from biography, but rather explores each as the condition of the possibility of the other.[38]

The Two Momoris

There were two friends. They were both called Momori. One day, the two of them sat down and decided that, because they were friends, they should go into business together. They became traders. They made about £30, and decided to use the money as bridewealth. They married the same woman. She then helped them, selling things in the market.

One day they said, "Well now, we are two, yet we have the same wife. How can this be?" One of the Momoris—his name was Gbeyekan Momori[39]—said: "My heart is white for you,[40] and it would be good if yours was as white for me. Since I feel nothing but goodwill toward you, and we have only one wife between the two of us, I am going to give her to you. Then we can work hard to get the bridewealth for me to marry." So the woman became the wife of the other Momori.

The two friends then continued trading. They continued until they had earned £20. But they needed another £10 to make up the £30 necessary to get a wife.

One day, traveling between towns, they came upon a flat expanse of rock (*faragbaran*), and decided to break their journey there. The other Momori told Gbeyekan Momori to go and fetch water to drink. Gbeyekan Momori said, "Eh, friend, we have worked hard and got a wife. Out of the goodness of my heart, I gave her to you. Now, instead of asking your wife to fetch water for you to drink, you are asking me. But no matter, I will go and get the water." So Gbeyekan took the water bowl and went to find water.

No sooner had he gone than the other Momori said to his wife, "When my friend returns, we will fall upon him, knock him to the ground, beat him up, and gouge out his eyes. Then the £20 will be ours." His wife said, "All right. There is nothing wrong with that."

Gbeyekan Momori returned. As he was setting down the water bowl, the other Momori fell on him. First, he called his wife to take Gbeyekan Momori's feet so that they could force him to the ground. The woman did as she was asked. Then they forced him to ground and beat him up. Finally, the other Momori took his knife and gouged out Gbeyekan Momori's eyes. The other Momori and his wife left Gbeyekan Momori lying helpless on the *faragbaran*.

Near that *faragbaran* was a great cotton tree. Gbeyekan Momori crawled to the foot of the tree and lay there until evening. He did not know that this was the meeting place of an old hyena and an old vulture. Whenever they met there, the vulture would tell the hyena what he had seen from the air during the day, and the hyena would tell the vulture what he had seen from the ground. That evening, the hyena and the vulture met. The vulture said, "Good evening, hyena." The hyena said, "Good evening, vulture." The hyena then asked the vulture what he had seen from the air that day. The vulture said, "Hyena, I did not go anywhere today. I was laying my eggs in the branches of this great tree. I laid five eggs before today. Today I laid the sixth. Now, whoever breaks these eggs will have his wishes fulfilled." Then the vulture told the hyena what had happened that day: "A woman and two men came onto this *faragbaran* today. When they came here, one of the men took a water bowl and went to fetch water. When he returned with the water, the others fell on him, forced him to the ground, and gouged out first one eye then the other. Then they went away. After they had gone I said to myself, 'This is a remarkable thing; I must tell the hyena about it.' So, have you heard me?" The hyena said, "I have heard you. But what a pity that the man is not here, because if he were to take the bark of this cotton tree, squeeze it, and wash his face with the sap, he would be able to see again."

All this time Gbeyekan Momori had been sitting under the tree, though the hyena and vulture were unaware of this. The vulture said, "Friend, I am sorry that I have no mouth with which to speak to that man. I would like to tell him to take a stone and dash it against the tree. The sap that flowed out could be washed over his eyes, and he could be made to see again. But I don't know where he is."

All night the vulture and the hyena rested there. In the morning they went away. As soon as they had gone the man crawled across the *faragbaran*, took a stone, and dashed it against the trunk of the tree. When sap began oozing from the tree, the man took some in his hands and bathed his eyes. Immediately he was able to see.

He cut a long pole, leant it against the tree, climbed up, and found the vulture's eggs. There were six in all. He took only three. Then he traveled far from that place to a level and fertile land. There he said, "You, egg of the vulture, if I break you here it is because I want a great town to be here." He dropped the egg on the ground and a large town sprang up.

Then he took the second egg. He said, "You, egg of the vulture, if I break you here it is because I want to be chief in this great town." He dropped the egg on the ground and became chief. Then he took the third egg. He said, "You, egg of the vulture, if I break you here it is because I want to be the wealthiest man in the world." He dropped the egg on the ground and instantly became very wealthy. He was chief there and had everything he wanted. He had many children, many wives. He had everything in great abundance.

In the meanwhile, that other Momori and his wife had become very, very poor. They didn't have a penny left of the £20 they had stolen. It seemed as if something was working against them. Whatever they tried to do, they failed. Then they heard people talking about a great chief. "He is the wealthiest chief in the world," people said. "He has everything in great abundance." The woman said, "My husband, why don't we go to that chief and ask him to give us something." The man said, "Ha, that is a good idea." So they started off.

It took them two days to reach that great town, but they could not approach the chief because they were dressed in rags. Still, they tried their best. By pushing ahead of others they at last managed to greet the chief. The chief looked at them. He looked at the man. His face seemed familiar. He looked at the woman. Hadn't he seen her before? Then the chief said, "I usually give strangers (*sundannu*)[41] lodgings outside my compound, but I am going to give you lodgings in the house adjoining mine." The chief sent them to their room where they remained until nightfall. The chief gave them food and other gifts.

In the middle of the night the chief went to greet his strangers. He went and knocked on their door. The strangers were afraid. The chief said, "I have come to greet you, don't be afraid." So they opened the door and he entered. Once inside, the chief said to them, "What town are you from?" They told him. The chief said, "How did you two come to be in the business of trading?" The man said, "Two of us started out in this business, but my companion died long ago." The chief said, "You say your friend died?" The man said, "Yes." The chief said, "How did he die?" The man said, "He had some kind of sickness. It came upon him one day as we were traveling across a certain *faragbaran*, and he died there. Since we couldn't take him with us we left him there." The chief said, "All right, let us tell some stories." They said, "But chief, we do not know any stories." They were afraid of the chief.

The chief began: "There were once two men in this world ..." The man said, "Nnhn." The chief continued: "They were close friends. One was called Gbeyekan Momori and the other was called Momori. They were such good friends that they went into business together. They made a little money ..."

The man said, "Eh!" He said to himself, "How does this chief know of these things?"

The chief went on: "Gbeyekan Momori and his friend Momori made about £30. They decided to use the money to get a wife. They married the same woman. Their wife helped them by selling things in the market. One day they said, 'Well now, we are two yet we have the same wife. How can this be?' Then Gbeyekan Momori said: 'Friend, my heart is white for you, and it would be good if your heart was as white for me. Since my heart is white for you, and we have only one wife between the two of us, I am going to give her to you. From now on, we can work hard to get a wife for me.' So they did just that."

No sooner had the chief said this than the man fell at his feet. He said, "You are my friend!" He shat his pants in fear. He said, "Eh! Are you not the one?" The chief said, "Be quiet, don't cry." But the man and his wife were prostrate at the chief's feet, begging for mercy. They said, "We are sorry, we are sorry, we have suffered disgrace and impoverishment because of what we did to you." The chief said, "When we first met I felt nothing but goodwill toward you. I will show you that I still feel the same. In this world, if you become friends and your friend's heart is white for you, then your heart must be white for him. If you have no goodwill toward him, then no matter how you conspire against him your conspiracy will fail and you will suffer disgrace because of what you have tried to do to him. It is best that people approach one another with open hearts. Now, I will show you that just as I once felt goodwill toward you, I feel goodwill toward you now. First thing tomorrow, I am going to divide my country into two. You will be chief over one part, I will be chief over the other." The man was very happy to hear this. The chief returned to his house to sleep.

When the chief had gone the woman said to the man, "Uncle,[42] rather than have this chief give you half his country, why not ask him how he came to acquire all his land and wealth in the first place? Then you can become as wealthy as he is." The man said, "Ha, that is true. I will go and ask him." He went to the chief's house. He was not afraid now, because the chief had cleared away the darkness between them. When he reached the chief he said, "Friend, I have come to you." The chief said, "What for?" The man said, "By what means did you acquire your chieftaincy and all your wealth? You, who we beat up and blinded and abandoned on the *faragbaran* … how did you become so powerful?" Gbeyekan Momori said, "Friend, you know that just as my heart was white for you in the past, so it is now. Well, at the place where you gouged out my eyes there stands a great cotton tree. I acquired all this wealth from lying under that tree. A vulture had laid six eggs in its branches. I took three of the eggs. If you take the other three, then whatever you wish will be granted. When you break the eggs, God will fulfill your wishes." Then the chief said, "Don't tell any of this to a woman."

But when the young man, the accursed man, left, he went and told his wife everything. He explained it all, just as his friend had explained it to him. The woman said, "Well, uncle, you must leave here very early in the morning."

Early next morning, the man went to the great cotton tree, climbed into the branches, and took the vulture's eggs. He returned to the town. He went straight to his wife. He said to her, "My companion, I have come with the three vulture's eggs." The woman said, "Let us go to some distant place in the bush. We are now chiefs." They traveled to a remote place. The man carried the three eggs. When they reached that place he said, "What will we do with these three eggs? What will we do with them?"

His wife said, "Well, if you want these eggs to be a boon for us, take one of them and break it on the ground, and wish for a great town to appear here." The man broke the egg and a great town appeared. Then he said, "What will we do with the second egg?" The woman said, "You must break the second egg on the ground and wish for a great river to appear here. No one can live without water." The man broke the second egg and a great river appeared. Then he said, "Now, what about the third egg?" The woman said, "Well, you know, if a man marries into a wealthy family he will never want for anything. You must break the third egg on the ground and wish for your wife's family to become very wealthy."

The man's affines indeed became wealthy, but his own kinsmen became poor. Therefore, if you try to extend goodwill toward someone and that person tries to deceive you, God will make him suffer disgrace and impoverishment. No sooner had the man's affines become wealthy than they took the woman away from him, leaving him without a wife. Therefore, it is always best to be honest and straightforward with your friends. If you try to deceive them, one day God will make you suffer impoverishment and disgrace. All the wealthy people in the world are descended from the family of that woman. All the poor people are descended from the family of that man.

The story of the two Momoris is a subtle exploration of the play of reciprocity and retribution in interpersonal life. In Kuranko thought, a moral person is one who gives life to others without ill-will or ulterior motives. The concept *morgoye* (personhood) condenses this ethic of "generalized reciprocity" into an ideal of being, expressed figuratively as *gbeye* (lit. "whiteness")—a disposition towards open-heartedness, plain-speaking, magnanimity, and honesty. But this notion of goodness does not imply some subjective essence that a person either has or does not have; rather, it rests on a principle of generative equilibrium in social life, whereby actions that sustain the life of others generally bring reciprocal blessings (*baraka*) back to the giver, while actions that sap or imperil the life of others—such as greed, stinginess, theft, sorcery, or witchcraft—generally entail retributive actions against the evil-doer. Symbolically marked by the color term *finye*, blackness connotes obscurity, darkness, duplicity, deviousness, uncertainty, enmity, and obstructiveness in interpersonal relations. To borrow another Kuranko metaphor, if positive intersubjectivity is a clear path through open grassland, negative intersubjectivity is a tortuous and obscure path through a dark forest.

Let us now consider in greater detail the logic that governs the interplay between good and evil. As already noted, Kuranko understand intersubjectivity in terms of a reciprocity of both actions and intentions. A gift that is honestly intended to augment another's well-being has the twofold effect of negating hidden forces of ill-will and inspiring positive reciprocation. Thus, gifts to a stranger or an ancestor "clear the path" or bring light to the darkness that tends to develop among people who are separated by boundaries of time, space, and ethnicity. Hence the adage: *morgo min bi wulai yan la, i sai yena, a sai yena, wo bi wo si dia kama* (a person who is far away for a long time, you don't sing, he doesn't sing, how could you both be friends?). However, suspicion, enmity, and animus are nullified by the purity of the subjective intentionality that finds objective expression in the gift. White, say Kuranko, forms a protective barrier against black. In the case of negative reciprocity, however, when what is given or mystically despatched to the other is a vehicle for ill-will, it is said that if the intended receiver is himself or herself innocent of ill-will (i.e. he or she is symbolically "white") then the evil intentions objectified in the malevolent gift will boomerang back and afflict the sender. This is precisely what happens in The Two Momoris, though Keti Ferenke, a Muslim, attributes to God/Allah the principle of retributive justice that is more commonly expressed by the notion of *hake*—an impersonal and neutral force that inheres in all human relationships and works to regulate the balance of goodness and evil according to the logic outlined above.

Good intentions are one defence against evil; plain speaking is another. To publicly confess ill-will or malevolent intentions is to dissipate and nullify their force, so bringing clarity and balance back into a relationship that has been at risk. It is not that confession salves individual conscience; rather, in the Kuranko view, it clarifies and readjusts relationships within the community, which is why confession must be performed publicly, before an audience, if it is to be effective.

While the Kuranko emphasis on good and evil as opposing forces within intersubjective life does not preclude a concern for the way good and evil impulses may contend *within* the individual psyche, it is intersubjective rather than intrapsychic relations that are generally the focus of Kuranko concern.[43] Nevertheless, these two dimensions of experience—the social and the psychological—must both be considered if we are to understand the transformations that occur in the story of the two Momoris.

Let us assume that the forces that in most human societies are polarized and designated as white/black and good/evil are reified expressions of contending human desires: on the one hand, the desire for individual agency and autonomy (enacted primordially, and reenacted symbolically, as a separation from natal dependency); and on the other hand, the desire for an enlarged and fulfilling existence with others (enacted periodically in rituals of collective and cosmic belonging). In the narrative imagination, these contrasted desires, though coexistent in the psyche of every individual, tend to be split into separate personae. In the story of the two Momoris, this splitting occurs, as it were, before our very eyes. Initially close friends and business partners, sharing the same name and married to the same woman, the two figures are virtually coalesced, and the black/white contrast between them disguised. The two Momoris then become dramatically polarized. Why?

The answer to this question may be found in the way in which the story is brought to a close and, more obliquely, by the way Kuranko men think about gender difference.

Like many people, Kuranko tend to essentialize the good, identifying it unequivocally with themselves, or with one group within their own society. Evil is thus displaced *elsewhere*. This is precisely what happens in the story of the two Momoris. First, different *dispositions* toward good and evil become split into two *persons*—the pure-hearted and the deceitful Momoris. Evil then appears to triumph over the good, with Gbeyekan Momori blinded and abandoned to die at the foot of a tree in a faraway place. But in Kuranko thought, goodness—particularly when bolstered by the wearing of symbolically "white" objects on the skin—will repulse evil intentions, causing malice to rebound and afflict the malefactor.

Accordingly, the other Momori becomes afflicted with the very adversity that he wished upon his virtuous friend.

At this stage, rather than conclude his story with two men at odds with each another, Keti Ferenke subtly displaces the blame for Momori's malice onto his scheming wife. In this way the story contrives to affirm the bond between men by making women—as outsiders—the root cause of the evil that constantly threatens to sow seeds of discord and division among them, as in the adages: *kele da ma si ban, koni musu ko kele ti ban* (all quarrels can be resolved, except those caused by women)*; yanfe dama si no, koni musu yanfe wo ti fo* (all conspiracies can be overcome, except those made by women).

Though spoken with the conviction of someone who has a personal axe to grind, and echoing a chauvinism shared by most Kuranko men, Keti Ferenke's story must, however, be placed in perspective. By turning now to a consideration of the ways in which storytelling sessions involve *various* narrators, sustained *series* of stories, and *several* points of view, it will be seen that storytelling tends to undermine rather than promote dogmatic and categorical identifications, and transcend rather than simply affirm normative boundaries.

Two Storytelling Sessions

Keti Ferenke Koroma recounted the story of the two Momoris on March 8, 1970, during one of my first visits to his village of Kondembaia. On this same occasion he related four other stories, all concerned, like the first, with problems arising from the give and take of interpersonal life. All affirmed that relations between friends and neighbors should be characterized by trust, cooperation, and mutual goodwill, despite the fact that people often deceive, malign, harm, and defraud others.

Because only I and my research assistant were listening to these stories, and because they were told in the daytime, this storytelling event was both artificial and atypical. In order, therefore, to convey something of the atmosphere and social dynamic of a more typical storytelling event, I will review briefly a night session in Kondembaia in February 1972 at which three gifted narrators were present—Keti Ferenke Koroma, Kenya Fina Mara,[44] and Sulimani Koroma—together with a sizeable audience of men, women, and children. Since I have described this session in detail elsewhere (1982, 64–66), I recall it now only to re-emphasize the significance of the theatrical or performative dimension of Kuranko storytelling, particularly the dialogical interplay of different storytellers. Not only did the three storytellers take turns to tell their stories, but each elected to tell stories that ironically counterpointed the story that had preceded his or her own. At the same time, each gave enthusiastic support to the stories that the others told, interjecting stock exclamations such as *ha, heh, eh, oho,* or *fiu,* or murmuring approval, astonishment, and emphasis. Indeed, in two stories about beguiling women, Keti Ferenke and Kenya Fina actually shared the narration and played the male and female roles. And when stories included songs, Kenya Fina encouraged and enhanced the singing with her mellifluous voice, and taught the audience the words of the songs before each story began.

This subtle alternation of voices and of various points of view means that Kuranko storytelling events play with rather than slavishly assert social dogmas. Moreover, this play maximizes audience participation, both in the telling and singing of the story, and in the elucidation of its ethical implications. For in counterpointing different standpoints, stories place in abeyance predetermined, conventional attitudes based on gender, age, and estate, and open up the possibility of dialogue and reflection on decisive questions of judgment and action. But Kuranko *tileinu* not only critique the rigid worldviews associated with established centers of chiefly power and male authority; they play and comment ironically upon each other. Thus, while individual stories, such as Keti Ferenke's "The Two Momoris," may take a dim view of women, such bias will seldom go unchallenged, either by other storytellers or by the audience. A pluralistic spirit prevails, encompassing both stories *and* persons, for, as Kuranko see it, stories are no more the same than people are. It is the adjustment and reconciliation of differences that storytelling attempts, rather than the strict imposition of unitary identifications. In this sense a storytelling event epitomizes the ideal of social intelligence (*hankili*), and conforms to a model of civility and conversability that is recognized in all cultures. Crucial to this ideal is the notion of a *complementary* relationship between different voices and different points of view, a complementarity, moreover, that implies that *anyone* may, in the event of an unjust use of privilege or power, take action to realign and reaffirm the social order. This is not to say that storytelling works toward unanimity or consensus, still less that it denies intrinsic and inherited differences in rank, gender, estate, and ethnicity; rather, it is to emphasize the ways in which storytelling, *simply by virtue of its being a shared action of speaking, singing, sitting together, and voicing various viewpoints*, makes possible a momentary fusion of disparate and often undisclosed private experiences. It is, therefore, not so much the *substance* of what is said or suggested in a story that affirms the ethic of openness and "whiteness" that Kuranko encapsulate in the notion of *morgoye*, but the very act of participating in a shared event that places diverse experiences in the context of a common humanity.

Let me now return to 1970, and a storytelling session I attended in Kondembaia on the night of March 11.

It will be recalled that when I visited Keti Ferenke four days earlier, he told me the story of "The Two Momoris" which, together with the other stories he told on this occasion, were concerned with the ideal of *morgoye*—how human relationships might be made honest, straightforward, and transparent, rather than dishonest, devious, and duplicitous.

The room into which we were crowded was shuttered against the tropical night. I was barely able to find a niche for my microphone. Children clambered over one another, trying to get nearer the storyteller. Babies slept, oblivious, on their mothers' backs. Old men, chewing kola, unmoved by the commotion, sat in the shadows of hurricane lamps. Young men's faces lost their brashness. And women smiled without inhibition, anticipating another of Keti Ferenke's irreverent and hilarious performances. Having boasted to me more than once that he could tell more stories than I would ever have patience to record, he began apace, partly to impress me, I think, and rattled off ten stories that immediately had everyone in stitches. Though all touched on familiar themes—the vaunting of self, looking down on others, taking unfair advantage of others, putting oneself before others, failing to keep promises, not heeding the advice of elders—they exploited ludicrous situations and played for laughs. Even when he broached his own obsessions—the wiles and wickedness of women—he used burlesque and grotesque to avoid too much gravity.

Then Kenya Fina signaled that she wanted to tell a story. Though it picked up on Keti Ferenke's themes of not lording it over others, and not using one's superior position to take advantage of those under one's care and protection, Kenya Fina's story focused on the relationship between junior and senior co-wives, and the unjust ways in which older women sometimes use their privileged position to abuse and exploit younger co-wives. "If you are the senior wife (*baramusu*), you should not look down on the ones under you, blaming them for whatever goes wrong in the house."

Now it was Keti Ferenke's turn again. Taking his cue from Kenya Fina, he also told a story about co-wives, but turned it into an indictment of the fickleness of women. Tricked and cuckolded by his wife, the chief in the story ends up ruefully observing that men should try to endure the wanton ways of women, just as the hardy leaf of the *kuron* tree endures high winds and driving rain.

It was at this point that Kenya Fina told what would become, for me, one of the most compelling stories I ever heard in Sierra Leone. But before relating it, I want to quickly comment on the six stories that followed, and brought the evening to a close, for this will help make clear the extent to which stories must be understood, not separately, as a disconnected set of entertainments, but as a strategic series that plays off points of view, one against the other, creating a polyphony of voices and enlarging one's understanding of how the recurring dilemmas of everyday life are experienced by the different people embroiled in them. As we shall see, Kenya Fina's story of Na Nyale is a plea for compassion and reconciliation, rather than harsh judgment. It was immediately followed by a story in a similar vein by Tina Kuyate, concerning the origins of ingratitude. A male ancestor, given great gifts by a magical bird, fails to give anything back to the bird when it is in need and, as a consequence, loses the bounty he had earlier gained. Keti Ferenke then told a story that pressed his point that women cannot be trusted. In a lighter vein now, Kenya Fina told a comic story about a seductress, showing that men can be as readily swayed by their emotions as women. The session ended with Keti Ferenke telling three more stories, the last of which affirmed the value of friendship. By reiterating the point of "The Two Momoris," though this time without any reference to women, it seemed to sum up all that he and Kenya Fina shared, a poignant demonstration that friendship may transcend lines of age and gender, not only in art but in life.

The Story of Na Nyale

There was once a very jealous chief. He allowed no man to see his wives. So the wives decided on a ruse. They wove several large raffia baskets that could be hung from the walls of the house. Whenever the women made ready to go from the town to the farm, each hid her lover in one of the baskets. The women also prepared food and put it in the baskets. Then they would set off to the farm to do the weeding, and in the evening return to the town, carrying their lovers in the baskets on their backs.

This went on for some time. Then one day, one of the wives, whose name was Na Nyale, decided to leave her lover in the farmhouse when she went out weeding, because he was too heavy to carry. What none of the wives knew was that the chief was going to visit them that day. Na Nyale had killed a chicken, prepared it well, and left it for her lover. But while all the other wives took their lovers with them to the place where they were weeding that day, Na Nyale left her lover in the farmhouse.

No sooner had the women left the farmhouse than the chief arrived. As he entered the house he saw that big basket hanging there. He touched it and said, "Eh, these women are amazing. What have they got in this big basket? I am going to have a look inside." When the chief said that he was going to look inside the basket, it started shaking, shaking, shaking. The chief said, "Eh, the basket is shaking! I must look into this." The basket shook twice. Then the chief took his machete and cut the rope. With the rope cut, the basket fell from the wall—*din*. The basket said, "Mm hmm." The basket hummed. The chief said, "Ah! So the basket can speak. I am going to open it this very day and see what is inside." He took a knife and cut the rope that held the mouth of the basket closed. And what did he see? Fara Mara. Then the chief said, "Who is in this basket?" The man said, "I am." The chief said, "Who are you." "I am Fara Mara," said the man. Then the chief said, "What did you come here for?" The man said, "Allah has destined that this should happen." The chief said, "Well, Allah has indeed destined that something should happen between us today. Now get out so that I may kill you." The man begged, "Oh chief, why don't you simply fine me. Whatever the amount is, I will pay it." The chief said, "No, I must kill you." Fara Mara got out of the basket and the chief seized him. He put one foot on Fara Mara's legs, the other foot on Fara Mara's hands, then he took out his knife and cut Fara Mara's throat. When his throat was slit, Fara Mara's blood splashed onto a cassava plant. The blood splashed over the leaves. The cassava leaf then changed into a little Senegalese fire finch.[45] The fire finch flew to the part of the farm where the women were weeding, to tell them what had happened. The bird found that the women had partitioned the area. Standing a little way in front of Na Nyale, whose lover had been killed, it sang:

> Na Nyale, oh Na Nyale, Na Nyale, oh Na Nyale
> Ni i wara sole to mansa, ni i wara sole to mansa
> Wara kemine ye m'bi yo, oh Na Nyale
> (Na Nyale, oh Na Nyale … If you have left the
> basket, then the chief has seen a man today,
> oh Na Nyale)

Na Nyale said to her companions, "Nnn, the bird is crying. I am not going to finish weeding my piece of ground. I am gone, I am gone, oh. The bird is saying something to us." The others said, "All right, go. We will see you later." She hurried quickly down the hill and arrived at the farmhouse. But what did she see? She saw the basket on the floor, all the ropes cut from its mouth. Then she saw the chief. She said, "Chief, what happened here?" The chief said, "Are you the owner of this?" She said, "Yes. But there is no need to be afraid. What did you do with it?" The chief said, "Well, I have not left any man in my farmhouse. If I found a man in the basket with the bones of a chicken and a pan with traces of palmoil on it, then it means that the food he eats is sweeter than the food I eat,[46] and I killed him." The woman said, "After you killed him, what did you do with him?" The chief said, "After I killed him, I burnt his body and threw the ashes in the river." The woman said, "Into what river?" The chief said, "The Seli."[47]

The woman went to the town and got some money. She said, "If I do not see this man today, then no matter what happens, I will not rest. I must find him." The woman then set off, following the river downstream. For two years she followed the river. She said she had to find her lover. Wherever she stopped she would find palmbirds in their nests. She would tell the birds to be quiet, that love was in the air and on the ground and under the water. She would say, "I am searching for my lover":

> I ya l moina, Fara Mara, i ya l moina? Dondo
> I ya l moi dondo? I ya saya soron n'de le fe
> Dondooooo. Don
> (Do you hear me, Fara Mara, do you hear me? All is quiet
> Do you hear quietness? You died because of me
> All is quiettttt. Quiet)

She heard nothing but the sound of her own voice. She would continue on her way. Wherever she stopped by the riverside she would sing the same song. For two years she followed the river, searching for her lover.

Then all the living things of the river met together and said, "That man who was killed and burned, and whose ashes were thrown in the river … whoever ate some should bring it forth now. There is someone searching for him, so desperate she cannot rest. All those who ate the bones should spit them out. All those who ate the flesh should regurgitate it. Those who ate the eyes should give them up. We should put all these parts back together again and make the man as he was." So everyone brought forth the different parts. All those who were able to reassemble the skeleton did so. All those who were able to put flesh on the bones did so. They put all the parts together again. Then they asked who had taken the life. The one who had taken it said, "I took the life." They said, "Well, go and get it." He went for the life. They told him to put the life back in the body. He did so.

Then they told the man that someone was looking for him, someone desperate to find him. At that moment, Na Nyale arrived at that spot. It was a place so fear-inspiring that no one ever ventured there. But so desperate was this woman that she cared nothing for her own safety. She stood there. There was dense forest all around. She heard the palmbirds chattering. She scattered some coins in the forest and said, "All you djinn who live here, this is my gift to you. I am looking for someone, for the man who was killed on account of me. If I do not find him I prefer to die by this river. I cannot live without him." Then she scattered some coins along the riverbank and said, "All living things in the water and on the land, listen to me." But silence surrounded her. She stood and sang (as before). Then the man sang in reply:

Ah, n'de Fara Mara; n'ya saya keni i le l le fe dondo (Ah, I am Fara Mara; I preferred death because of you … all is quiet)

The woman leapt into the river—*gbogbon*. She said, "He is here. No one knows my song, except Fara Mara. He must be here." Then she saw him.

The creatures who dwell under the water took care of them for two years. They were well fed and provided for. In the third year they were given a xylophonist.[48] A horse was given to the lover, and the woman was given two boxes of dresses. Then they were carried to the surface. The water creatures said, "Well, we have to tell you that when you return you should immediately find the man who killed you and take your revenge. If you don't do this, we will kill you. Here is what to do: when you return, ask for him, and spend a night lodged in his house. Next morning, tell him you want to dance. Invite him to dance with you. Sit on your horse and let him sit on his. Then, as you dance, take your sword and cut off his head, thus paying him back in his own kind.[49] By cutting off his head you will satisfy us." The man and the woman said, "All right," and set off.

In every town they came to, they asked, "Is that chief still there?" People said, "What chief?" "That chief who killed a man that year, the man who was hidden in a raffia basket on the farm." Then people said, "He is there." Finally the couple reached the town where that chief lived. But they did not recognize the *luiye*. They asked, "Is that chief still here?" People said, "What chief?" "The chief that killed a man on his farm on account of his wife." They said, "Yes, he is here."

Then the man said, "Well, he raised me, so I have come to thank him." People said, "He is here." The man said, "Well, can you show me the way to his *luiye*?" They led him right into the chief's house. Everyone was looking at the two strangers. Then one of the chief's wives said, "Eh! This man's wife resembles Na Nyale, the one whose lover was killed by the chief. She looks like her." The woman went and greeted Na Nyale. But Na Nyale said, "I am not Na Nyale." The other woman said, "Well, people really can look alike!" She went away. But then she said, "But the man looks like Fara Mara." The talk went on, but the strangers said nothing.

Then the man took £15 and gave it to the chief. He said, "You raised me. You have forgotten, but you did." (The chief had no idea that a plot was being hatched against him, to make him do what the strangers wanted.) The woman then gave two lapas and two head ties to each of the chief's wives. Then they retired for the night.

In the morning the man told the chief that he was going to offer a sacrifice, because it was a long time since he had done so. He said, "I did not know that I would find my big man here." Then the chief mounted his horse. The man mounted his. The old women crowded around them, clapping, and the *jelebas* played their xylophones, singing the praises of the chief. The man scattered coins on the ground. People scrambled to get them. Even Fara Mara's mother did not recognize him. But he did not go to her place. The *jelebas* were playing. Everyone was happy. But Fara Mara had a sword hidden under his gown. He put his hand under his gown and grasped the sword. He said, "Oh God, I did not start this. This man killed me. My body was burned and my ashes strewn in the river. If this all happened, oh God, help me take my revenge." As the chief passed him, he drew his sword and with one blow cut off the chief's head. His head fell there. His body fell there. There was a great commotion among the people. Everyone was crying. Fara Mara said, "Heh, heh, heh, heh, everybody be quiet. Everyone can tell me soon why he or she is crying." (A killer's word is always feared.)[50] Then everyone fell silent.

Next day he sacrificed two cows, one for himself and the other for the dead chief. He became chief in that town. All the chief's wives became his wives. Therefore, be you a chief or a nobody,[51] if you should find your wife with another man, fine him but do not kill him. To kill is not our custom. That is not what we have met.

Since these events occurred, a stop was put to killing. No one does it now.

To understand violence intersubjectively, it is necessary to stress that the principle of reciprocity operates both at the level of being and of having, for being is in all societies cathected onto and distributed among the *things* which people call their own and with which they identify. What one *has* objectifies who one *is*. The Kuranko notion of *miran* helps make this clear. *Mirannu* (pl.) refer both to material possessions—particularly those that contain and protect, such as a house, clothing, water vessels, and cooking pots—as well as to personal attributes that give one a sense of self-possession, presence, and substantiality of being—such as forceful speech, physical skill, and social adroitness. But *miran*, in both senses of the term— material possession and personal disposition—is never a fixed property or attribute. In practice, a person's *miran* may be bolstered by fetishes that symbolically enclose, contain, and protect the vital spaces that define his or her being—body, house, village, chiefdom—in exactly the same way that in a consumer society material possessions bolster and define a person's sense of well-being, substantiality, and standing. But self-possession may be undermined, sapped, or lost. Just as a person's property can be stolen, a pot broken, and a house fall into disrepair, so a person can lose self-possession and confidence. Moreover, a person's *miran* can be "taken away" by more powerful others (such as autocratic parents, forceful public speakers, and powerful bush spirits) whose voice and power "press down" with great weight, diminishing the *miran* of those in their presence. Ideally, a balance is struck in which everyone's voice, presence, and property is accorded due recognition in relation to his or her role, age and gender. But some people assert themselves beyond their due station—as in the case of a chief who exploits his position to take advantage of people, a senior co-wife who abuses her junior partners, a man whose jealousy overrules his better judgment, or a woman whose emotions are not held in check. A kind of intersubjective logic then comes into play, based on the principle of reciprocity, according to which one has the right to counter in kind any action that has the effect of directly nullifying, diminishing, belittling, or erasing one's own being, or indirectly doing so by taking away properties that one regards as essential to and as extensions of one's being. The phrase *ke manni a nyorgo manni* reveals the kinship between the social logic of partnership and the abstract calculus of retaliation. But in the case of *lex talionis*, when the party that feels that its being has been violated takes identical counteraction against the violator, can we call such action violent?

According to Kuranko reasoning, no.

If one is innocent, one has every right to avenge oneself against anyone who seeks to do one harm. This is why, before avenging himself, Fara Mara declares before God that since he had done nothing to justify the violence of the chief, he now has every right to do to the chief what had been done to him. Not only is this not, in the Kuranko view, a violent act; it is a necessary and honorable one, rewarded by Fara Mara inheriting all that the chief had once possessed. Violating the being of someone who is believed to be responsible for violating one's own is not violence but retributive justice. Which is, on the evidence, what the RUF rebels believed, who severed Fina Kamara's hands in Kondembaia, for was she not part and parcel of the being of *ferensola*—of the party and people that threatened to rob them of their power?

However, Kenya Fina's story juxtaposes this retaliative attitude (associated with the djinn, the beings of the wild) with another, based on the notion of personhood as magnanimity. These two ethics are also co-present in the previous story where Gbeyekan Momori's goodwill and generosity of spirit breaks the cycle of vendetta and payback by focusing not on the immediate situation that has caused such grief and pain, but invoking a more abstract point of view. In this same vein, Kenya Fina makes a case for indemnification without death—a form of redemption in which something of comparable value is given to replace what was taken, but without the taking of a life. "Fine him but do not kill him."

I have argued that Kuranko stories open up discussion of varying points of view, and help restore faith in common sense and conciliation in a world plagued by division. Folktales and historical memory both preserve, I suspect, traces of two quite different strategies of coping with violence—vengeance and forgiveness—and so leave open, at all times, the possibility of choosing how one will react to evil. But at the same time they reveal the irreconcilable differences and contradictory potentialities that inhere in every being and in every human situation—as when the spirits of the wild demonstrate *morgoye* ("humanity") in empathizing with Na Nyale and assisting her on her quest, only to later demand the death of the chief as the price of their goodwill. In dramatizing extreme possibilities, stories may all too easily deceive us into thinking that the world is quintessentially and categorically divided into good and evil, the deserving and the undeserving, the human and the non-human, and that we—exemplars of the good, and the just—will win out in the end. But in exchanging one standpoint for another, and testifying to the way life is actually lived rather than merely thought, stories also cross and blur such boundary lines, revealing—as in the stories of the two Momoris and of Na Nyale—the potentiality of amity and enmity, love and hate, selfishness and generosity, vengefulness and forgiveness inherent in all relationships, an ambiguity that Primo Levi, writing of the paradigmatically most black and white situation of our times, calls "the gray zone"—"indecipherable because it did not conform to any model; the enemy was all around but also inside, the 'we' lost its limits, the contenders were not two, one could not discern a single frontier but rather many confused, perhaps innumerable frontiers, which stretched between each of us" (1989, 38).

At this point, these two traditional Kuranko stories, so apparently distant and imaginary, merge imperatively with contemporary events in Sierra Leone. For the tension between retaliation and reconciliation that we have traced out in these stories defines one of the most critical political and ethical issues of the postwar period. Not only is it now clear that many of the RUF rebels were driven by a desire for revenge and retribution after decades of political persecution, economic exclusion, and personal humiliation under a collapsing patrimonial regime (Richards 1996, 51–52); many of those who have suffered brutal losses at the hands of the rebels, now demand payback, not compromise, while still others fear that the Lomé peace agreement on July 7, 1999, that granted amnesty to the rebels and guaranteed them positions in both the army and government, simply licenses and perpetuates a politics of violence. Consider, for instance, Edward Karuma's explanation of why he has enlisted in the new postwar army. "I joined for revenge. I lost everything, so I joined because the only way to make up for what has happened is with a gun. I wanted to kill those who have killed us and made our lives miserable. I didn't even think to protect the country, just myself and my family" (McGreal 1999a, 5).

The misgivings that many Sierra Leoneans feel about amnesty and reconciliation have been echoed in the UN, where it is asked whether justice is being sacrificed on the altar of peace. Some argue that those who committed atrocities against civilians must be brought to justice if Sierra Leone is to come to terms with its recent horrendous past and if the international community is to be consistent in its refusal to grant amnesty to crimes against humanity and to flagrant violations of international humanitarian law (Pour 1999, 29). But emphasizing the moral imperative of justice over the pragmatics of reconciliation smacks of Eurocentrism, and risks overlooking efforts being made by the Kabbah government in Sierra Leone and the Obasanjo goverment in Nigeria to initiate more equitable, non-patrimonial, regimes. As the Nigerian lawyer Tunji Abayomi observes, "the issue is: can we secure the future by closing our eyes to the past? Or should we set an appropriate standard so it never happens again by holding people to account? Some people say, "Forgive. It will help to heal." But holding people responsible can heal too. Justice heals" (McGreal 1999b, 3).

As a general rule, it is easier to take revenge than to accept reconciliation. This is partly because the process of reconciliation requires the intervention and mediation of a third, neutral party, or the acceptance of a transcendent set of values, or elaborate ritual techniques. But it is partly because reconciliation is impeded by the difficulty of substituting values that belong to essentially opposite domains. Revenge is governed by the law of an eye for an eye and a tooth for a tooth. As with any other form of direct exchange, vengeance seeks to cancel a debt by demanding the equivalent of what has been taken—whether property, life, or a scarce existential good such as dignity or honor. Reconciliation, by contrast, depends on *a substitution of values*—financial recompense for loss of face or honor, a verbal apology in return for property stolen, forfeiting one's freedom (incarceration) for taking a life. The trouble is, however, that in every human society mutually exclusive and mutually inimical domains of value make this kind of substitutability difficult. "Blood" and "money," for instance, symbolize two very different domains of relationship—the first encompassing family values, the second encompassing the world of commerce (Schneider 1968). The two domains are ordinarily kept strictly apart. Business relations based on "blood" relations equate to nepotism, and monetary considerations can easily destroy "blood ties." Parker Shipton's study of Luo values provides another example of mutually exclusive domains of value. Unearned windfalls, lottery winnings, rewards for mercenary acts, stolen money, and profits from the sale of ancestral land, are all spoken of as *gueth makech* ("bitter money") in contrast with wealth gained from traditional social activities such as farming (Shipton 1989, 28). Such incommensurable domains of value often work against reconciliation, as when people reject monetary compensation for grievous personal loss, or when contrition and apology are deemed inadequate compensation for the loss of honor or a life. Even when rituals of reconciliation employ external authorities or mediators, as well as transcendent sanctions, inequality may prove to be an insurmountable obstacle. In the event of a killing among the Acholi, redress is ritualized (*mato oput*—"to drink the bitter root"). This reconciliation between clans involves apology, reunion, and compensation, mediated by "the influence of independent elders" rather than blood vengeance. In the words of one Acholi elder: "If you kill a person, you compensate, you reconcile—by paying heavily of course, but not death to death" (Finnström 1999, 50). Citing a young informant, however, Sverker Finnström notes that ongoing warfare and inequality may make such reconciliation impossible: "The rebels cannot accept anything as long as they are denied equality. The more ignored they are; the more determined [to fight] they will be. *Mato oput* comes in only at a later stage when equality is established. There can be no *mato oput* as long as there is inequality between the fighting parties" (personal communication).

Sierra Leone has a long history of conflict, in which strategies of retribution and reconciliation are equally evident—as in the stories analyzed in this chapter—and the discursive counterpointing that this implies between particularizing and universalizing tendencies is paralleled by numerous forms of social, ritual, and political organization in Sierra Leonean societies that effectively cut across identifications based on descent, locality, ethnicity, and estate, in order to define broader, more open-ended modes of collective identity. In this context may be cited the adoption of Islam (Jackson 1998a, 74–75), the use of cooperative and neighborhood work networks (Jackson 1977, 9, cf. Richards on "agrarian creolization" 1996, 83), the invocation of cross-tribal ties of totemic clanship to affirm universal human ideals (Jackson 1998a, 37–49), the creation of "multicultural bonds" through initiatory rites and cult associations (Jackson 1977, 238–41, cf. Richards 1996, 78–86), and the use of Krio as a *lingua franca* (Richards 1996). As Paul Richards reminds us, speaking of the civil war, "The hope of reconciliation … is that all parties share a heritage of cultural compromise forged over many centuries of social and economic flux. There are many articulate ideas in local cultures about the importance of forgetting the past, the danger of over-defining the present (concisely summarized by the Krio proverb *tok af ief af*—i.e. don't say all you know) and the positive virtues of political compromise, religious syncreticism and the hybridization of material culture. Within these cultural resources it is possible to discern a neglected but positive potential for making peace" (70).

However, to propose the possibility of peace when so many are suffering in a seemingly endless war may be construed as a kind of blasphemy. For even if traditional strategies, including the kind of storytelling I have reviewed here,[52] have in the past played some part in healing the wounds of conflict, all such discursive, ritual, and imaginary tactics remain empty unless the grievous injustices and inequities of everyday life are simultaneously addressed and radically changed.

And this is a matter not of art but action.

FROM THE TRAGIC TO THE COMIC

> The hero of a tragedy represents individuality unique of its kind ... No one is like him, because he is like no one ... Altogether different is the object of comedy. ... Comedy depicts characters we have already come across and shall meet again. It takes note of similarities. It aims at placing types before our eyes.
>
> —HENRI BERGSON, *Laughter*

Thus far my argument has been that Kuranko storytelling—and folktales in general—must be understood relationally and transgressively—as the expression of a "visiting imagination" that crosses discursive boundaries that ordinarily mark off "town" from "bush," private from public space, and past from present time, while infringing many of the social conventions that define male and female, old and young, rulers and commoners as possessing categorically different subjective essences. We have seen how journeys to and fro between these antithetical domains are enacted in storytelling sessions—various narrators taking it in turns to tell tales that suggest different slants on similar themes, in a spirit not of competition but of tolerant coexistence. It is in this hermeneutic openness and probing, in this straying beyond the bounds of orthodox viewpoints, that stories inspire judgment and critique—the ability to see one's immediate situation as it appears from another vantage point. When Kuranko observe that *tilei* are means of moral instruction, dramatically bringing home to small children the negative consequences of bad behavior, it is not because stories dogmatically lay down the law; rather that they foster the same abstract attitude that initiation seeks to instil, an attitude that leads individuals beyond their own subjectivity, their own self-interest, and their own situations, toward a comprehension of the social as a field of *inter-est*, made up of complementary and cooperative groupings rather than contending factions.

In building my argument, I have, however, given the impression that because Kuranko stories are often about incipiently tragic situations—the betrayal of friends, the brutality of an authority figure, the bitterness of sibling rivalry, the sorrow of an unhappy marriage—storytelling is inevitably serious. In fact, it is anything but. Just as loosely connected sequences of stories told by different narrators foster different points of view, gifted storytellers such as Keti Ferenke Koroma alternate trivial with tragic tales, and mix, within a single story, sadness and absurdity. The task I set myself here is to analyze this interweaving of the tragic and the comic, and to explain why human beings should so universally have recourse to comedy as a way of coping with adversity, and why laughter is so close to tears.

Rigid Virtues and Flexible Vices

I begin with an observation, based on an analysis of 230 Kuranko narratives recorded in the course of ethnographic fieldwork in northeast Sierra Leone in 1969–70, 1972, and 1979, that Kuranko stories all begin with an initial situation of imbalance between "town" and "bush." Either people find themselves blocked, bound, or bewildered by an overdetermination of rules, constraints, obligations, and limiting conditions—a parodic image of social, civic, or religious *order*—or overwhelmed by an excess of emotion, appetite, speech, and energy—manifestations of the "wild" powers of the bush. That most stories fall into the first category, may be because, as Henri Bergson has observed, "a flexible vice" is less easy to ridicule than "a rigid virtue" (1911, 177).

Here is a story told by Kenya Fina Kamara of Kondembaia in March 1970 that exemplifies the first of these two cases:

The Drummer and the Muslims

There was once a town where all the Muslims[53] lived, and there was a law there that no one should beat a *yimbe* drum. But there was a drummer who, wherever he went, could not stop himself from drumming. He came to that town during Ramadan. As he neared the town he tightened the skin of his *yimbe* drum. Just as the Muslims were about to pray he began drumming, tagban tagban tarara tara tagban tagban tagban. The Muslims cried out, "Who is this? Who is this? Who is this?" The drummer only turned to them and sang:

> *Eh, morgo ti yimbe fo morenu bare yan*
> (Eh, nobody should beat the *yimbe* in the Muslim's place here)
> Chorus:
> *Horo nyima ara n'keni yo horo nyima*
> (A free-born woman is like me, all right, a free-born woman)
> *Morgo ti yimbe fo sinkari sama*
> (Nobody should beat the *yimbe* at Ramadan)
> Chorus (as before):
> *Horo nyima ara n'keni yo horo nyima*
> (A free-born woman is like me, all right, a free-born woman)
> *Eh, morgo ti yimbe …*
> Etc.

At once the Muslims began following the drummer, dancing to his tune. They forgot their prayers. And by the time they realized what was going on, Ramadan was over and the drummer had gone on his way. Then they began crying, "La illaha illallah, Mohammad rassout Allah! This good-for-nothing made time pass so quickly that we forgot to pray."

Here is a second story, told by Keti Ferenke Koroma of Kondembaia in February 1972, that complements the first.

The Seductive Woman and the Muslim

There was once a Muslim who lived in a forest. He never came to town. Many people went to the forest to try to get him to come to town, but they all failed. Then a certain woman said, "I am going to get that Muslim to come to town." People said, "Heh, that Muslim will never come to town. Many of us have tried to persuade him, but we have all failed. That is why we have no one to lead us in prayer." The woman said, "Just you wait, I will get him to come."

The people said, "Ah, you. That Muslim will not come." The woman said nothing. But she spent the whole of the next day threading beads. Black and white, black and white, black and white. Then she plaited her hair, and tied the strands of beads around her waist so that the Muslim would be attracted by them.

The following morning she said, "I am going to get the Muslim." Everyone said, "He will not come."

Before leaving the town the woman bathed herself, and asked four other women to accompany her to the forest to help her sing. Then, as she neared the Muslim's place, she folded a headkerchief three times and tied it around her waist.

As she approached the Muslim, she half-untied the headkerchief around her waist. The Muslim was sitting down, reciting *suras* and telling his beads. But he was soon distracted by the woman, and began to count the beads around her waist.

As the woman came closer, she sang:

> Sefu, Sefu, this is what they have in town, Sefu.[54]
> This will not pollute Islam.

As she sang, she lifted and let fall, lifted and let fall the headkerchief around her waist. Immediately, the Muslim got up and followed her, saying, "Let us go, let us go, let us go."

The woman began to back away from him, still singing, and in this way the Muslim followed her all the way back to the town.

Well, Eve's descendants! May we be saved from the descendants of Eve. Whatever plan they lay against men, they succeed in it.

In Gregory Bateson's terms, the initial situation in these stories is one of schismogenesis—an unbridgeable gap, a breakdown of communication, an absolute division between two nominally different though ideally complementary spheres of life. Though the key opposition in these stories is between Muslim and non-Muslim estates, an identical polarization may be described in other stories between men and women, parents and children, elder and younger siblings, senior and junior co-wives. Having established the initial situation as one of imbalance—in which a strict condition, dogmatic attitude, closed frame of mind, or abuse of a privileged position has brought relations between two persons or groups to a standstill, the stories proceed to ingeniously break the impasse and redress the imbalance.

Typically this is achieved by having recourse to dispositions, talents, and forces associated with the extrasocial sphere of the "wild." In the two stories above, cleverness, cunning, singing, drumming, dancing, laughter, lust, and desire break the Muslim's thralldom to religious rules and regulations. The liberating effect of these emotions is compared, in the story, to the status of a free-born woman—someone not a slave to any man. In other stories, bush spirits and socially marginal persons—generally clever and courageous youngsters, or wise old women—are the agencies of correction. But in every case, that which has become too rule-bound, rigid, and dogmatic is loosened, lightened up, opened up, and made susceptible to influences and energies that belong symbolically to the bush.

It is clear, however, that the images of boundary-crossing in these stories coalesce two frames of reference—the personal body and the body of the world at large. In this sense, sexuality connotes *both* an experiential and conjugal blurring of the line between two lovers *and* a crossing of the line in social space between two lineages or two communities. Similarly, images of bodily incontinence (farting, vomiting, dribbling, gossiping, giggling, laughing) simultaneously suggest a relaxation of control over the orifices that connect home spaces and the space of the world (cf. Lévi-Strauss 1970, 134–35). In crossing and blurring the lines between different spheres of life, stories heighten anxiety and ambivalence, for while the unruly energies that are allowed to burst through the boundaries that ordinarily separate bush from town have a redressive function in the stories, they are, when not controlled, potentially destructive to social order.

The Comic

We have now reached the point where we may venture an explanation of the comic power of these stories. The explanation draws first upon Arthur Koestler's notion of "bisociation" (1964)—in which two usually distinct frames of reference are suddenly brought into close conjunction—and second upon the customary way in which anthropologists have understood joking relationships as strategies for managing social situations in which two categories of persons find themselves related in mutually contradictory ways—simultaneously dissociated and associated—as in societies with leviratic inheritance, where a man and his elder brother's wives are potential spouses and intimates, yet must, while the elder brother is alive, maintain a respectful and formal distance. Just as ritualized joking or play (*tolon*) is a way of both marking this anachronistic situation and releasing people from any obligation to take the contradiction seriously, so, as forms of play, stories both open up communication between the opposed worlds of "town" and "bush" and release people from becoming too anxious about the ambiguous and antinomian situations that ensue. Laughter is both an objective marker and subjective expression of this liberating sense of distance from a radically contradictory situation.

Before pursuing this further, however, let us consider some stories of "flexible vice."

The Promiscuous Woman

There was once a woman who would go with every man that passed her way.[55] Her mother told her that it was not right to accompany every man that visited their village. The girl paid no heed. Her father told her the same thing. She ignored her father too. One day she saw a stranger on his way through the village. The girl told her father that she was going to accompany the stranger on his way. Her father told her not to go. She said she was going. She went and told her mother that she was going to accompany the stranger. Her mother told her not to go. She said she was going. Her mother said, "If you keep on like this, you will one day regret it," and she told her daughter that on the very road she planned to travel there was a great rock that could swallow up a human being. The girl said, "Never mind that, I am going." So her mother said, "If you are bent on going despite your father's advice and my advice, then heed this warning: do not stand on that rock. If you stand on it, it will swallow you up." The girl said, "Never mind that, I am going." Finally her father spoke to her. "You should not follow your lover blindly. If your lover says goodbye, stay where you are, and say goodbye in turn. Do not follow him far from your own place."

The girl went with her lover far into the bush. When she came to that great rock she leapt up onto it and stood there, despite all the warnings she had been given. Immediately, the rock began to swallow her up. She struggled to move, but could not. She then cried out (singing):

> My mother told me and my father told me
> My mother told me and my father told me
> That if I came upon this rock
> That if I came upon this rock
> I should not stand on it
> I should not stand on it …

Before long she was half swallowed by the rock. "Eh, my mother told me but I paid no heed, my father told me but I paid no heed. Now look at me. The rock has half swallowed me. I did not know that in saying, "do not go," they were trying to protect me from harm. If I had listened to their warning, the rock would not have swallowed me. And she sang (as before).

Soon the rock had swallowed her up to her neck. Again she sang.

Finally, the rock swallowed her entirely. And there was only silence.

The Man Who Made Love to His Mother

There was once a great dancer. Nobody was his equal. When he had tired of dancing in his own town he went about the chiefdom dancing.

Now his father had two wives. The dancer was attracted to his father's younger wife, and wanted to make love with her. One day he told her how much he desired her. She said she also desired him. But though they wanted to be together, there was no way they could arrange a tryst without being discovered. So the dancer went to another village, and from there sent a message to his younger mother, saying that she should visit him while his father was away.

This happened. Indeed, whenever her husband was away the woman would go and sleep with the dancer. But the husband consulted a diviner, who said, "Hnn, your wife has done something bad, and will not bear you any more children."

The dancer was now staying in a village like Bendugukura. One day, his father announced that he was going on a journey. The woman was very happy, because she would be able to go and sleep with her lover. But her husband was not really going on a journey. His announcement was a ruse to find out what his wife was up to.

No sooner had he left than the woman caught and killed a big rooster. She cooked a large pot of rice, and put the rice in a large basket. Then, before setting out on her journey to see her lover, she went down to the streamside to bathe. While she was bathing, her husband came and quickly untied the basket, took out the rice and put it under the bed, then climbed into the basket, calling to his small son to tie it up again. He told his small son not to tell the woman. The boy tied the basket exactly as it had been, and sat down.

When the woman returned she picked up the basket, put it on her head, and set off. As she approached the other village, her lover slipped away from the crowd of people he was with and went to his room. The woman soon joined him there. She said, "Come and help me here." He helped her lift the basket down from her head. Then she said, "I don't think you love me as much as I love you, because I am always coming to visit you and you never come and see me." He said, "Don't blame me. You know my mother is your co-wife, and that we are lovers. If I went to your village and people saw that we were lovers we would be both disgraced and shamed. That is why I left your village and came here. No one here knows that we are lovers. They simply think it is my mother coming to visit me."

As they were speaking, the man's father was listening to every word. The woman said to her lover, "Well, I have brought food for you." The man said, "Then untie the basket." She went and untied it, and saw her husband lying there. He whispered, "Put the lid back, tie it on, and take me home." The woman was so ashamed that she did as her husband asked. When she returned home, her husband said, "Come and untie me." She did so, and her husband climbed out of the basket. But the woman was so ashamed that she sat down and was changed into an anthill. From that time forth it has been prohibited for men to have sex with their mothers.

The Bereaved Husband

A man and his wife had six children. Then his wife died. Before she was buried, the man cut off her breasts and hung them in the rafters of his house, thinking they would not decay. When mourners came to the house crying, he said, "Don't cry, my wife did not leave me empty handed." People thought he was referring to his children, but he was thinking of his wife's breasts.

Thirty-nine days passed. On the fortieth day,[56] he went to look at the breasts but found that they had decayed. He was distressed. Though he had all but forgotten about his wife's death, he now began crying for her: "Yeneba, ah Yeneba!"

People said, "Be quiet. Trust in God." He said, "Ah yes, you can say that because you are lying beside your wives."

That night he got up and went to his wife's grave and started singing:

Greet me here, Yeneba, Yeneba, my wife Yeneba.

He put his hand into the grave as he continued singing:

Look at the children, Yeneba, Yeneba, my wife Yeneba
Greet me here, Yeneba, Yeneba, my wife Yeneba
Greet me today, Yeneba, Yeneba, my wife Yeneba
Look at the children, Yeneba, Yeneba, my wife Yeneba
Look at the water pots, Yeneba, Yeneba, my wife Yeneba
Look at the fishing nets, Yeneba, Yeneba, my wife Yeneba
Look at the cooking pots, Yeneba, Yeneba, my wife Yeneba

Everyone became fed up with this. Two strong men said, "This man disturbs our sleep. As if his wife is the first wife to die in this world. We are going to put a stop to this today." So they climbed into the man's wife's grave and sat there and waited. That midnight, the man came, and started crying for his wife (as before). But when he put his hand in the grave, the men there grabbed it and began to pull him into the pit. The man was frightened, and cried out, "Eh, Yeneba, are you joking? Who will take care of the children? Yeneba, can't you take a joke? I was only joking. Why have you taken it so seriously? Yeneba, think of the work we did together, and think of our love, and leave me. I beg you, please leave me."

The men released his hand and the man fell back on the ground. Then he picked himself up and ran back to his house. Next morning he took a hoe, filled the grave with rubbish, and closed it. He was quiet that day, and for many days afterward.

Henri Bergson writes that comedy is corrective (1911, 157). And so it is here. An excess of desire, a lack of self-control, or an overweening emotional attachment signify, in Kuranko terms, an encroachment of the "wild" on the civil space of the town, and must be countermandered by restraints, rules, and regulations. Comparable stories involve other excessive passions, such as greed, covetousness, jealousy, and unregulated speech (gossip, rumor-mongering, and the inability to keep secrets). If the agency of correction in stories concerning "inflexible virtues" is something that loosens and lightens—such as drumming, dancing, singing, seductiveness, incontinence, laughter, and trickery—the very opposite is true of the second set of stories, in which a lapse of self control is countered by extreme constraint. These transpositions are expressed by means of ontological metaphors of extreme subjectivity and objectivity. Thus while volubility leads to deathly silence (as in the story of the bereaved man), uncontrolled movement ends in stillness or petrification (as when the dancer's lover/"mother" is transformed into an anthill, and the promiscuous woman is assimilated into a rock).

Folklorists often interpret such transformations in terms of the moral lessons they teach and the social order they uphold. Being turned to stone is thus seen as a supernatural punishment for heedlessness or lack of self-control. But such a view essentializes the antisocial and condemns it out of hand, failing to see that, as trickster stories so vividly demonstrate, the antisocial can be both a destructive *and* regenerative faculty. Thus, in situations where power is abused, it is the antisocial, antinomian genius of the trickster that redresses injustices and revitalizes the social order.

Such a dialectical understanding informs Lévi-Strauss's argument that the social and moral content of myth is largely incidental to the *logical* transformations and resolutions that myth contrives. But it is possible to analyze narrative without reducing it either to an external "social" function or an internal logic. While it is my aim to place stories in social context *and* clarify their structural transformations, my overriding concern is with the ways in which stories facilitate an intersubjective dynamic in which the condition of social viability is shown to depend on a balance that people strike between being subjects-for-themselves and objects-for-others.[57] This dynamic is governed by strategizing, not by rules (either intrapsychic or social), and its polar terms are not society and mind but subject and object—the extreme possibilities of human being and non-being that Sartre characterizes as *pour-soi* and *en-soi*, and Heidegger as *vorhanden* and *zuhanden*. While this kind of existential contrast is artic-ulated in Kuranko thought as a relationship between the free or "wild" powers of the bush and the rule-governed order of the town, it finds expression in European traditions in contrasts between humanity and animality, freedom and constraint, libido and superego, and the organic and mechanical.

Since the contrast between the organic and the mechanical is so central to Bergson's work on laughter, I will make it my starting point in spelling out why the Kuranko stories are funny.

I have already alluded to the idea that laughter springs from an ambig-uous or equivocal situation in which two or more contradictory images are collapsed into a single frame of reference (Bergson 1911, 96; Koes-tler 1964, 35).[58] Such situations characterize all Kuranko stories, and stem from a crossing or blurring of the boundaryline between bush and town. As we have seen, this symbolic contrast encapsulates a set of other con-trasts—between bodily incontinence and self-control, between raw emo-tion and social intelligence, between "wild" and secular power, between dispositions (such as cleverness and courage) and social positions, and between different subjectivities (male/female, ruler/commoner, Muslim/non-Muslim, elder/younger). But the crossing of lines and the switching of positions that bring these opposed spheres of life into incongruous con-junction is simply the condition of the possibility of laughter, and not its cause. If people are to laugh at such situations, they must *at the same time* recognize it as familiar *and* feel at a safe distance from it. Laughter catches us on the cusp of identification. For Bergson, laughter is our response to a situation that "encrusts" thing-like images of mechanical, robotic, or auto-matic action on vital images of energy and life.

In Kuranko stories, mechanical imagery is, in the strict sense of the word, absent, but the juxtaposition of rigidity and elasticity finds expression in the close conjunction of images of mobility and stasis, incontinence and control. Whereas, for Bergson, the paradigmati-cally funny story might involve an absent-minded individual with airs, walking blindly into a lamppost, or a toff slipping on a banana skin and instantly losing his superior composure, the quintessentially comic story for Kuranko draws far more directly on the visceral and emotional body.

The Great Farter

The father of a very beautiful girl declared that he would only give her in marriage to a suitor who could split a stick with a fart. Many men came and tried and failed. Finally, one man came, farting, farting, farting, and said, "Pa! My farting is going to get me a wife." He forthwith split the stick and married the girl.

That Kuranko find this story uproariously funny is undoubtedly because of the ludicrous conjunction of images of rigidity (the absurd stricture the father places on his daughter's marriage) and of unrestrained bodiliness (the fart). But, laughter is never a response to an objective contradiction; it wells up from the sudden recognition that though the situation is too absurd to take seriously it nonetheless discloses a serious truth. This is why laughter can only be understood in terms of its close relationship to tears.

What, then, is the tragic element in the story of the Great Farter? The answer is that tragedy is an outcome of being arrested, stuck, immobilized, or trapped in a situation *that one is powerless to do anything about*. The comic, by contrast, is defined by the relief, release, and distance it provides from just such binds, which is why laughter may be compared with the freedom of being able to breathe, speak, or move again after a moment of suspense. In the story of the Great Farter, the image of the suitor splitting a stick with a fart immediately distances and distracts us from the far more recognizably real, and potentially tragic, situation in which attachments to the natal family threaten the freedom of a child to grow up, leave home, marry, and begin her own family.

The comic is not the opposite of the tragic so much as a strategy for countermandering the tragic with distance and indirection. Tragedy befalls us like a bolt from the blue, as "natural" disasters, physical accidents, or social violence. Such traumatic events overwhelm and diminish us, and we withdraw into ourselves, feeling singled out, silenced, and powerless in the face of forces we can neither comprehend nor control. Though tragedy is suffered in solitude and silence, comedy opens up the possibility of subverting the original event by replaying it in such dramatically altered and exaggerated form that it is experienced as "other." It is often said, of tragedy, that healing takes time. With distance comes release. The comedic is the ultimate expression of this kind of distancing and release, and entails three critical transformations in our experience. First, the comedic restores a sense of agency. Second, it fosters a sense of emotional detachment. Third, it entails shared laughter, and thus returns us to a community of others. In taking us from ourselves and our own emotions, comedy returns us to the world, allowing us to see that we are a part of it, rather than the center of it. In this sense we are able to review the human condition from a general rather than exclusively personal standpoint (Bergson 1911, 4–6, 165). This is why comic characters are always stereotypes—"the mother," "the daughter," "the senior co-wife," "the dancer," etc.—rather than particular individuals, why they are often depicted as animals rather than persons, why they have one-track minds rather than mixed emotions, why their personalities are unidimensional rather than complex, and why that which they have in common is given more weight than their idiosyncratic features. Moreover, in so far as they transcend private and particular identifications, funny stories can be more widely shared than tragic ones. Accordingly we can coalesce Arendt's private and public spheres and Bergson's particularizing and generalizing idioms, schematizing the relationship of tragedy and comedy as follows: private : public : : particular : general : : tragedy : comedy.

In her study of everyday life in Sarajevo during the Bosnian war, Ivana Macek provides compelling examples of how caricature and gallows humor generated this kind of "shared experience," this sense of solidarity, while at the same time helping people distance themselves from the oppressive realities of life under siege. "Jokes were a typical way of commenting upon situations of destruction and humiliation," Macek writes. "For example, the joke that runs: 'How does a smart Bosnian call a stupid one?—From a phone abroad!' was basically only expressing one of the most acute dilemmas during the war—to leave or not to leave. By sharing the joke, people were letting each other know that they shared the same problem" (Macek 2000, 61). Much of this joking play had recourse to two stock characters, Mujo (Muhammed) and Suljo (Suleiman), whose stupidity and shrewdness are legendary in the former Yugoslavia. In some jokes "snipers were made into fools, as in the joke where Mujo killed Suljo with his sniper rifle."

The astonished people asked, "Mujo! Why on earth did you kill your brother [in faith, Muslim] Suljo?" "Well, you never know these days," answered Mujo. "I saw Suljo and when I looked through the sniperscope I saw a big cross on his forehead. So I fired" (Macek 2000, 61).

The cross was of course in the telescopic sight of the rifle, and not a sign that Suljo had become a Christian, an enemy.

It may be true, as Marx averred, echoing Hegel, that "all facts and personages of great importance in world history occur, as it were, twice ... the first time as tragedy, the second as farce (Marx 1934, 10). But he forgot to add that what is true of history is also true of biography: in replaying tragic events as a farcical story we preempt and decide how we will construe those events, and thereby put them behind us.

The Body as Common Ground

Kuranko joking relations and comic stories exemplify a mode of imagery that Bakhtin calls "grotesque realism." As in medieval traditions of carnival, with their Rabelaisian celebration of uncensored bodiliness and emotionality, Kuranko storytelling reveals the common ground of human existence to be bodily, rather than conceptual or spiritual—to reside in commonplace desires and needs, and not in some narrative of divine salvation, individual emancipation, intellectual transcendence, or material success.[59] Accordingly, Kuranko storytelling celebrates not the individual subject but the indivisible whole we call Everyman—the common clay. "In grotesque realism, therefore, the bodily element is deeply positive. It is presented not in a private, egotistic form, severed from the other spheres of life, but as something universal, representing all the people" (Bakhtin 1968, 19). Liberating people from the dogmas of hierarchy, the spirit of carnival brings everyone down to earth, irrespective of his or her birth, wealth or breeding.

In so far as tragedy has the effect of sending one deep into oneself, it is characterized by social withdrawal, silence, and retreat. Storytelling brings one out of oneself. It involves a decision to speak out, to share one's story with others, to see one's situation as from afar, and even, in time, to see its comic side. Accordingly, the tragic and the comic cannot be treated as distinct genres, but as terms that mark the opposite ends of a continuum, charting a passage from subjectivity to intersubjectivity, from the retracted and particularized world of private thoughts and feelings to the expanded sphere of public life. Comedy puts things in perspective, we say. Experientially, this implies the restoration of a balance between a sense that one is singular and alone (in good fortune or in ill) and a sense that one is essentially no different from any other human being in the world.

How then are we to understand assertions that storytelling belongs to traditional societies, and that science has eclipsed storytelling as a way of coping with the world in modern societies? Is there, in fact, a very different relationship between private and public spheres, or subjectivity and intersubjectivity, in societies like the Kuranko and our own? And what of the disparagement of the comic in modern societies as a lesser or popular tradition, and the demise of grotesque realism? Does this mark a divide between radically different societies and worldviews?

Walter Benjamin observed that we don't tell stories any more because, with the advent of new technologies of communication, "experience has fallen in value" (Benjamin 1968, 83–84), and Jean-François Lyotard has argued similarly that as a result of the burgeoning techniques and technologies of communication since the Second World War, narrative has lost its credibility as a way of legitimating meaning (Lyotard 1984, 37).

In fact, storytelling has not been occluded by science; rather it has come to occupy, like religion and art since the Enlightenment, those shadowy and peripheral spaces of our social worlds that Fredric Jameson calls "our political unconscious" (1984, xii). Thus, in times of personal tragedy, crisis, and transition—sickness, death, birth, dislocation, divorce—it is not the legitimacy of science that we demand but the need for a sense of agency, voice, and belonging. And the answer to these existential imperatives is not science per se, but storytelling. It is the story told to a medical specialist or nurse, the story one tells oneself, the story one shares with those one loves or with whom one identifies, that keeps one in the world and allows one "to persevere in one's being" (Spinoza 1982, 109). All that differs between our times and the times of Rabelais, or our world and the world of the Kuranko, is the content and context of the stories with which we create and recreate the ties that bind us to the world.

Turning Tragedy Around

To tell a story is to immediately put a distance between oneself and the events with which the story is concerned. A degree of agency is recovered, a version of the truth is contrived, a balance restablished between our need to determine the world to the same extent that it is felt to determine us. The comic is the consummation of this distancing. It unites us with others in a visceral community of laughter, it throws the tragic back in its own face, changed, and releases us from our thralldom to the past through a subversive mimesis that makes us its authors and arbiters. But does the comic ever completely efface the tragic and obliterate the past, or is it in its very nature a temporary displacement, a momentary respite, unstable and fugitive? Consider the following Arabic story that N. J. Dawood includes in his edition of *The Tales from the Thousand One Nights* as "typical of the amusing folktales still current in the Middle East" (1973, 12).

The Historic Fart

Abu Hassan's wife died when she was young. After many years as a widower, during which time he became a merchant of considerable wealth, Abu Hassan yielded to the persuasions of his friends and decided to marry again. His bride was ravishingly beautiful, and his wedding attended by kinsmen and friends from far and near. After hours of banqueting and festivity, the time came for Abu Hassan to go to his new bride. But as he rose from the table, bloated with meat and drink, he let go a long and resounding fart. His embarrassed guests pretended to have heard nothing, but poor Abu Hassan was so mortified by shame that he wished the ground would open up and swallow him. Hurriedly leaving the room, he went not to the bridal chamber but to the courtyard where he at once saddled his horse and rode off into the night. For several years he journeyed far and wide, before settling into exile on the Malabar coast. But filled with longing for his native land and his young bride, Abu Hassan decided he could bear his isolation no longer. Disguising himself as a dervish, he set off for home. After a year of hunger and deprivation, he finally came to the edge of his natal village. Uppermost in his mind was that he should not be recognized, that he had by now been consigned to oblivion and might, perhaps, return anonymously to a new life. Under cover of dusk, he cautiously made his way through once-familiar streets, hoping to overhear some gossip that would confirm his hopes. But as he sat outside a hovel, he heard a young girl questioning her mother. "Please, mother, what day was I born on? One of my friends wants to tell me my fortune."

"My daughter," replied the woman, "you were born on the very night of Abu Hassan's fart."

Abu Hassan fled. He traveled back to India. He lived in exile until his death.

From Abu Hassan's point of view this story is nothing if not tragic. If comedy rests on distance and indifference, the tragedy of Abu Hassan's situation lies in the impossibility of distance. And the full force of this impossibility is brought home by the fact that the great *geographical* distance Abu Hassan puts between himself and his shame makes no difference whatsoever to his doomed social and emotional identification with a primal event which cannot be forgotten, to which he is drawn back continually, and in which his life is finally consumed. Abu Hassan's tragedy is the tragedy of shame. Shame is a transgression, deliberate or inadvertent, that causes one to stand out from the crowd, a sore thumb, a misfit, an undesired reminder of something collectively repressed, an object of the gaze of others, arrested and ostracized, possessing no will or reality of one's own. For one so shamed at home, there can thereafter be no place to stand except elsewhere, in exile, among others who are equally anomalous. But Abu Hassan's real exile is from agency. Stuck forever in this defining moment of the past, imprisoned in his own subjectivity, lost to the world, separated from his bride and the family he might have had, Abu Hassan is socially dead.

But for us, who read or hear this story, and recognize or remember comparable embarrassments in our own lives, our cultural and historical distance saves us from taking the story too seriously, and so we laugh. However, we do not laugh because the story is intrinsically funny; we laugh because we are caught *between* empathy and neutrality. Between seeing Abu Hassan as a type and as an individual. Our laughter marks the instability of the line we are tempted, by the exotic framing of the story, to draw between ourselves and the other. In Abu Hassan's loss of self-control, of honor, and of community, we glimpse the loss that we our-selves most fear. In all comic situations, writes René Girard, we are really laughing at something that might happen to ourselves, and our laughter is an oblique attempt to ward off this existential threat (1966, 127–28). In laughing at others, we secure for a moment a sense of being in control of our own lives, of not being playthings of fate, mere puppets or victims.

This is dramatically conveyed in Anne Fadiman's book about a family of Hmong refugees who came from the highlands of northwest Laos to the US in 1980 and settled in Merced, California. Although this is a book about adversity and suffering, reading the following passage I could not but smile, for at the same time that the misadventures of newly arrived Hmong in the US seemed so ludicrous, they rewakened memories of the shameful mistakes I made when I first came to the US, and reminded me how vulnerable we all are when we are strange to a situation, lacking knowledge of the local language, ignorant of local protocols, and confused about our rights:

> The customs they were expected to follow seemed so peculiar, the rules and regulations so numerous, the language so hard to learn, and the emphasis on literacy and the decoding of other unfamiliar symbols so strong, that many Hmong were overwhelmed. Jonas Vangay told me, "In America, we are blind because even though we have eyes, we cannot see. We are deaf because even though we have ears, we cannot hear. "Some newcomers wore pajamas as street clothes; poured water on electric stoves to extinguish them; lit charcoal fires in their living rooms; stored blankets in their refrigerators; washed rice in their toilets; washed their clothes in swimming pools; washed their hair with Lestoil; cooked with motor oil and furniture polish; drank Clorox; ate cat food; planted crops in public parks; shot and ate skunks, porcupines, woodpeckers, robins, egrets, spar-rows, and a bald eagle; and hunted pigeons with crossbows in the streets of Philadelphia (Fadiman 1997, 187–88).

But it does not take long before the refugee begins to put some distance between himself and his initial situation. The self "goes visiting." And sto-ries are told, not solely from the privatized, subjectivized space of the self that has suffered, but from the space of the other, from the standpoint of the American that you feel you are beginning to become.

Joua Chai Lee had arrived from Thailand two weeks ago, carrying one piece of luggage for all eleven members of his family. "I asked Joua what he thought of America," writes Anne Fadiman. "'It is really nice but it is different,' he said. 'It is very flat. You cannot tell one place from another. There are many things I have not seen before, 'like that'—a light switch—'and that'—a telephone—'and that'—an air conditioner. Yesterday our relatives took us somewhere in a car and I saw a lady and I thought she was real but she was fake.' This turned out to have been a mannequin at the Merced Mall. 'I couldn't stop laughing all the way home,' he said. And remembering how funny his mistake had been, he started to laugh again" (202).

Reenacting events in a comic vein does more than simply distance individuals from events that may have troubled or humbled them; it fosters an image of the world as a stage, and of life as a game—a theater in which the agonic and the ludic are brought together and made to coexist. As Michael Gilsenan has shown in his study of storytelling and power-holding in rural Lebanon, fantastic, excessive, and theatrical modalities of verbal play create a sense of self-esteem, agency, and control, not through the *private* reworking of lived events but through decidedly *public* enactments and negotiations of power relations in which men make "themselves out to be" in the eyes of others (1996, 231). Power ultimately resides, as Hannah Arendt insisted, not in what we may imagine for ourselves but in what we may make happen in the divided world we share with others (1969).

PREVENTED SUCCESSIONS

If, in the fantasy of early growth, there is contained *death*, then at adolescence there is contained *murder* ... because growing up means taking the parent's place. *It really does.* In the unconscious fantasy, growing up is inherently an aggressive act.

—D. W. WINNICOTT *Playing and Reality*

In the dry season of 1979 I was living in the Kuranko village of Firawa with my family. After nightfall, when we had eaten, we would sit together on the porch of Abdul's house, sometimes in silence, sometimes talking over events of the day. One moonlit evening, Tilkolo and Mantene, two of Abdul's wives, began quietly singing:

Muse dila den koe le la:
ni i wara ba denke sorona
i kana fo i ma lui soron;
ni i wara dimusu
i kana fo i ma bon soron

Roughly translated, the song exhorts a woman to be grateful for her children, and not anguish over the hardships of conceiving, bearing, and raising them, for a male child will give her a courtyard (*luiye*) and a girl child will give her a house (*bon*).

As Abdul's "younger brother," I had a joking relationship with Tilkolo, and I later asked her, provocatively, "What is more important, courtyard or house?"

"It is the courtyard, of course," said Tilkolo, "because the house is contained within the courtyard. That is why people always say, "*m'bi tala m'fa luiye ma*" (I am going to my father's courtyard).[60]

In many respects, this vital Kuranko distinction between house and courtyard corresponds to the anthropological distinction between domestic and politico-jural domains (Goody 1962), which in turn reflects the long-standing European distinction between private and public spheres. Thus the Kuranko house—or more precisely the back rooms and backyard—are walled and fenced off from the gaze of the community, and never freely entered by outsiders, while the *luiye* is open to the village as a whole, and dusty paths lead from it toward the village plaza where the chief and his council of elders meet to discuss legal and political affairs. But more emphatically than in any contemporary European situation, domus and polis are identified in Kuranko as gendered spaces, and *musu dugu* (women's space) and *ke dugu* (men's space) define quite separate spheres of labor and social activity. While women have little freedom of speech, movement, or action within the polis, men have commensurably little influence in domestic life, though men are nominally "masters" or "owners" (*tiginu*) of the household. Just as women cannot sit or speak in the *luiye*, men cannot freely enter the backyard or back rooms of their houses, for these are exclusively women's spaces.[61]

This gendered balance of power is made explicit at the very outset of a child's life: seven days after birth, a baby girl is brought out into the world for the first time through the back door of the house, while a baby boy is brought out through the front door (Jackson 1977, 38–53).

While these spatialized and ritualized gender divisions are symbolically condensed in Tilkolo's observation that the courtyard (the space of men) contains the house (the space of women), her comment was tinged with the same irony and innuendo that finds expression in many Kuranko women's stories, for every woman knows that the field of female influence is never determined or contained by the fences, physical or conceptual, that men build around them. Although men's rules may determine hierarchies of power, the forebearance, influence, and passion of women determine the fortunes of children, and the way of the world.

Oedipus in Africa

Hannah Arendt observes that the relationship between private and public realms is mediated by storytelling. It is through storytelling that people transcend their differences as private individuals, families, and households, and create, as in rituals of initiatory rebirth, a public sense of "sheer human togetherness" (1958, 180)—a coexistence in plurality (8). In Africa, as Victor Turner has shown, this sense of communitas is achieved ritually by playing down particularizing identifications of kinship and descent and playing up "universal constants and differentiae of ... age, sex, and somatic features" (1970, 265). Storytelling and initiation rites effect comparable ethical and political transformations. Just as initiation transmutes, by means of a symbolic death and rebirth, a child's natal identifications and attachments into a new understanding of his or her identity in a wider community, so storytelling takes people out of themselves, and by fostering alternative points of view drives home the truth that the body politic is always more than the sum of its individual parts.

In every society, these transformations—from domus to polis, from kinship to community, from childhood to adulthood—are experienced with deep ambivalence and accomplished with great difficulty. While initiation enacts them as a terrifying sequence of ordeals, including seizure, symbolic death, genital mutilation, and scarification, oedipal narratives dramatize the conflicting imperatives in violent images of incest and murder. Indeed, initiation rites and hero myths may be said to encapsulate the central drama of all political life, if by political we mean the volatile relation, both imagined and enacted, between the secure, intimate, and nurturing space of natality, and the comparative anonymity of a pluralized public realm. In the following pages, I explore this force-field through an analysis of a series of closely-related hero myths, all of which disclose the profound ambivalence that marks this borderline between home and the world.

The Story of Yata

My starting point is a Kuranko narrative whose manifest themes are the rivalry between half-brothers (*fadenye*) and problems of intergenerational succession. I will analyze this narrative, first by placing it in social context, second by exploring its analogues in West Africa and elsewhere, third by showing how the *structural* transformations it effects may be compared with *intrapsychic* strategies for coping with the anxieties of growing up as well as with *social* strategies, both ritual and political, for dealing with the vexed relationship between private and public realms. This discursive progression, from a single Kuranko story to universal existential themes, thus echoes the Arendtian argument of this book—that by enlarging our horizons of understanding, storytelling helps reconcile singular and plural worlds.

Yata

A certain chief had two wives. The two women became pregnant at almost the same time. So they gave birth on the same day. Both babies were male.

Before the births, the chief had appointed two *finabas*,[62] one to each wife, so that he would be notified of the births as soon as they occurred. The *finaba* appointed to the first wife went to announce the birth of her child to the chief. When he arrived at the chief's house he found the chief eating. Instead of delivering the message and informing the chief that his son was born, the *finaba* sat down and accepted an invitation to partake of the food. The second wife also sent her *finaba* to tell the chief about the birth of her child. He went and found everyone eating. He too was invited to eat. But he said, "I was sent to deliver a message first: your wife has given birth to a baby boy." Then the chief said, "Good, that is the child to whom I shall give my father's name." So that child was named after the chief's father. Thus the second child became the first.[63]

Then the first wife's *finaba* said, "Oh chief, I came to deliver the same message: your wife has given birth to a baby boy." But by then it was too late. So the first child became the second.

Now, before the birth of these children a diviner had told the chief that one of his sons would prove eminently capable of succeeding him. The children lived together. But the first wife was never content. She was always unhappy about the position of the second son, who had been proclaimed the first. During this time the children were growing up and receiving instruction in the same household.

There came a time when the second son (who had been proclaimed the first) began to walk. The first son could only crawl. This went on for several years. The mother of the first son (who had been proclaimed the second) began telling her son that God had seen his inadequacy and so had made the boy's father proclaim him second. "Now look at my co-wife's child, he goes about gathering wood and doing everything for his mother, but here you are, lame and unable to do a thing for me. And every time I have to send your brother on errands for me, his mother tells me that she is not responsible that my own child is lame."

The woman continued to upbraid her child. But his was no ordinary lameness. The reason for it was that on the very day he walked his father would die. But as a result of his mother's persistent nagging he got up on his knees and went to a monkey-bread tree, seized it, shook it, and uprooted it. He brought the entire tree trunk and laid it at his mother's door. He then told his mother's *finaba* to go and tell his father to send him the iron bow. They brought the iron bow. When he drew back the bow it broke. He sent for another. The same thing happened. Then he announced that he would go himself. He stood up. His mother sang:

> Yata tamanda, Yata tamanda, keliya le kake,
> Yata tamanda; bi yo, bi yo, bi yo, ma bi nyorgoye.
> (Yata walked, Yata walked, envy made Yata walk; today oh, today oh, today oh, there has never been a day like today)

As soon as Yata stood up a serious illness befell his father. So the boy sat down. But his mother was laughing at him, taunting him. So he finally stood up, walked straight to his father and took his father's gown and cap and put them on. As he walked away his father died. Because of his great strength he became ruler. But the other wife was jealous and urged her son to go away rather than be ruled by the proclaimed younger brother. The second son who had been proclaimed first went away. But he never ceased to resent his brother's position. Since that time *fadenye* (rivalry between brothers) has existed.[64] Up to the present time brothers of the same father but of different mothers are rivals and competitors.

To Be or Not to Be

Noah Bokari Marah, my field assistant, told me the story of Yata in Kabala, July 1970, unaware that it was an episode from the widely dispersed epic of Sundiata—the political charter myth of the nuclear Mande. Though this indicates the way myths frequently become fragmented and pared down in the course of migration, surviving only as folktales, with their original cosmological, metaphysical, and natural oppositions reduced to parochial homilies (Lévi-Strauss 1977, 128), my interest is less in how myth and folktale may be formally distinguished than in the interplay between the social contexts to which each belong.

In so far as the story of Yata is evidence of a retraction of narrative from the public realm (the Mande epic of Sundiata is a charter myth, legitimating the status quo) into the private realm (the story of Yata belongs to a genre of playful, antinomian, *family* tales), our understanding of the meaning of the story of Yata must begin with the biographical circumstances of the one who tells the tale.

I have described elsewhere Noah's deeply ambivalent, "oedipal" relationship with his elder brother (a prominent political figure in Sierra Leone), and Noah's fantasy that had his elder brother not "tampered with my destiny" he too could have proven his mettle in national political life. "I could," he commented, "easily have been someone else" (Jackson 1998a, 102–3). Although Noah's frustrated political ambitions and craving for public recognition find expression in this story about fraternal rivalry (*fadenye*), the motif has wider ramifications, for, as we shall see, sibling rivalries arise from rivalries among co-wives, and between father and eldest son, while all may be understood in terms of each person's struggle to exist as a person in his or her own right, free from the shadow of more powerful figures, with independent standing in the world. Accordingly, Lévi-Strauss's *structural* question about the distinction between tale and myth may be fruitfully rephrased as an *ontogenetic* question: how can a person strike a balance between *Eigenwelt* ("own world") and *Mitwelt* ("with-world")—the contrasted social spaces that Hannah Arendt compresses into her dichotomy between private and public realms?

The Mande Connection

In turning now from biography to history, I remain mindful that the one converts continually into the other, and that each appears, in any narrative, as tenor to vehicle.

My first task, then, is to consider some of the numerous versions of the Sundiata epic, respecting Lévi-Strauss's injunction that the understanding of any narrative requires that we compare the structural transformations *within* single narratives with those occuring *among* sets of narratives over a wide cultural area.

Most Kuranko share Noah's ignorance of the origin of the Yata story. Even among the Kuranko in Guinea, where "the name Sundiata is vaguely known, his legend is practically ignored" (Person 1973, 207), and the hero of Kuranko epics is invariably the ancestral hunter, Mande Fa Bori, though his name is never linked to Sundiata as it is in the Mande epic. The sole version of the Sundiata epic that I heard in Sierra Leone was related to me by a *jeliba*, widely traveled in Guinea. This version, narrated by Yeli Fode Gibaté in Kabala, August 1970, was given in explanation of the origins of the xylophone and of praise-singing. Relevant passages are abstracted below:

> The ancestor of the Mansare [clan] was called Mande Sundiata … He first demonstrated his powers of witchcraft[65] against his mother. After his mother conceived, she remained pregnant for four thousand, four hundred and forty years, four months and four days. During this time Mande Sundiata would leave his mother's belly at night. He would go into the bush and hunt. He was a great hunter. At dawn he would return to town and leave the animals there. Then he would return to his mother's belly. At night his mother would look at her belly but see nothing; but during the day her belly would be swollen. This confused her. She went to a diviner and said, "By day I am pregnant, by night I am not." The diviner said, "You must prepare riceflour (*dege*) for sacrifice and offer it to four elderly women. There is something in your belly that will conquer and command the entire world."

The woman carried out the diviner's instructions. Then the elderly women told her that when she next woke at night and found her belly empty she should take a mortar and place it on her sleeping mat. They also told her to cover the mortar with her bed sheet and then leave that place and sleep elsewhere. They said, "God willing, you will give birth to your child tomorrow; that child is older than its own mother."

That night Mande Sundiata left his mother's belly. When she saw that he had gone she did just as the old women had told her: she took the mortar and covered it with her bed sheet, then went and slept elsewhere. Very early in the morning, at cockcrow, Mande Sundiata returned. He wanted to re-enter his mother's belly but the mortar prevented him from doing so. He knocked his head against the mortar and cried out. Then everyone exclaimed, "Oh, Mande Musukoro has delivered her child." Mande Sundiata was crying like a baby. But when the people came to see him they found that he had teeth. Although he cried like a baby he was a grown man. Everyone gathered round. A chicken was killed and cooked. The baby, Mande Sundiata, ate it all. Everyone was astounded. The wise men came and said, "You should not be worried, this is no mere baby, this is something great."

When other boys went to gather leaves, Mande Sundiata would go too, crawling like baby to gather leaves for his mother. When the senior hunters came to town with meat for sale, Mande Sundiata would disappear. When he went into the bush he would be a grown man, but when he came back to town he would be like a baby again. So when they speak of Mande Sundiata, they are not speaking of an ordinary man. He was a djinn (*nyenne*).

The narrative continues with a description of how Mande Sundiata continued to live a double life—a child by day, a supreme hunter by night—while the villagers never suspect that he is the provider of their abundant meat supplies. On one journey into the bush, Mande Sundiata steals the xylophone from the spirits of the wild (the *nyenne*), shooting and killing them. Then Sira Kaarta takes up the xylophone and becomes Sundiata's praise-singer. He gives Sundiata the title *keita*, which, according to Kuranko folk etymology, means "property-seizer," or possibly "heart-burner," from *sun* ("heart") and *ya* ("dry" or "searing"). According to Yeli Fode, another praise name of Sundiata is Sumaworo, said to derive from *sume* ("elephantiasis of the scrotum") and *woro* ("calf of the leg"):[66]

> His name is made up from his deeds. They named him for what he did. Sundiata, because he could strike fear into people's hearts; Keita, because he could seize anyone's property; Mande Sumaworo, because when he became angry he would make others so afraid that they would be afflicted by elephantiasis of the testicles. These were the words with which Sira Kaarta praised Sundiata (Yeli Fode Gibaté, from his 1970 narrative).

One of the most lengthy and detailed versions of the Sundiata epic is that of Djeli Mamoudou Kouyaté, recorded and published by D. T. Niane (translated from the French, 1965). The following synopsis of events preceding Sundiata's exile highlights similarities and differences between the Kuranko narratives and the "Niane version" of the Mandingo epic.

Sundiata's father, Maghan Kon Fatta, had three wives: the first, Sassouma Bérété, mother of the heir and future king, Dankaran Touman, and his sister, Nana Triban; the second, Sogolon Kedjou, mother of Sundiata and his two sisters, Sogolon Kolonkan and Sogolon Djamarou; the third, Namandje, mother of Manding Bory (or Manding Bakary), best friend and half-brother of Sundiata.

A soothsayer informed the king that his true heir was not yet born, even though Dankaran, his eldest son, was eight years old at this time. The soothsayer foretold the coming of a hideous, humpbacked woman whom the king must marry, for she "will be the mother of him who will make the name of Mali immortal for ever" (Niane 1965, 6).

The king marries, as predicted, but his wife—Sogolon Kedjou—repulses his advances. To his griot, the king confesses his inability to possess Sogolon; moreover, he doubts that she is a human being because, "during the night her body became covered with long hairs," striking fear into his heart. But the "wrath" that possesses Sogolon is finally subdued and she conceives the king's child.

The king's first wife—Sassouma—becomes envious and afraid of Sogolon whose son, it has been predicted, will rule over her own. Sassouma uses sorcery in a vain attempt to kill Sogolon.

Sundiata is born and named (Sundiata is a contraction, according to the narrator, of Sogolon and the boy's name, Djata). His development is difficult and tardy. At three years of age he still cannot walk or stand. Sassouma, whose own son is now eleven, derives malicious pleasure from the adversity of her co-wife's child. She taunts the child for being retarded and "stiff legged." At seven years of age Sundiata still cannnot walk or stand.

When the king dies, Dankaran succeeds him. Sassouma continues to persecute Sogolon and her backward child. Sogolon weeps because of the public ridicule she has to endure:

Sogolon's son was spoken of with nothing but irony and scorn. People had seen one-eyed kings, one-armed kings, and lame kings, but a stiff-legged king had never been heard tell of. No matter how great the destiny promised for Mari Djata might be, the throne could not be given to someone who had no power in his legs. … Such were the remarks that Sogolon heard every day (Niane 1968, 18).

One day Sogolon happens to be short of condiments, and asks Sassouma for some baobab leaf. Sassouma points out that her son picked the leaves for her, and laughs derisively at Sogolon, mocking the uselessness of her son, Sundiata. Humiliated and enraged, Sogolon strikes her son with a piece of wood, blaming him for her misfortunes and for the insults she has had to suffer. Sundiata then declares, "I am going to walk today." He sends to his father's smiths to have them make the heaviest possible iron rod. In order to wipe out the insult she has suffered, Sogolon asks that Sundiata bring the entire baobab tree (not just the leaves) to her house.

The iron rod is forged, and a praise-singer cries, "Today is a day like any other, but it will see what no other day has seen." The iron rod is brought to Sundiata. Sitting up, then standing with the aid of the iron rod, he bends it into the shape of a bow. Sogolon sings the praise of God who has given her son the use of his legs. Sundiata then uproots the baobab and takes it to the door of his mother's house.

Quickly, people begin to compare Sogolon with her senior co-wife, Sassouma.

It was because the former had been an exemplary wife and mother that God had granted strength to her son's legs for, it was said, the more a wife loves and respects her husband and the more she suffers for her child, the more valorous will the child be one day. Each is the child of his mother; the child is worth no more than the mother is worth. It was not astonishing that the king Dankaran Touman was so colourless, for his mother had never shown the slightest respect to her husband and never, in the presence of the late king, did she show that humility which every wife should show before her husband. People recalled her scenes of jealousy and the spiteful remarks she circulated about her co-wife and her child (Niane 1968, 22).

Sassouma now attempts to kill Sundiata by witchcraft. Sogolon, fearing for the safety of her daughters and her son's vulnerable half-brother, Manding Bory, decides to take her family into exile.

Other versions of the epic, treated in an essay by Pageard (1961), supply details which are also found in the Kuranko narratives. According to one of these versions which Pageard collected in Segou:

Soundiata, the eldest of [Sogolon's] children, could not walk before the age of seventeen. When he got up for the first time, it was to avenge the honour of his mother and he had to lean against a huge iron bar which gave way. It was on that occasion that the father of the KOUYATE griots (Dionkouma Doga) and Soundiata's two half-sisters, SOGOLON (KOLONGA) and SOGOLON (SOGONA) invented the song beginning with "Soundiata was able to get up to-day" (Pageard 1961, 56).

Pageard also stresses that Sundiata's voluntary exile is "justified to the extent that it prevents a brotherly struggle and everyone knows the strength of the *fadenya* (a rivalry between sons born of the same father but of different mothers) in the Manding country" (1961, 63).

It is also worth noting a synoptic account of Sundiata's birth, given by Bird (1971). In this account (hereafter referred to as the Bird version), details of Sundiata's birth conform even more closely to those in the Yata narrative.

After Fasaku Magan's marriage to Sogolon, both women become pregnant and both give birth on the same day. Saman Berete's son, Dankaran Tuman, is the first born, but Sunjata's birth is announced first to the king. He joyfully proclaims Sunjata his heir over the protest of Saman Betere. Saman Betere has a spell cast on Sunjata as a result of which he is paralyzed for nine years. The spell is eventually broken and Sunjata walks, giving rise to a magnificent series of songs (Bird 1971, 21).

Finally, we should remark the Mandinka versions of the "Sunjata" epic from the Gambia, published by Innes (1974). In one version, recited by an elderly griot—Bamba Suso—the following episodes occur:

Sunjata's mother, Sukulung, is pregnant with him for seven years. Sunjata's father, Fata Kung Makhang, declares that he will give his kingdom to his first-born son.
Sunjata Sunjata is born first, but the birth of another son is announced first

because of the first messenger's delay in bringing news of Sunjata's birth. Sunjata crawls for seven years.

When the time comes for Sunjata's initiation, the smiths make iron rods for him, but they break under his weight.

Sunjata then puts his hands on his mother's shoulders and stands up. Soon after Sunjata's initiation, his father dies (Innes 1974, 35).

Having now established this epic's range of variations within the Mande-speaking area, I want to focus on episodes within the epic concerning difficulties in the hero's conception, gestation, birth, or maturation—namely prolonged infancy (reluctance to walk) in the Yata narrative and the Niane, Pageard, Bird, and Innes versions; delayed and difficult conception in the Niane version; prolonged gestation (reluctance to be born) in the Gibate and Innes versions.

The Yata Narrative: An Analysis

In the Kuranko narrative, the *finaba*'s failure to transmit the message from the chief's senior wife to the chief precipitates an ambiguous situation. The proper status distinction between the two sons is reversed, although the superior ability of the rightful heir, albeit disguised, remains unchanged. Equally relevant is the *finaba*'s error of allowing his appetite for food (personal gratification) to deflect him from his social duty as a message bearer.

Myths from throughout Africa attribute the breakdown of social unity and continuity to a failure to communicate a message, and death and affliction are often shown to have their origins in a message garbled or information incorrectly transmitted (Abrahamsson 1951). In the Yata narrative, the *finaba*'s error has two consequences. First, since the rightful heir is named second in line of succession, the delayed transmission of the message has the effect of *increasing the distance* between the chief and his senior wife's son. The second consequence of the *finaba*'s error in delaying transmission of the message is that the *distance is decreased* between the two brothers. Instead of becoming unequivocally status-differentiated, the senior wife's child becomes the junior (but will claim the chieftaincy by right *and* by virtue of superior ability) while the junior wife's child becomes the senior (but will fail to claim the chieftaincy because of his inferior birthright and inferior ability).

These transformations have the effect of playing down the nascent conflict between incumbent and heir, and playing up the tension between first and second sons. This "displacement" has been noted by Otto Rank in his study of hero myths: "The duplication of the fathers (or the grandfathers) by a brother may be continued in the next generation, and concern the hero himself, thus leading to the *brother myths*" (1959, 90). M.J. Herskovits (1958, 88–89) has also referred to this kind of displacement in Dahomean narratives, where intergenerational conflicts become transmuted into intragenerational ones. Indeed, among the Kuranko it is freely admitted that a father's feigned rejection and overbearing criticism of his eldest son is an attempt to disguise the actual line of succession. The father's delegation of authority to the eldest son over the latter's younger brothers is interpreted similarly—as a way of deflecting attention and envy away from the privileged relationship between father and eldest son. Both stratagems are seen as ways of preventing *fadenye* (Jackson 1977, 164–68).

Thus far we have focused on tensions between men, but perhaps the most significant transformations in these myths involve a shift of emphasis from male-male to male-female dyads. Let us first contrast two crucial episodes in the Yata narrative:

1. The senior wife's *finaba* delays transmitting a message. As a consequence the status distinction between the chief's two sons is reversed, and the social distance between the chief and his rightful heir is increased.

2. The senior wife berates her son because of his backwardness. As a consequence the status distinction between the chief and his eldest son is reversed since, as soon as Yata walks, his father dies and Yata becomes chief.

The first episode involves male-male oppositions while the second involves female-male oppositions. They are linked by virtue of the fact that both *finaba*s and women occupy marginal, mediatory, message bearing positions. When they exceed the passive, mediatory functions ascribed to them, calamity follows. The second episode is thus a transformation of the first, but while it reiterates the same moral stricture (message-bearers should not be message-senders) it has the effect of displacing blame from the *finaba* onto the senior wife.[67] The narrative thus implies that *she* is ultimately responsible for the chief's death. Despite her son's reluctance to reveal his powers lest his father die, his mother goads him into walking.

The preceding analysis establishes the basic transformational pattern of the Yata narrative: intergenerational (parent-child) conflicts are transformed into (or displaced onto) intragenerational (sibling) dyads, and the source of conflict located in male-female rather than male-male relationships. This displacement of tension away from "central," "vertical" relationships towards "peripheral," "lateral" relationships is also characteristic of everyday Kuranko modes of explaining interpersonal conflict. Indeed, the pattern is so characteristic of traditional African societies that it is important to explore in greater depth the interplay between institutional and fictional variations of it.[68]

Aspects of Succession

The Freudian concept of displacement implies that emotional stress is deflected from relationships that are considered pivotal to those that are deemed to be peripheral. In Karl Abraham's formulation, "The least important is substituted for the most important and is transposed into the focal point of interest" (1909, 188). Freud himself referred to this process as "the inversion of all values."

Logically, male and female perspectives will, of course, tend to be diametrically opposed: while men prioritize their roles in the politico-jural domain, women emphasize their power and influence in the domestic domain. Accordingly, it is important not to universalize the Yata narrative as "a Kuranko myth," but place it within the specific context of male discourse.

Bearing this in mind, let us consider some of the problems associated with vertical systems of agnatic succession in Africa.

In his landmark study of succession to high office, Jack Goody refers to what he calls the "Prince Hal complex":

Where office passes between close agnates of adjacent generations, there is a potential heightening of tension within a relationship that usually carries the burden of the whole process of socialization. To the ordinary conflicts between father and son are added those arising out of the transmission of office; this is one of the problems Shakespeare sees in the uneasy relationship between Henry IV and Prince Hal (Goody 1966a, 34).

Goody observes that one "solution" to this problem is the custom of the "banished heir." For example, even though Mossi custom decreed that the eldest son of a previous incumbent be made Mogho Naba, the heir customarily lived away from the palace with his mother's kin, guarded and educated by palace servants. If his father was on the throne at Ouagadougou when the boy reached ten, he was formally installed as chief of the Djaba district, the traditional seat of the Crown Prince (Skinner 1964, 45). Strict formality obtained between the ruler and his sons. Skinner observes that "the Mogho Naba was not expected to enjoy seeing his son and heir, because of the Mossi father's traditional anxiety regarding those individuals who would profit from his death" (48). Younger sons were also given district chieftainships or assignments away from Ouagadougou. In the Mossi case, it is noteworthy that although the most capable person (in the royal minimal lineage) acceded to power, the emphasis placed upon the *principle* of primogeniture was considerable. This is equally true of the Kuranko, and it is worth remarking the parallel between the following Mossi "folk rumor" reported by Skinner and the Yata narrative (Kuranko)—though the similarity is even more striking in the case of the Bird version (Mande):

> If the child was a boy, the ruler or Crown Prince was notified immediately, because the important privileges of a first-born hinged upon this notification. Since several wives of the Mogho Naba might be pregnant at the same time and errors might be made about the onset and duration of pregnancy, primogeniture had to be established immediately to forestall dynastic conflicts. For example, it is commonly believed that the present Doulougou Naba was born several days before Mogho Naba Sagha II (1942–1957) but was deprived of the *nam* ["the power first possessed by the ancient founders, which is described by the Mossi as 'that force of God

which enables one man to control another"' (Skinner 1964, 13)] because the messenger who brought the news of his birth reached Mogho Naba Kom after the messenger who announced Sagha's birth (45).

A second "solution" to the Prince Hal problem is to avoid or delay making public the identity of the heir. The Swazi (who also sometimes "banish the heir") are quite explicit about the value of this strategy. "The heir's position is coveted, and ambition for the power and wealth it brings often leads to strife—strife in the homestead between father and sons, between brothers, between co-wives, between women and their husbands" (Kuper 1947, 89). Identical ramifications are traced out in the narratives we have referred to.

Goody also refers to a "basic alternative" (and thus a third solution) to the problems inherent in the vertical system, namely a "horizontal or fraternal one" (1966a, 35).[69] He points out that by including brothers among the eligibles there is less strain on the father-son relationship; "a wider range of kin acquires a direct interest in the throne; and you have older office-holders and shorter reigns" (ibid.). For example, although the Kuranko place considerable ideological emphasis on the principle of primogeniture, actual successions involve manipulations of both vertical and lateral possibilities in order to elect to office the most capable individual. For it is readily accepted that the attributes of leadership are not always found in the heir, and that both brothers and sons of an incumbent may regard themselves as potential successors.

Finally, it should be noted that a system of rotating or circulating succession has the effect of shifting political conflicts away from the domestic domain and shifting the tensions of intergenerational succession on to more distant relationships (Goody 1966a, 39, 1966b, 165).

All the institutional and "official" solutions summarized above have parallels in the narrative schemes earlier discussed. These parallels can be tabulated as follows:

Institution	Narrative scheme
1. Banishing the heir; avoidance relationship between incumbent and heir.	1. "Distancing" the heir by reversing the status distinction between first-born and second-born sons.

2. The identity of the heir is masked or uncertain.	2. The heir's development is retarded; there is uncertainty about his capability to accede.
3. Increasing the number of eligibles to include brothers.	3. Succession does not conform to the ideal pattern (primogeniture); in the Niane and Bird versions Sundiata is second-born.
4. Circulating succession; conflicts are shifted from close to distant kin.	4. Displacement of conflicts from father-son to brother-brother to half-half-brother.

We have now reached the point where we can bring structural analysis and psychoanalysis together, for it is clear that the strategic solutions to recurrent problems in intersubjective life that are imagined and articulated in narratives have direct analogues with the strategies implemented and institutionalized in other contexts of social life, as well as in other societies. This insight underpins George Devereux's argument for the psychic unity of humankind; what is backgrounded in the social imaginary or in the myths of one society will be foregrounded in the customs of another (1978a, 63–85). By implication, that which is marked "private" in one society, will find expression in the "public" life of another, and vice versa. Moreover, as we have seen, in any one society, espoused ideals will tend to be compromised in practice, although all such compromises will be played down or denied. The significance of "good character" as a factor in Swazi succession is a case in point. "Occasionally an outstanding son has won for himself such affection that he is appointed with his own mother over a child whose mother is of nobler birth. *But this is not put forward as a general principle by any family council*" (Kuper 1947, 103, emphasis added). The "fundamental principle" underlying the selection of an heir is that power is inherited from men but transmitted through women, whose rank determines the choice of successor (91).

Heracles

In order to explore further the ontogenetic complexities of the Yata narrative, I turn now to a consideration of certain parallels between the Mande narratives analyzed above and the Greek myth of the birth of Heracles.

The circumstances of the conception, gestation, and birth of Heracles bear remarkable similarities, both at the level of detail and structural organization, to the Yata narrative. The following genealogy and synopsis (from Kerényi 1959) will assist further exposition.

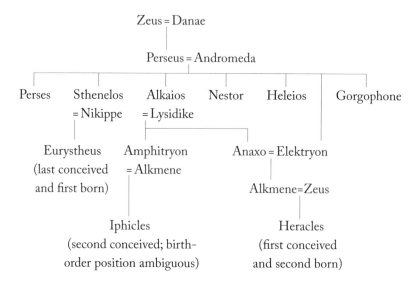

It will be recalled that Zeus impersonated Amphitryon on his wedding night. Zeus slept with Alkmene, and the night was of the length of three. Heracles, child of this union, was thus called triselenos ("child of the triple moon"). Later, during this same artificially prolonged night (some versions say the following day), Amphitryon returned and Alkmene conceived his child—Heracles's twin brother Iphicles. Nine months later Zeus boasted about the imminent birth of his son, who would rule the House of Perseus. Hera made him promise that any prince born before nightfall to the House of Perseus should be High King. Hera now hastened the birth of Nikippe's son, Eurystheus, and artificially delayed the birth of Heracles. When Heracles appeared, "one hour too late, he was found to have a twin named Iphicles, Amphitryon's son and the younger by a night. But some say that Heracles, not Iphicles, was the younger by a night; and others, that the twins were begotten on the same night, and born together" (Graves 1955, vol. 2, 86). The parallels between the myth of the birth of Heracles and the Yata narrative should now be clear:

Heracles	Yata
First conceived, second born (thus seeming to have lost his right to rule the House of Perseus).	First born, proclaimed second (thus seeming to have lost his right to succeed to his father's position).
Artificially delayed birth. Great physical strength (contrasted with his brother's greater power: Eurystheus, whose name means "the widely powerful," becomes king).	Artificially delayed growth. Great physical strength (contrasted with his brother's superior position).

Both myths may be seen as examples of contrived ultimogeniture, since both heroes are deprived of their rightful first-born status. The person artificially made younger/junior ultimately succeeds to a high position because of his superior strength and ability (Heracles becomes a god).

George Devereux has drawn attention to this theme in his study of the relationships between the Heracles myth and the myths of the founding of the Scythian royal dynasty. In the Scythian myth proper (as distinct from the version of the Pontic Greeks[70]), the first inhabitant of Scythia was Targitaos (or Targitaus). Targitaos=Heracles. Targitaos fathered three sons: Lipoxais, Arpoxais, and the youngest, Kolaxais. Four golden objects fell from the sky: a chariot, a yoke, a war-axe, and a cup. The oldest sons were unable to take hold of the objects, but Kolaxais the youngest picked them up and became the founder of the *senior* royal dynastic line. The objects subsequently became the insignia of Scythian royalty (Devereux 1972, 263–64). Summarizing the Heracles myth, Devereux stresses certain key episodes and themes:

The important thing, here, is that the myth explains how the child who was the last to be conceived, but who was going to be the first to be born (after only 7 months of pregnancy) can become king—a cruel and cowardly king, who is a tyrant towards the one who, having been conceived first, was born after him, as the pregnancy of his mother was artificially prolonged. In this tradition, an evil miracle confers on the biologically youngest child the dynastic rights of the eldest. In other words, the succession effectively conforms to the principle of ultimogeniture, fraudulently disguised as primogeniture (1972, 268–69, my translation).

Ontogenetic Approaches

The common theme of the narratives and institutions discussed in the preceding pages is the delaying or disguising of the rightful succession. From this point of view the *retarded birth* of Heracles has the same significance as the *retarded maturation* of Yata. A device with similar implications—the artificial prolonging of a pregnancy—while not present in the Yata narrative, occurs in several other Kuranko narratives including the "Gibate version," and yet another comparable device, present in both the Heracles myth and the "Niane version," is difficulty in conceiving. These devices for delaying or disguising the rightful succession can, of course, be compared with the various customs discussed above—banishing the heir, suppressing the name of the heir, implementing an avoidance relationship between father and eldest son. Clearly, that which is institutionalized in one society may be found in the fictions of another.

But institutional and phantasmagoric dimensions of social reality are also coalesced in core ontological metaphors, particularly metaphors of being-in-time.

Whether a myth emphasizes a son's reluctance to grow up or a father's reluctance to be displaced, the social consequences are the same: a prevention of succession and a breakdown of lineage or social continuity. Moreover, a father's desire to retain omnipotent control, or an heir's desire to remain a child, will have the same social consequences as a father's refusal to give his daughter in marriage or a daughter's reluctance to marry. The latter is, of course, a widespread theme in myth and folklore (Acrisius and Danae; Aleos and Auge; Indo-European tales in which almost impossible conditions attach to the winning of the King's daughter), and numerous examples exist in Kuranko.

A girl decrees that she will only marry a man without a navel (a *clever younger sister* realizes that the young man who comes courting is a djinn, and warns her sister in time to save her life); a girl declares that she will only marry a man who can dig bush yams with his penis (such a man appears); a girl says she will only marry a man as clever as she is (she meets her match and is obliged to marry); a beautiful and much sought-after girl feigns death to avoid marriage (a young man sings her awake); a chief lays down impossible conditions to prevent the marriage of his daughter (a resourceful suitor meets the conditions); a chief determines that no one will succeed him (his wife bears a child who has superhuman powers, or a djinn intervenes on the child's behalf, and the chief is displaced and killed).

If prevented succession leads to a breakdown of continuity *within* a lineage, prevented marriage leads to a breakdown in the alliance networks *between* lineages. This structural equivalence may help explain why Oedipal and incestuous themes are frequently found together in myths concerned with relations between familial and communal domains (Jackson 1982, 123–56).

Time is the key to this relationship. For the transformations that turn a child into an adult, and that maintain a cyclical to and froing between the private domains of family and the public domain, rest entirely on accepting the passage of time. Existentially, this means accepting that every birth presages a death, that every child foreshadows the demise of its parent, and that the condition of founding one's own family is separation from natal attachments. Though social necessity and human mortality set these limiting conditions, human beings everywhere tend to regard them with deep ambivalence. That which is socially imperative and biologically inevitable is often felt to contradict the individual's will-to-be. This contradiction is lived in the bodymind, and it is to this complex of ambivalent imagery that I will soon turn. But first, let us summarize the conclusions we have already reached.

Social continuity and social life (images of physical strength, agility, and potency) imply the *progress of time*, which implies the *succession of genera-tions*, which implies *individual mortality*.

Social discontinuity and social death (images of physical weakness, retar-dation, and delayed birth) imply the *arrest of the progress of time*, which implies *no succession of generations*, which implies *individual immortality*.

Preventing succession—either by the father hindering the birth or devel-opment of his son, or by the son hindering his own development—can be understood as an attempt to annul time. So too can the themes of *difficulty in conceiving and prevented marriage*. In the Yata narrative, circumstance allows Yata to prolong his childhood, to postpone coming into his own. This "psychosocial moratorium" implies a double-bind. If the precocious hero reveals his nascent identity, then his father will die. If he continues to camouflage his identity, then a false and incompetent heir will assume his father's position. This impasse is broken by the mother's behavior, which obliges Yata to get up and walk. The mother thus enables time to pass again. The son displaces the father, the chief is strong, the continuity of the ruling lineage is assured.

The narrative suggests a profound contradiction between biolog-ical time (which is irreversible) and social time (which is reversible). It emphasizes the need for the intergenerational transmission of power and knowledge over personal desires to arrest the passage of time. Individual growing up (even though the second birth leads to a death) is thus the basic precondition for social continuity.

Psychophysical Imagery

For the purposes of cross-cultural analysis, it is important to free the notion of the Oedipus complex from its Freudian emphasis on "the nar-rowly sexual problem of lust and competitiveness" (Becker 1973, 35; cf. Fromm 1973, 59–60, 103–4), as well as its patriarchal bias toward "blaming" incestuous and aggressive impulses on the child rather than the parent (Devereux 1953, 132; Fromm 1973, 61–62, 101). That the will to be finds expression in some cultures in images of incestuous or patricidal desire should not distract us from seeing that what is universal about the Oedipus complex is, as existential psychoanalysts argue, the imperative desire to become one's own person, to negotiate one's freedom in relation to the freedom of others in the public sphere (Brown 1959). A boy's desire to become his father is not necessarily born of hatred for the father or a desire to dispossess him and possess the mother; it is more likely to have its source in his growing need to be an autonomous person with a life beyond the confines of the natal family. As Merleau-Ponty puts it, a person's "sexuality" cannot be reduced to his or her genital life; rather, it symbolizes and expresses "the whole life of the subject," encapsulating his or her "manner of being towards the world" (1962, 158). Thus, against Otto Rank's argument in *The Myth of the Birth of the Hero* (1959, 77) that the Oedipus complex is basically *sexual*, I want to emphasize here the *existential* imperative that the child separate himself or herself from the parents in order to become an independent being. This transition to independence is difficult and painful, since many children are reluctant to grow up if this means relinquishing the security and succor their parents have given them, while many parents are loath to let their children come of age if this means losing the fulfillment that parentage has given them. The Oedipus complex has, therefore, on the one hand a *complementary* character in which the father's possessiveness toward all that he is and has is countermandered by his son's ambitions to possess those very same objects, and second, an *ambivalent* character, for this possessiveness and ambition come into conflict with the love that binds father and son in a common desire to honor each other's life.

This ambivalence gives rise to the conceptual and bodily distortions that comprise the core images in hero myths. But these images are not intellectually contrived. They arise from the lived relationship between conceptual and bodily being. This is to say that the struggle to be finds expression in a struggle to balance the boundless energy of youth (associated with strong limbs and virility) and the bound energy of the old (whose strength is symbolically displaced from the body and essentialized as wisdom, or vested in cultural objects and accoutrements of power, such as robes, maces, orbs, thrones, bodyguards, and armies).

This being so, it is easy to understand why psychological ambivalence should assume the symbolic form of physical retardation.

Elsewhere (Jackson 1979, 116–17), I have published numerous examples of the mythical child-adult: the Nyanga culture hero Mwindo, Sundiata (especially in the Gibate version), Maui (the youngest of five brothers but the most able), Heracles (the infant with the strength of a man), Krishna the "infant god" (Kinsley 1975, 13). These heroes display great precocity *and* various infantilisms. The anomalous character is nicely summarized by Wendy O'Flaherty, referring to the mythology of Krishna the baby. The mythology, she notes, "plays constantly upon the contrast between appearance and reality—the apparently tiny mortal (the dwarf, the infant, the individual soul) which occasionally reveals its true nature as the infinite immortal (the giant, the god, the universal godhead)" (1975, 214). These infantilisms may be interpreted variously: as devices to foster and emphasize the value of caring behavior (Eibl-Eibesfeldt 1975, 490–91); as images of fetalization in human evolution (Dobzhansky 1971, 95–196); as fantasized regression (Rank 1959, 84); as ways of establishing the hero as a mediator between childhood and adulthood. But only the last interpretation emphasizes the fusion in the one person of childlike and adult characteristics.

Undoubtedly, different values attach to the same mytheme in different societies and for different individuals. In the Yata narrative, however, I suggest that the hero's spurious retardation is a consequence or expression of excessive filial piety. His conviction that his father will die on the day he walks is a projection of his fear that his own growing strength will automatically entail his father's growing weakness. Yet it is imperative that Yata "forget" his father in order to "become" him. Because of the failed message, the distance between Yata and his father is greater than it would ordinarily be. This allows Yata to remain a child for longer than usual, to delay his detachment from his parents. His procrastination is, moreover, associated in his mind with keeping his father, the chief, alive and in office. This attitude is remarkably similar to that of a psychiatric patient whose retrospective insights into the sources and rationalizations of his own infantilisms are discussed by Devereux.

The patient commented:

> If I remain a child forever, if my very existence continues to depend on the presence of my parents, I can arrest the progress of time. By staying a child, I prevent my parents from becoming old and dying. If I am a dependent child, they simply have neither the right, not even the possibility, of deserting me by dying (Devereux 1964, 185).

Devereux cites a parallel case from Chinese sources, originally given as an exemplary case of filial piety:

Lao Lai-tsu was a man of the country of Ch'u. When he was 70 years old, his parents were still alive. His filial piety was very strong. Constantly clothed in a medley of garments [like children], when he carried drink to his parents, he pretended to stumble on arriving at the hall, then remained lying on the ground, uttering cries after the manner of little children. Or else, with the object of rejuvenating his old parents, he remained before them playing with his long sleeves, or amusing himself with chickens (185).

Such parallelisms between exemplary tales, clinical cases, narrative schemes, and individual biographies[71] from quite unrelated cultures makes a compelling case for the psychic unity of human kind, and the validity of psychoanalytic interpretations of culture (Devereux 1978, 64). But my interest here is the methodological entailment of this view, namely, to quote Devereux again, "that a single detailed study in depth can yield universally valid conclusions" (67). Let us then summarize the competing imperatives and contradictory identifications we have discerned thus far in the Yata narrative.

If the continuity of the lineage is to be assured, the father must accept the inevitability of his own death and displacement, and the son must assume the responsibilities of the paternal role.

A son can only realize his own identity by establishing his independence from his father. This change of identification and this independence are difficult, and require "more or less sanctioned intermediary periods between childhood and adulthood, often characterized by a combination of prolonged immaturity and provoked precocity" (Erikson 1968, 156). This "psychosocial moratorium," as Erikson terms it, is characterized by a delay of adult commitments, and by selected permissiveness. Such is the period of initiation in Kuranko society, and adolescence in Western societies. And everywhere, images of death and birth accompany this transformation of identity. As Winnicott puts it, "If the child is to become adult, then this move is achieved over the dead body of an adult" (1974, 170).

In both cases, socio-moral imperatives conflict with subjective factors: the father's reluctance to be superseded, the son's reluctance to come of age and assume his adult responsibilities. These double-binds generate ambivalent attitudes, and the hero commonly embodies this ambivalence as the "child-adult," though other symbolically equivalent images may be noted:

- Youngest of several brothers, yet the most able (Maui; Kolaxais).
- A baby confined to the domestic world by day, yet by night, in the bush, a great hunter (Sundiata in the Gibate version).
- Apparently weak and retarded, yet actually strong and precocious (Yata; Sundiata in the Niane, Pageard, Innes, and Bird versions).
- Human, yet a god (Heracles).
- Babbles and cries like a baby, yet has teeth at birth and eats solid food (Sundiata in the Gibate version).
- Stiff-legged, yet potentially strong and fleet-footed (Sundiata in the Niane version).

Given these contradictory traits, the hero may mediate structurally between conflicting imperatives and different worlds. He may thus, as a discursive figure rather than as a real person, facilitate the fictional resolution of recurrent problems arising from a contradiction between social necessity and personal inclination. That the heroic tale records the crises and binds involved in achieving a mature identity ("second birth") makes explicable the hero's bizarre parentage: both human and divine, both human and animal, from one parent only.

We may now consider the ways in which this ambivalence is embodied. In the Yata narrative, the Kuranko word used to describe Yata's retarded development is *namara*. Ordinarily the word means "lame" or "limping"; here it connotes "inability to walk." I regard Yata's lameness as far more than a physical image of his psychosocial immaturity. It signifies, in my view, the hero's ambivalence, for he desires simultaneously to remain a child (so preserving his father's life and position) *and to* realize his potential away from his natal family (so achieving status and authority equal to his father). These contradictory urges literally immobilize him.

The frequency with which hero myths from cultures throughout the world incorporate references to limping and to the legs as loci of power has often been remarked. Lévi-Strauss has observed that limping, as a mythological and ritual sign, is "everywhere associated with seasonal change" (1973a, 463). He observes that a normal gait is a symbolic representation of the periodicity of the seasons; limping is a "diagrammatic expression" of a desired imbalance—a desire for more rain or less rain, for a longer summer or shorter winter, etc. (464). In an earlier study, Lévi-Strauss commented upon the "universal characteristic of men born from the Earth that at the moment they emerge from the depth they either cannot walk or they walk clumsily" (1963, 213). Citing Pueblo Indian and Kwakiutl parallels to Oedipus ("the One with Swollen Feet"), he establishes a connection between ambulatory difficulties (particularly lameness in one leg) and a doctrine of autochthonous origins (only one parent). Although there are myths from Africa that are open to these kinds of interpretation, Yata's lameness has little to do with either seasonality or parentage. But it is an image (a "diagrammatic expression"), nevertheless, of a desired imbalance with regard to the succession of the generations. The slow-maturing, stiff-legged hero signifies impeded or prevented succession.[72] And his sudden maturation, signified by suppleness and strength, presages his father's death. In a version of the Maui myth from Rennell and Bellona, the son's vengeful killing his father, 'Ataganga, is preceded by the following incident:

'Ataganga defecated, and a child fell out there from. He raised [it], and the child grew up. He called [him] Mautikitiki. 'Ataganga looked at Mautikitiki; [he] was stiff, the body members were not pliant. And he told [Mautikitiki] to climb into a tree and jump down from it. And [Mautikitiki] fell down and his legs and arms broke, and so his arms and legs became pliant (Elbert and Monberg 1965, 113).

The Icelandic hero Grettir, we are told, was "not of quick growth in his childhood" and fumbled feminine tasks (Magnusson and Morris 1869, 28). And the Trobriand Island mythological hero, Tokosikuna of Digumenu, is initially crippled (according to one version he has no hands or feet), lame and very ugly (Malinowski 1972, 308). These examples of partially immobilized heroes are paralleled by narratives in which the father tries to hobble or otherwise immobilize his son in order to prevent the succession. The example of Laius ("the Left-Handed One") who pierced Oedipus's feet with a nail (and, according to some versions, bound the feet) before abandoning the baby on Mount Cithaeron is perhaps the best known.

The notion that strength, power and potency reside in the leg is universal. The Riddle of the Sphinx itself refers to the legs and to walking as a dramatic way of signifying the ages of man. But what is important to my discussion here is that immobilization may be connected not only with preventing succession but with preventing the "second birth" in which the son becomes detached from his father and initiated into the wider male community. Bunker and Lewin have traced out the philological and "unconscious" connections among such words as "knee," "know," "narrate," "generate," "generation," and suggest that the leg (particularly the knee) is a kind of "male womb" of the "second birth" (1965, 364). Devereux has suggested the same symbolic equation of knee and penis (1970, 1231) and ankle and penis (1980, 145–47). Onians, who has made an intensive study of such connections in Roman and Greek thought, concludes that suppleness and fluidity in the legs connoted potency and strength (1973, chapters 4 and 5), and Popper remarks that the pro-Socratic terms for the sense-organs ("the body") were *melea* and *guia*, i.e. "limbs" (Popper 1969, 410). In Africa, a Masai narrative recorded by Hollis tells of an old man who has no wife and lives alone; his knee becomes swollen, and six months later, thinking it to be an abscess, he lances it and two children emerge: a boy and a girl (Hollis 1905, 153). Among the Moi clan of the Nandi there is a similar tradition that one of the first men (the Dorobo) gave birth to a boy and a girl. His leg became swollen, and when it at last burst open a boy emerged from the inner side of the calf and a girl from the outer; these two are the ancestors of everyone on earth (Hollis 1909, 98). The Wakulwe, who live in the region between Lakes Nyasa and Tanganyika, believe that Ngulwe (God) "caused a child, known as Kanga Masala, to come out of the [first] woman's knee" (Melland and Cholmeley 1912, 21). Alice Werner notes that this idea reappears in a Khoisan myth where the name of the supreme being is "Wounded Knee" or "Sore Knee," a being capable of repeated rebirths and resurrections (Werner 1925, 157). The same author cites a similar example from Junod's collection of Baronga narratives, in which the mother of Bokenyane, the culture hero, was afflicted with a boil on her shin bone; the hero emerged from the boil when it finally burst (222). A Sonjo myth relates how the culture hero Khambageu was born from his father's swollen leg (he had no mother) (Gray 1965, 56), and a comparable Kuranko narrative tells how the hero Gbentoworo (whose name derives from *woro*—"calf of the leg") was miraculously conceived in the calf of his mother's leg, where he remained for more than seven years until the day a splinter of wood lanced open the leg and he emerged as a mature, strong, though small-statured person (Jackson 1982, 127–32).

The same motif occurs in contemporary writing from Africa. In Amos Tutuola's *The Palm-Wine Drinkard* (1952), the hero spends three years with his father-in-law in the latter's town. When he has passed three years there he notices that his wife's left-hand thumb has become swollen. One day, punctured on a palm-tree thorn, the thumb bursts open and a child emerges, able to talk "as if he was ten years of age." Within an hour the child has grown to a height of three feet, and asks his mother, "Do you know my name?"

On Walking into the World

The significance of walking is clearly related to the pivotal moment of ontogeny when a child is separated from family and childhood, and becomes an autonomous adult, a fully-fledged member of his or her community—a moment that also symbolically presages the movement from the private into the public sphere. But all mythological images or figures are over-determined, and it is the irreduciblility of their meanings to any one field of experience or social action that gives them their power to assume a second life beyond the particular social fields in which they have their origins.

It is thus important to expand our horizons, and consider the wider spectrum of meanings—phylogenetic as well as ontogenetic, private as well as political—associated with images of the legs, the knees, and walking.

Our species evolved in the Pliocene, bipedal and well adapted to plains' living. Dexterity, physical agility, fleet-footedness, and suppleness of limb must have had survival value and supplied, on the intellectual plane, some of humanity's primordial metaphors for socially adaptive behavior. Long after the evolution of semi-permanent settlement and sedentary habits, physical mobility and agility continued to serve as images of culturally valued traits: quickness of mind, strength of purpose, flexibility and vitality of thought. Infirmity, lameness, dragging the feet, and physical imbalance served, similarly, as images of social breakdown and discontinuity.

In contemporary English, lameness is a vernacular synonym for ineffectuality. Among nomadic and semi-nomadic peoples, physical immobilization (particularly of the aged) meant abandonment and death.[73] A Kuranko clan myth that I have published elsewhere (Jackson 1974) refers to a period when the ancestors of two clans are journeying together from Mande toward Sierra Leone. When one ancestor is impeded by an impassable river (his companion is able to change into a crocodile and has thus crossed the river), the other cuts off his calf and gives it roasted to the first so that he will not perish of hunger. The significance of this self-sacrifice is appreciated only when one realizes that mobility was crucial, both for the survival of the individual ancestor and his lineage.

Walking is, as I suggested in the Introduction to this book, one of the grounds of narrative itself. Walking carries us into the space of the world, an image of an evolutionary transition as well as the transformation that is effected in every generation from childhood to adulthood. Accordingly, ontogeny recapitulates phylogeny, and every biography conserves and recapitulates the course of history. This is why any account of hero myths and Oedipal narratives is incomplete while it remains focused on the private space of family relations or subjective experience. Life stories only assume the full measure of their meaning in the space of the world, as allegories of public life, of plural existence, of intersubjectivity. The link between these realms is disclosed by the fact that the structural transformations within the stories are universally paralleled, on the one hand, by intrapsychic operations (or "defence mechanisms") such as "displacement," "representation" (or "symbolic disguise"), "scotomization" and "projection," and, on the other, by ritualized social patterns of avoidance, denial, banishment, and separation.

Myths effect a fusion of biographical and historical horizons; in myth, the agentless and epic events of social time provide the crucial elements with which each individual articulates his or her own life story (Young 1983), while each individual life story becomes in turn "the prepolitical and prehistorical condition of history, the great story without beginning and end" (Arendt 1958, 184). It is in this unceasing two-way movement between private and public space, between *Eigenwelt* and *Mitwelt*, that the purpose of storytelling is consummated, which is why it is absurd to speak of stories as *either* personal or social, for their meanings inevitably depend on a fusion of both horizons, such that the one is always the condition of the possibility of the other.

PART III

HISTORIES

PREAMBLE

Marguerite Yourcenar's *Souvenirs pieux*[74] begins, much like any memoir, with the birth of the subject. "The being I refer to as *me* came into the world on Monday, June 8, 1903, at about eight in the morning, in Brussels." But after her first perfunctory paragraph, the author moves back in time, recounting her paternal and maternal family histories in such depth and detail that she is herself quickly eclipsed. Yourcenar's avoidance of self-centeredness is, of course, deliberate. By freeing the personal *voice* from the conventional autobiographical burden of tracing the development and career of a personal *identity*, she is better able to go "beyond the confines of individual history and even beyond History" and explore "the hopeless tangle of incidents and circumstances which to a greater or lesser extent shape us all" (1991, 3).[75]

Living in a society where we customarily enclose autobiography within the brackets of birth and death, and narrow it down, despite allusions to historical circumstances and external influences, to a unique trajectory, Marguerite Yourcenar's memoir is an ironic reminder that one of the most difficult and urgent problems we face whenever we attempt to account for the course of any human life is how to project a sense of its singularity while also doing justice to the historical, biogenetic, genealogical and social forces that shape it.[76] In implying a critique of the very genre in which she relates her story, Yourcenar's "pious memories" bring home to us the extent to which all stories embody a complicated interleaving of personal, interpersonal, and transpersonal frames of reference. The "complicated play of causes" that this implies (107) is, however, rarely represented without distortion, for in recounting the stories of their lives people tend to construct events according to cultural stereotypes, personal bias, and strategic interest. In some instances, individual life stories are so completely assimilated to normative scenarios that any trace of their unique character is all but lost. This is the extreme that Leslie White describes in his pejorative comment on Pueblo biographies: "The autobiography of a Pueblo Indian is about as personal as the life history of an automobile tire" (1943, 327). At the other extreme, the focus on the individual may be so intense that constraints of history and forces of circumstance tend to be reduced to the status of mere obstacles, heroically surmounted in the course of each person's journey toward selfhood. These contrasted models imply quite different strategies of attribution: in the first, the individual tends to fatalistically assign cause, will, and knowledge to sources outside himself or herself; in the second, the individual becomes a *causa sui*, heroically arrogating agency entirely to himself. Both these models, and the theories of attribution that go with them, obscure the complex *intersubjective* relationship between individuals, and the way in which personal, transpersonal, and impersonal identifications are simultaneously at play in every society and every story. Empirically speaking, the identity of the self is never so clear-cut as to justify the modern novel's assumption that human existence is a struggle between "the individual" and "society," and in no society can the collectivity be justifiably conceived as a real entity, possessing consciousness and will. Nonetheless, both views are incipient and mutually entailed in all human experience, which is why I find it ironic to recall, a propos Leslie White's image of the automobile tire, that in Central Australia, Aboriginal people track the imprint of tires on dusty desert roads as assiduously as they track human footprints, pointing out that though all tires appear alike to the unobservant eye, each has an idiosyncratic tread and unique pattern of wear and tear that make it readily identifiable as belonging *to a particular vehicle, a particular person.*

THE SOCIAL LIFE OF STORIES

> If every event which occurred could be given a name, there would be no need
> for stories. As things are here, life outstrips our vocabulary. A word is missing
> and so the story has to be told.
>
> —JOHN BERGER, *Once in Europa*

It is a truism that all stories get subtly reshaped and reconstrued every time they are told. To extend Heraclitus's metaphor of time and the river, one might say that it is impossible to ever tell the same story twice. And this applies to rumors and folktales, as well as the most rigorously documented events. Even when print promotes an illusion of fixity, and fosters the ideal of an authorized version, stories are inevitably revised in memory and reworked as they pass through the hands and minds of a community. Accordingly, such antinomies as the "personal" and the "social" or the "private" and the "public" do not define distinct genres of narrative, but only moments in a drawn-out dialectic in which individual life stories become interleaved with the narratives of a nation, and shared stories assume new meanings in the uses to which each individual puts them according to his or her particular experiences and predilections. It is in this two-way transformation of private into public personae, and shared worldviews into personal allegories, that narratives attain their power—their seeming ability to fuse Then and Now, Here and There, the One and the Many. As Walter Benjamin observed (1968, 92), stories are like vessels shaped from wet clay under a potter's hands. While each pot conforms to the stylistic and utilitarian conventions of a single society at a certain moment in time, it simultaneously bears the tell-tale traces of an individual potter's hands.

In this chapter, I trace the social life of a single narrative over a period of almost eighty years, exploring this interplay of lives and stories, and the contending notions of narrative truth it has generated. As with the heroic narratives of Odysseus, Oedipus, and Troilus that have survived for several centuries by changing under the impress of changing times, it sometimes happens that the story of a story is as fascinating as the story itself, and that what has been made of it more compelling than the life that originally inspired it or the original author's motive for recounting it.

The Blind Impress

When, in 1997, I published *The Blind Impress*, my aim was both to recount the story of John Joseph Thomas (Joe) Pawelka—one of New Zealand's most notorious and mythologized criminals—and to lay bare some of the other stories, historical as well as biographical, that had become connected with it. As such, my method followed the example of Sartre's great biographies of Genet and Flaubert—an attempt to demonstrate that while every human situation is subject to limiting conditions that lie largely beyond the reach of anyone's will and understanding, no two individuals ever experience or react to these conditions in exactly the same way.

The most widely known story begins in 1910, when 22-year-old Joe Pawelka is arrested in the Manawatu and remanded on charges of housebreaking, arson, and theft. His escape from police custody triggered the most intense manhunt in New Zealand since the military pursuit in the late 1860s of the Maori resistance leader Te Kooti. During the weeks that Pawelka was on the run, two men were shot dead, buildings were set on fire, shops and homes burgled, and panic engulfed a province.

Recaptured and brought to trial, Joe Pawelka got twenty-one year's hard labor, a sentence many considered vengeful and unjust, and on the wintry August day in 1911 when Pawelka escaped from The Terrace gaol in Wellington, never to be heard of again, there was a widespread feeling that poetic justice had been done.

The story first emerges in newspapers of the time, with journalists making the most of the dramatic events taking place in a region where the commonest crimes were riding a bicycle at night without a lamp, being drunk and disorderly, rigging scales and using false weights, playing hooky, and allowing stock to stray onto a public thoroughfare. But within a year of Pawelka's escape, the story is retold by a Wellington newspaperman, Albert William Organ, and for seventy years, until another Wellington journalist, Des Swain, recasts the Pawelka story in a quasi-fictional way, celebrating Joe as a hard-done-by romantic hero, Organ's *True Life Story of Joseph John Pawelka: His Crimes, Sentences, Prison Career, and Final Escape* (1912) remains the account on which encyclopaedia articles, TV scripts, and the Pawelka legend are based. In part the story of Man Alone, it belongs to the diffuse and dimly lit world of New Zealand's collective imagination, blurring with countless other popular stories, pub yarns, and anecdotes, and resembling a kind of national self-portrait on which New Zealanders work tirelessly, unselfconsciously, and without much sense of the finished picture.

I first heard of Joe Pawelka from my grandfather, who was a policeman in Levin in 1910 and among the police reinforcements brought to the nearby Manawatu region for the Pawelka manhunt. An immigrant himself, with working-class roots in the north of England, he had a lot of sympathy for Joe Pawelka. Sharing his reminiscences with me, his young grandson, was one way in which he came to terms, in his retirement, with the questions of social justice and human dignity that had preoccupied him all his life.

Stories have a habit of generating stories. They come to nest, one inside the other, like Matryoshka dolls, each a window onto another's world, so it was not surprising that when, in 1973, I went to live in the Manawatu, places where Joe Pawelka lived, worked, and took refuge became part of my life too. In a poem I published in 1978,[77] I alluded to some of the ways in which my story and Joe Pawelka's story were beginning to come together in my imagination:

> This poem has been written before;
> it has been written by men and women
> who never read a line of poetry all their lives;
> it has been said and imagined many times;
> it is the poem of the labyrinth,
> of the other way, of forgotten roads
> and of the wheel of chance
> and today, travelling the Pahiatua track
> to Scarborough, I think of Joe Pawelka
> and what went wrong for him,
> of my grandfather's story of a hunted man

who vanished from the cells
in which he was condemned
for burning down a school,
housebreaking and escape,
for bothering his wife when the magistrate
ordered their separation,
who scrawled a note with the lead of a bullet
and signed it "a man against the world."

Though I'd always wanted to find out "what went wrong" for Joe Pawelka it wasn't until the winter of 1994 that I set about the task. But my search did not stop with Joe Pawelka. It led me from the past into the present, and brought me to consider questions of fate and belonging that are as pressing now as they were at the turn of the nineteenth century. Inevitably, too, my research implicated my own story. In looking for Joe Pawelka I began to come to terms with my own small-town New Zealand upbringing, and rethink my own New Zealandness in the light of my increasingly attenuated relationship with the country I still called home.

Background Research

In the National Library and Archives I covered ground that previous researchers had covered, and formed a picture of a close-knit family of working-class Catholic Moravian migrants struggling to make a living in the predominantly Protestant and Anglo settlement of Kimbolton a hundred years ago. Joe was the first-born, a "smart boy," but given to "morose moods." Pampered by his mother and at odds with his quick-tempered father, he felt bitter and bereft when obliged to leave school at thirteen and become a butcher's apprentice. A letter to his mother, written in the winter of 1905, gives us a glimpse into his life at this time.

My Dear Mother

I suppose you are wondering where in the world I have got here in a place a little smaller than Palmerston   Since I came here I have got a job butchering in the town and intend to stick to it if I don't have a row with the boss This place is not so bad to live in and since I have been here I have met Cruden and his missus the Richardsons and the Gensons who are all living here Cruden is as big a skiter[78] as ever he was his Mrs has grown like her mother about as broad as she is long Well Mother how have you been getting on I hope you are quite happy and well and am not working too hard I suppose the kid[79] gives you enough bother though Oh Mother what about the Photo you promised me I should like to have a separate one of the lot of you Agnes Jack and yourself Tell Agnes to get her Photo taken as soon as she can and you too mother for I often wish for a separate Photo of you all so try and satisfy my wish if you can I hope you got that Photo of mine all right I have been wondering whether it went astray or not Dear Mother I wonder whether you have been why I asked for my school certificate in such a hurry for the truth is I had a chance of obtaining a government billet as Guard on the Railway train at Masterton, but I would not take the billet on account of the wages too small If I had been 21 years of age I would have received 8 shillings a day to start but being young they would not give enough to suit me and so I threw it up I have been travelling about aimlessly ever since and as you see luck brought me here and I struck work at my own trade Dear Mother you always complained about Kimbolton being a cold place but I believe this is worse here I do not know if it is always like this but the weather is something terrible since I have been here I have seen three snow falls all ready. I suppose Kimbolton is nearly as bad now too I am glad I am not in that miserable hole I wonder when I shall see it again How is young Jack getting on I expect he is getting quite a big lump of a fellow by this time and the baby too you havent told me its name yet Mother I feel quite proud to have a little sister like that Have you got a Go Cart for her yet If not write and let me know How are all the people getting on around you now I expect if I were to go back I should find nearly all strangers in the town and all the young fellows married by what I have heard on occasions The fools are mad and don't know what they are doing never mind we have all got to go through the mill once they find women out as well as I have they wont trouble their heads about them How is Agnes getting on with the tailoring it is a good thing for her to learn something in that line it is far easier than going out to service Well Mother it is getting dark and I cant see very well to write I would like to tell you a little more but I cant see so I think I shall close this little letter I hope to hear from you as soon as possible so write immediately and let it be a long letter with any amount of news in it   Good by Dear Mother my best love to you and Agnes and Jack

>   from
>   Your loving Son
>   J Pawelka

Written five weeks before he turned eighteen, the letter is from a solitary young man with little joy in his life. He feels rejected, displaced, alone. His father does not figure in his affections. His unhappiness has embittered him, making him judgmental and cynical. He has the habit of getting into arguments with his employers, and changes jobs often. He has been wounded in love. The world is a cold and inhospitable place.

On his twenty-first birthday, Joe was admitted to Palmerston Public Hospital with typhoid fever, and barely survived the operation on his lungs. After convalescing under his mother's care, he took work with a Palmerston butcher, only to be soon sacked on account of his habitual lying. Ten days after losing his job he stole some meat and a steel from another butcher, and three weeks later burgled the house of a Palmerston lawyer. Then, after a brief courtship, he married Hannah Elizabeth Wilson. The marriage lasted only two months. Possibly Lizzie feared her husband's mood swings, his histrionic threats against those who had crossed him, the revolver he had hidden in the house. Though pregnant, she filed a court application for "summary separation" and went back to live with her widowed mother in Ashhurst. In an attempt to win back Lizzie's love, Joe tried to drown himself in the Manawatu River, but all he got for his pains was a fine and a court order to pay his estranged wife maintenance. Unable to imagine or endure life without Lizzie, Joe now began to fill their vacant house with stolen furniture and furnishings. It was as if the empty dwelling embodied his loss and served as a sore reminder of the bourgeois world in which he had failed to find a place. As if he imagined that by filling the house with things taken from the family homes of others, his stolen happiness would be magically restored. In fact, Joe lost everything. Charged with numerous thefts of furniture and furnishings from houses in Palmerston, he was remanded in custody.

Two weeks later he escaped and made it back to Kimbolton only to be rearrested the following day and taken to Wellington for trial. Again he escaped, and returned to the Manawatu. Breaking through police cordons, he tried to see his wife, and one windswept night left a note in a milk can in Ashhurst protesting his innocence of the crimes that the papers were daily attributing to him. Scrawled with the lead of a bullet, the note was signed: "J Powelka, a man against the world."

The rest is history. Arrested in a hay barn outside Ashhurst where he had taken shelter from torrential rain, he railed against false accusations and then, in custody, defeated and weeping, begged to see Lizzie. When told she would not come he asked to be given poison to finish himself off. At his trial in Wellington he was charged with a string of break-ins and burglaries, with burning down a furniture store and high school, with escape, and with the murder of a policeman. Though found not guilty of murder, he got the maximum sentence the law allowed. But within six months, after four unsuccessful attempts at escape, he broke out of Wellington's maximum security prison in The Terrace with the help of other prisoners, and was never recaptured.

The Past in the Present

At this point, the subject of my research was snared by the stereotypes and stories that had gathered around Pawelka and taken on a life of their own. One such stereotype is immediately recognizable in the photo on the 1910 police poster that still conditions our image of him. The rigidity of the mugshot, with its formal placement of the hands, and the prisoner literally up against a wall, evokes an image of a body in death. Made over as a criminal type, Pawelka suffers our gaze and our judgment. His name, his history, his background, his thoughts, his voice are invalidated. The frozen image has taken him over. He is trapped inside the frame as in a cage, and even today we find it hard to see him otherwise.

To know another person's soul, to read another person's mind, one must find that person within oneself. One has to locate in one's own experience something that corresponds roughly to the other person's experience—that can provide common ground and assist comparison. This is why, from the outset of my research, I found myself digressing into my own life. But a second strategy for finding one's way into another person's life is to trace the ways in which that life has impinged upon and shaped the lives of others.

Having finished my archival research in Wellington, I went back to the remote Aboriginal settlement in North Queensland, Australia, where my wife and I had been living for half a year. But the Pawelka story had me in thrall, and three months later I returned to Wellington to pursue the story further.

Contrary to the expectations I had had at the beginning of my research, I began to realize that the full story and its conclusion were not facts of history, finalized years ago, but events still in the making—events that included me. And as I moved from archives into the world of the living, I came to see that Joe Pawelka's story was as much the story of his family over several generations as his own, and as much that family's shameful secret as part of the nation's mythology.

My first step was to visit Ray Carter, a retired senior constable who had interviewed members of the Pawelka family when researching his history of the Palmerston North police district. Ray had met Joe's sister Agnes in 1985, a few months before she died, and Agnes had not disguised her contempt for journalists. Sensitive to her hurt, Ray did not even broach the subject of her brother's fate. "It was the same with my interview with Jack Hansen," Ray told me. "I began to interview him but never followed it up."

Jack Hansen was Agnes's son and Joe's nephew. He had run a store in Kimbolton, established by his father in 1891, but was now retired and living in the back of the shop.

One of the leads I was following was a photograph. Apparently, some time during the First World War, Joe's parents received a photo of a group of soldiers clipped from a newspaper. There were about thirty soldiers in the photograph. They were in a desert somewhere. Around one of the soldiers in the back row a circle had been drawn. The family were unable to decipher the postmark on the envelope, and there was no letter to indicate who had sent the photo or why.

When I met Jack, I mentioned the photo Ray had described to me. Jack said he remembered the photo, but had no idea what had become of it. It was actually a photo Joe's mother Louisa had clipped from a newspaper—of a group of American or Canadian soldiers in France. Louisa was convinced that one of the soldiers in the photo was Joe, but Jack was inclined to think this was wishful thinking, something for her to hang on to. That Joe had never contacted his mother, that he had broken his promise to write her and broken her heart, was something Jack could never forgive.

I asked if Joe's family ever spoke of him.

"Seldom, if ever," Jack said. It was only when he was in his twenties and asked outright that he was told anything. The family kept its own counsel. Partly it was fear of prosecution for having aided and abetted the fugitive. Partly it was shame—because of the ill-repute Joe brought upon them. "It was hard," Jack said. "It was always hard for the mother."

Jack explained how the family sheltered Joe during the six months between the spring of 1911 and the summer of 1912. Apparently, Jack's father, Willie, who was married to Joe's sister Agnes, organized everything. Joe's mother cooked meals. Willie smuggled them to an old grainstore across the road from his shop where Joe was in hiding. But the entire community was complicit. When, years later, the Kiwitea County Council bought the old grainstore to convert it into a garage, some musty old prison clothes were discovered under the floorboards. Supposing them to have belonged to Joe Pawelka, the Council presented them to Willie Hansen as a souvenir.

When and how did Joe leave Kimbolton?

According to Jack, Willie Hansen planned everything. He got a friend, a local farmer, to buy train tickets to Auckland and a boat ticket to Vancouver. The Pawelkas, the Hansens, and Willie Hansen's friend scraped up the money for the fare and arranged for a young man called Ted Lawrence, who worked on the farm, to accompany Joe to Auckland. Joe's father took him to Mangaweka on February 15, 1912, hidden under grain sacks in a dray. Ted Lawrence traveled on horseback separately. The two men boarded the Auckland train in the evening. Next day, Ted and Joe had only a short walk from the Auckland railway station to the new Queen Street wharf where Joe was to board a ship for Canada. Having got Joe onto the boat, Ted went ashore. But when he returned to say goodbye not long before the boat sailed, he couldn't find Joe anywhere. So there was no certainty that Joe had actually sailed.

After my conversation with Jack Hansen, I went back to the National Archives in Wellington. I figured that since Joe Pawelka would not risk sailing under his own name, his assumed name might contain some small clue as to his true identity. So I began combing shipping lists.

At five in the afternoon of February 16, 1912—the day Ted Lawrence and Joe Pawelka reached Auckland—the *R. M. S. Makura* (4920 tons) sailed from the new Queen Street wharf, bound for Vancouver, via Suva and Honolulu. Arriving early that same morning from Sydney, the Makura loaded a large consignment of butter and hides for Vancouver, as well as ten tons of general cargo for Suva and Honolulu. She carried 246 passengers, 149 of whom embarked in Sydney.

In Auckland that day the wind was fresh and from the south. The afternoon air temperature was 70 °F.

My heart was pounding as I scanned the names. On the strength of what Jack had told me about people scraping together money for Joe's fare, I assumed he would not have had a saloon or second-class ticket, so gave my most careful attention to the steerage passengers, fifteen of whom had boarded in Auckland. In the lists, they were designated "labourers and domestics." Of the twelve men, one was traveling with his wife. The destination of another, Mr Peterson, was Honolulu. The ten remaining names, written in longhand and difficult to decipher, suggested nothing.

Despite drawing a blank, I decided to photocopy the *Makura* passenger lists, as well as lists for the *Morea* which sailed from Auckland for Sydney and London the same day. Unfortunately, there was, an archival assistant informed me, a "blanket restriction" on photocopying shipping lists.

I asked if I could speak with the archivist.

I was told it would be a long wait.

The delay proved fortuitous. With time to kill, I went back to the Shipping Indexes. When was the next sailing from Auckland?

The *Makura* sailed on Friday. The next sailing was on Monday, February 19th. The *S. S. Wimmera* (1871 tons) crossed the Tasman twice a month.

I now worked my way through the names of the steerage passengers on the Wimmera. Seventy-six were men. One was a Mr J. Wilson.

I was sure I had tracked him down. He must, I told myself, have had recourse to his second name, John. The thought that he might assume Lizzie's maiden name had already occurred to me. But what really seemed to clinch the matter was my discovery, next day, in the shipping advertisements of *The New Zealand Herald* for February 1912, that tickets purchased for sailings on Union Steamship Company boats were interchangeable with Huddart Parker—the company that owned the *Wimmera*.

Was it possible that Joe Pawelka had not sailed for Canada after all? Keeping his plans to himself, had he come to a decision to cover his tracks, cut off all ties with his past, and never look back? When he gave Ted Lawrence the slip in Auckland, was it his intention that no one, not even his family, would know where he was going? As an escaped and hunted criminal, there was no future for him in New Zealand. His wife had washed her hands of him. His family had been obliged to farewell him forever. Under these circumstances, did he choose to die to the life that was now dead to him? Did he turn against the world that he imagined had turned against him, in an act of symbolic suicide? An act of spite as much as it was an act of survival.

Many of the men who crossed the Tasman in steerage each summer were shearers. Joe Pawelka could have fallen in with them, disembarked in Sydney, and gone inland. When war was declared, he may have enlisted. There was a real possibility that he numbered among the thousands of ANZAC casualties at Gallipoli.

However, nothing would come of this line of inquiry, despite my extensive searches in Australian war archives and Registers of Births, Deaths and Marriages. I tell myself now that it doesn't matter. But I did not want to bring my story to an end, as others had done, by imagining what happened.

Yet was I not a writer, a storyteller. And don't all stories demand closure?

Moving On

It was almost a year before my story found its ending. It happened in Kimbolton, where Joe began, and where I had returned to see Jack Hansen one more time.

During my year away in the US I had written a draft of my book and sent copies to Jack, as well as to Anne Harris, Joe's granddaughter, whom I had met in Wellington during a previous visit. I told them there were pieces missing from the mosaic, and that these pieces belonged not to the past but to the present. I was already aware that the most compelling thing about Joe Pawelka's story, the thing I wanted to write about, was the way his story had become transmuted into others. The real story was the story of the people who had survived Joe's disappearance, who had had to deal with the stigma of loss, humiliation, and disgrace: Louisa, who, in Jack's words "took to her garden and rosary beads," Joseph senior, who "took to the grog," Lizzie who bore his child and tried to erase his name, Agnes, Jack and Helen, Joe's siblings, who bore the brunt of gibes and gossip in their turn. Their stories were the way I would bring my story to an end.

In August 1995 I returned to Kimbolton, to a "round table conference" Jack had arranged to "solve the remaining pieces of the puzzle."

It was the weekend of the America's Cup, and when I saw the Marque Vue sparkling wine in Jack's fridge I thought our conference would be overshadowed by this event. But no, the champagne was to celebrate what Jack called the family reunion. This would be the first time all of Joe's living descendants had come together. Anne drove up from Wellington, and John and Fay—Helen's children—came from Wellington and Wanganui with their spouses. Everyone had files and boxes of photos, genealogies, and family memorabilia. There was even a revolver Joe had made when he was a boy—a sawn-off .22 rifle, with the patent mark of H. Pieper's, Liège, Belgium engraved on the beveled barrel.

Though my research had been the catalyst for our meeting, Joe Pawelka did not dominate it. For Joe's nephews and niece, clearing up the mystery of his disappearance eighty-three years ago was far less urgent than affirming their survival as a family. As John, Fay, Jack, and Anne began to share their stories, photos, and memorabilia, the talk was less of Joe than of his sisters, Agnes and Helen, who had struggled to escape his shadow.

Fay recalled some of her mother's memories—of when she was eight and came home from school at lunchtime with a friend one day to find Joe in the kitchen with Louisa; of the police poking pitchforks into the haystack behind the house, but too afraid to go into the hay shed lest Joe was hiding there.

But mostly Helen said nothing of her brother.

"Any time I mentioned the name Pawelka, the walls came up," John said.

"She felt shame," John's wife, Maria, added. "It ruined her life. You can't imagine what it was like back then. Joe's brother Jack never married because he carried the Pawelka name. He didn't want his children to be stigmatized by having to carry it too."

"We were never allowed to mention his name," Fay said. "Mum didn't keep some of the things she got from Louisa. She destroyed a lot of things that had to do with Joe. She was ashamed of the memory."

When she was 87, Agnes wrote her nephew about a television film that was being made about her brother. She said: "When Joe disgraced us, we lost touch with everyone, thinking they would not want to have anything more to do with us. I suppose we were too sensitive; and now it's all going to be dragged up again in a film. I wish God I was dead and out of it. There is no doubt about the innocent having to suffer for the guilty unto the third or fourth generation. People are so cruel."

Joe's *guilt* had become metamorphosed into the family's *shame*.

Despite everything, Louisa kept a faithful record of every rite of passage in the life of the family, and when Fay showed me Louisa's prayerbook it was like being given a glimpse into the family's soul.

The small, battered Catholic missal measured about three inches by five. The boards were covered in purple cloth. There was a tarnished metal cross on the front cover. The binding was broken. I had to turn the dog-eared, age-blotched, brittle pages with care.

In several pages in the front and back of the book, Louisa had, over the years, written details of births, deaths, and marriages. Here was the date of her arrival in New Zealand, and of her marriage to Joe senior when she still called herself Louise König. Here were the birthdays of her sons, Joseph John Thomas (Joe) and John Alfred (Jack), and of her daughters Agnes and Florence Helen. Here also were the dates on which her children left home.

One page arrested me. Though the right-hand edge of the page was tattered, making it impossible to decipher two of the dates, here, at last, was confirmation of the date of Joe's final leave-taking. His name, Joseph John Thomas, was reduced to initials, possibly to disguise a potentially incriminating fact:

J.J.T left home 15th
Feb 1912

A later entry reads:

Joe left home 15th
Feb 1912

"She wrote him out of her life," Jack said.

Stories Within Stories

Our lives are storied. Were it not for stories, our lives would be unimaginable. Stories make it possible for us to overcome our separateness, to find common ground and common cause. To relate a story is to retrace one's steps, going over the ground of one's life again, reworking reality to render it more bearable. A story enables us to fuse the world within and the world without. In this way we gain some purchase over events that confounded us, humbled us, and left us helpless. In telling a story we renew our faith that the world is within our grasp.

Consider the stories occasioned by Joe Pawelka's life.

A psychotherapist might discern in the circumstances of Joe Pawelka's childhood, in his recorded remarks, and in his behavior under stress, a clinical picture of wounded narcissism. Convinced that fate has singled him out as a victim of injustice, this individual will do anything to draw attention to himself. To this end, heroism and notoriety, affection and contempt, are on a par. Deep down he remains a resentful child who thinks he deserves to be pandered to, and when the going gets rough appeals to others for rescue and care. Thus the overweening and remorseless need for acceptance. The habits of feigned illness and sham dementia. The threats of suicide, the manipulative confabulations, the downright lies. Such aggressive narcissism is an attempt to bend the world to one's will. One's sole reality is one's own need, one's own feelings, one's own state of mind. By contrast, the world of others is weightless and colorless; affectivity does not exist.

There may be grains of truth in this picture. But it is only a picture—underexposed and poorly developed.

Of all the stories which invoke fact, perhaps none are more tenacious than newspaper stories. Written in the confident if naive belief that "getting the facts right" will also settle the attendant moral, legal, and political issues, such stories quickly take on a life of their own. When *The Weekly*

News commissioned an article on Joe Pawelka in 1936, the rationale was that the facts be given precedence over personal sensibilities and possible slights. Thus, despite assuring Louisa that the story had been killed when she objected to its publication, the editor defended his right to publish it. Writing to Joe's younger brother, Jack, he argued: "I can understand your unwillingness to have the case needlessly re-opened to go over the facts as they have been published before, but I would point out to you that the author has had full access to police and other records and has gone to great trouble with his story with the object of doing your brother justice. Surely Joseph Pawelka has a right to have his name cleared. There is no shame for his family in this."

The editor went on to stress that the public was fascinated by the Pawelka story, and urged Jack Pawelka to appreciate the need to have "the facts put straight" in "the interests of pure history."

The Pawelka family rejected this argument, and fifty years later was still opposed to the idea of raking over dead coals.

In 1987, broadcaster and freelance journalist Des Swain began his research on Joe Pawelka, and met with the same resistance.

In a letter to Iris McGaffin—Joe's and Lizzie's daughter—whom he had traced through a birth certificate, marriage records, and electoral rolls, Swain sought to mollify her by painting a flattering portrait of Joe and pointing out that he could not have killed McGuire and did not shoot to kill Pauline Kendall. Testifying to the "positive aspects of his character," Swain wrote: "I am satisfied that a large number of comments about Joe Pawelka had no basis in fact: that he was a much better man than people are led to believe."

Iris was elderly and ill when she received Swain's letter. Not wanting to confront the specter of the past, she did not reply. But her son Terry wrote to his uncle, suggesting he contact Swain. Terry made one stipulation: "Mum requests that you do not involve the newer generation, i.e. her children, and grandchildren."

Not long after Des Swain began work on his "historical novel," Anne Harris learned of her kinship with Joe Pawelka. And the story she came to tell was also steeped in romanticism. "I'm a terrible romantic," Anne told me. "Lizzie and Joe must have been so in love." In Anne's view Joe couldn't do enough for his young bride, but had very little money, "so when he had a chance to acquire some inexpensive furniture he jumped at it." Anne was, however, aware that this was very likely not what happened. "It's my theory," she said. "It's based on the sort of thing I'd do."

For Joe's parents and siblings, such heroic nostalgia would have been as futile as the argument of the editor of *The Weekly News*: that proving Joe innocent of the violent crimes of which he was accused would alleviate his descendants' shame and stigma. The fact is that for Joe's immediate family there was no redemptive myth. While Joe's maternal grandmother told herself that Joe's tragic life was divine retribution for his parents' decision to marry against her will, Louisa and Joseph could never bring their son's story to a close. It had a beginning, a middle, but no end, though Louisa may have imagined some God-given resolution in the afterlife. Until their own deaths ended their self-questioning, they kept their silence and implored others to do the same. For the children's sake. In the hope that in forgetfulness and the fullness of time their pain might ease.

What then of the story I came to tell?

Walter Benjamin observes that "death is the sanction of everything that the storyteller can tell. He has borrowed his authority from death" (1968, 94). In a similar vein, John Berger explains that "any story drawn from life begins, for the storyteller, with its end." Most stories, he goes on to say, "begin with the death of the principal protagonist. It is in this sense that one can say that storytellers are Death's secretaries. It is Death who hands them the file" (1985, 239–42).

At Jack's "round table" in Kimbolton I had been a ghostly eavesdropper, registering a story that at times brought tears, at other times laughter. But though I was privy to these unrehearsed recollections and shared memories, I was an outsider. Almost a voyeur.

What had brought us together? And why now?

Our meeting had little to do with vindicating Joe. If anything, it was a celebration of being free of his legacy. Greater than any sense of his presence was the sense of Helen's absence. If shame is a kind of perpetual grieving, then the family, working through their grief over Helen's death, had at last begun to unburden itself of the shame it had shared with her.

Helen had been the last of Joe's generation. "An afterthought," Fay said. Much younger than the others, she was the last to have known Joe in life. Though Jack liked to tell me that if Helen had been alive my research would have been easier, I knew that it would have been harder, because I, like the others, would have been bound by the same taboo against talking about the past—the sole defense Helen and the others had against further hurt. The generosity with which John and Fay showed me Helen's heirlooms, and confided to me what they remembered of her and Joe, expressed their freedom from an old constraint.

But this was only my guess. For Jack and the others, our meeting was a mystery. "It's strange that after all these years everything is coming together," he told me, and mentioned how one of the South Island Pavelkas got in touch at the very same time I began work on the story. But as soon as we tried to clear up the mystery, we found ourselves again standing in Joe's long shadow.

Anne was convinced that Joe's spirit had brought us together. John's wife, Maria, agreed. Joe's spirit had presided over our meeting. It was Joe who inspired Barbara Blyth (nee Pavelka) to contact the others last year. And it had been Joe who had moved me to write my book.

In some ways, these spiritualistic suggestions come close to the truth. No life is sufficient unto itself. A person is singular only in the sense in which astronomers use the term: a relative point in space and time where invisible forces become fleetingly visible. Our lives belong to others as well as to ourselves. Just as the stars at night are set in imperceptible galaxies, so our lives flicker and fail in the dark streams of history, fate, and genealogy. One might say that we are each given three lives. First is our conscious incarnation, occupying most of the space between our birth and death. Second is our existence in the hearts and minds of others—a life that precedes the moment of our birth and extends beyond our death for as long as we are remembered. Finally there is our afterlife as a barely remembered name, a persona, an element in myth. And this existence begins with the death of the last person who knew us in life.

Translated into the language of storytelling, these transformations suggest a vast pool of ever widening intersubjective circles, possessing multiple centers of consciousness. The nucleus of each such center may be compared to the private realm, while the entire pool, with its overlapping ripples, its areas of turbulence, its stretches of calm, and its ebbing circlets of disrupted water, may be compared to the public sphere. Hannah Arendt's principal interest was in the ways in which private passions, thoughts, and experiences were "deindividualized" in the process of becoming "fit for public appearance" (1958, 50). But the process whereby idiosyncratic or private experience is pared down, selected, and sorted in ways that make it conform to conventional wisdom or make it accessible to the collectivity is countermanded continually by the ways in which individuals draw on this "cold store" of tradition, charging extant stories with meanings of their own, and using public narratives as "intrapsychic alibis" for the expression of private concerns (Devereux 1961, 378–79). It was in this way that I discovered, in Joe Pawelka's story, a way of telling my own story, an "objective correlative" as it were, of my own childhood isolation and marginalization.

It is, I think, in this elusive intercourse between public stories and private experiences that redemption may be possible.

In *The Life of Reason* (1905, vol. 1, ch.12), George Santayana observed that those who cannot remember the past are condemned to repeat it. But the past cannot be simply "found" in the same way that we unearth a stone—as my research into Joe Pawelka's life and my interviews with his descendants made very clear. The past has to be reinvented and retold. And this is something the living must do together.

Stories are thus like ancestors. In many societies, death signals the beginning of a ritually managed metamorphosis, often linked to the physical decay of the body itself, in which the idiosyncratic personality is erased. Personal property is destroyed, personal names put out of circulation, and the flaws and foibles of the individual's worldly life are forgotten so that the deceased may become an ideal type, embodying the essence of a *collective* ethos. So too, in time, do stories become ancestral, abstracted from our individual preoccupations so that they may articulate, as myths, a vision of a shared humanity.

Stories are redemptive, then, not because they preserve or represent the truth of any individual life but because they offer the perennial possibility that one see oneself as, and discover oneself through, another, despite the barriers of space, time, and difference.

STORYTELLING AND CRITIQUE

But who is that on the other side of you?
—T. S. ELIOT, *The Waste Land,* 1922 (l. 365)

On May 28, 1971 Hannah Arendt wrote her friend Mary McCarthy from New York: "I wish you would write about What it is in people that makes them want a story. The telling of tales. Ordinary life of ordinary people, Simenon-like. One can't say how life is, how chance or fate deals with people, except by telling the tale. In general one can't say more than—yes, that is the way it goes. For better or worse, of course, but the worst certainly is what people used to tell you, especially in this country [:] Nothing ever happens to me. Think of the craze for operations in middle-aged women. We seem unable to live without events; life becomes an indifferent flux and we [are] hardly able to tell one day from the next. Life itself is full of tales. What makes the tales disappear? The overpowering events of this century which made all ordinary events that concerned only you look too puny to be worth being told? Or this curious neurotic concern with the self which in analysis was shown to have nothing to tell but variations of identical experiences—the Oedipus complex, as distinguished from the tale Sophocles had to tell—?" (Brightman 1995, 294–95).

Writing from Paris the following month, Mary McCarthy shrugged off her friend's searching questions: "I'll defer taking up many points in your letter," she wrote, "we'll leave the tale-telling business; perhaps I shall write that next, if I ever start writing again. Anyway, it will be fun to talk about" (298).

I felt disappointed when I read Mary McCarthy's somewhat offhand response. For Hannah Arendt had not assumed that her friend had the answers to her questions and, strangely, Mary McCarthy seemed not to realize how profoundly Arendt's notion of critical understanding took its bearings from storytelling. Nowadays, however, given the academic industry that has been devoted to the subject of knowledge and narrative since Hannah Arendt's death in 1975, one is tempted to conclude that the questions Arendt put to Mary McCarthy in the Spring of 1971 make up an agenda that we have unwittingly yet faithfully followed for the last thirty years, and that, moreover, the numerous authors who have contributed to this industry share a single genealogy, traceable to her.[80]

While this is a conceit postmodernism no longer allows, it nonetheless reminds us of the emphasis Arendt placed on storytelling as part and parcel of the *vita activa*—the activities, both conceptual and physical, through which human beings produce and reproduce themselves in the world. Stories and storytelling, she insisted, are shared activities— unlike the novel that, according to Walter Benjamin, is born of solitariness (1968, 87). Stories take us out of ourselves. Stories belong to the in between spaces of intersubjectivity—a domain of "conflicting wills and intentions" (Arendt 1958, 182–84). As with other forms of labor, storytelling is a modality of working with others to transform what is given, or what simply befalls us, into forms of life, experience, and meaning that are collectively viable. This *vita activa* of which storytelling is so much a part is very different from the *vita contemplativa*. Unlike polemic, which cultivates a disinterested, objective, abstract, and authoritive view from afar, stories are a form of "situated thinking"[81] that brings philosophy down to earth, working within the everyday lifeworld of human struggle, encompassing a plurality of perspectives, in order to gain an enlarged view of human experience.

The work of such philosophy cannot be anything but political.[82] But Arendt's notion of the political is profoundly existential. Even when storytelling belongs conspicuously to hearth and home, its breadth of identifications and its allegorical layerings extend its significance into the public domain. Against the view that storytelling is a homespun, traditional, and conceptually unsophisticated art that conveys conventional wisdom but not objective truth, Hannah Arendt (1958, 1973), like Walter Benjamin before her, argues that storytelling is a modal form of social critique. In most societies, those who belong, through birth or privilege, to the establishment presume a superior *understanding* of the world—an Archimedean or god's-eye view from above or from afar. But instead of a spectator's standpoint, that seeks conclusions after an action has taken place, the storyteller's point of view remains *within* the world, moving from one particular place or person to another, and resisting all claims to ultimate truth by reminding us that truth is relative to where we situate ourselves, to where we stand (Arendt 1965, 52). Stories reconcile us to this variousness, rather than seek to transcend or condemn it. Indeed, it may be argued that in as much as those who invoke reason to legitimate their rule tend to separate themselves and their understanding from the world of everyday experience, storytelling is both dialectically imperative and perennially redemptive. For in telling stories we testify to the very diversity, ambiguity, and interconnectedness of experiences that abstract thought seeks to reduce, tease apart, regulate, and contain in the name of administrative order and control.[83] Storytelling achieves "distance," to be sure, but not through rhetorical tricks that purge the phenomenal world of the immediacies of raw experience, but through rhetorical devices that transport we the listeners or readers, into another space-time that remains, however, recognizably the same as our own. The journey away always brings us back to where we began, though with a transformed understanding. It is in this sense that once upon a time is always the here and now.

Judging

On Thursday, December 4, 1975, five days after completing the second section of her book *The Life of the Mind*, Hannah Arendt received two old friends—Salo and Jeanette Baron—for dinner in her Riverside Drive apartment in New York City. After dinner, the three friends retired to the living room. As they were talking over coffee, Hannah Arendt suffered a brief coughing fit, then slumped back in her armchair and lost consciousness. A heart attack had killed her instantly.

For the next three years, Mary McCarthy devoted herself to editing and publishing her friend's unfinished book. Working until late at night, and even in her dreams, Mary McCarthy would speak of this labor of love as sustaining "an imaginary dialogue ... verging sometimes, as in life, on debate."

Arendt's book, Mary McCarthy explains in her editor's postface, had been conceived in three parts—Thinking, Willing, and Judging—but the faculty of judgment had been, for Hannah Arendt, the "linchpin in the mind's triad" (Brightman 1995, 391), for judgment brings home to us our connectedness to the world we inhabit with others; it is judgment that makes intellectual activity worldly and wise. At the time of her death, Hannah Arendt had written only scattered notes toward this third and final section of her book. These were found on her desk. Threaded into her typewriter was a sheet of paper, blank but for the title, "Judging," and two epigraphs that gave little clue as to what she had intended to write. *The Life of the Mind*, then, resembled a story without an end (Beiner 1982, 90).

Yet its conclusions were presaged in Arendt's lectures on Kant's political philosophy, delivered at the New School for Social Research in the Fall of 1970.

In Hannah Arendt's view, judgment presupposes "the human condition of plurality" (1958, 7). Unlike pure reason, judging does not consist in a silent Platonic dialogue between me and myself, but springs from and anticipates the presence of diverse others (Arendt 1968, 220). More than any other mode of thought, it is socially situated and socially mediated, taking its bearings from incidents in our lived experience and finding expression in stories (14). The faculty of judgment, however, requires distance from "subjective private conditions," though this distance is not achieved through the kind of social and affective disengagement that scientific rationality demands—assuming "some higher standpoint ... above the melée" (Arendt 1968, 220, 1982, 42). Remaining faithful to its essentially *social* character, judgment seeks distance through imaginative displacement—reconsidering one's own world from the standpoint of another.[84] Reminiscent of Jaspers's notion of "border situations" (*grenzsituationen*), where philosophy gives up the search for bounded and coherent theories of the whole and seeks the conditions under which it may be unsettled or agitated (Arendt 1994, 182), Arendt's interest is in how thought may venture beyond itself. However, she is at pains to point out that the practical and experiential mimesis that one looks for when adopting the standpoint of others neither eclipses one's own being, nor supposes an understanding of what actually goes on in the minds of others. Distancing oneself from one's own customary point of view is not, therefore, a matter of exchanging one's own prejudices for the prejudices of others (43). Nor does it imply passivity. Unlike classical empiricism, where the observer makes himself a *tabula rasa* in order to register his impressions of the observed, judging requires active engagement and conversation—submitting *one's own thoughts* to the thinking of others. Accordingly, judging implies a third position, reducible to neither one's own nor the other's: a view from in-between, from within the space of intersubjectivity itself:

> Imagination alone enables us to see things in their proper perspective, to be strong enough to put that which is too close at a certain distance so that we can see and understand it without bias and prejudice, to be generous enough to bridge abysses of remoteness until we can see and understand everything that is too far away from us as though it were our own affair. This distancing of some things and bridging the abysses to others is part of the dialogue of understanding for whose purposes direct experience establishes too close a contact and mere knowledge erects artificial barriers. Without this kind of imagination, which actually is understanding, we would never be able to take our bearings in the world. It is the only inner compass we have. We are contemporaries only in so far as our understanding reaches (Arendt 1994, 323).

But isn't there something too idealistic in this notion of judgment that is neither an empathic merging of one's own identity with the other nor an abstract conceptualization that sets one apart from others, but depends, rather, on a lateral displacement that puts oneself in the place of others even though their views and tastes may be repellent? Doesn't Arendt's view tend to play down the entrenched divisions in the public realm that militate against "communicative transparency" and make it practically impossible to accept what Bill Readings has called "dereferentialization" (1996, 122–24, 166–67). To inhabit a "dissensual community"—thinking without identity, thinking without a priori assumptions, "thinking without a banister"—may be within the reach of those who have nothing to lose, but is it possible in situations where difference is not a matter for academic debate and edification but a matter of life and death? For example, in Veena Das's moving account of a woman called Shanti, who survived the death of her husband and three sons during the Delhi riots that followed the assassination of Indira Ghandi in 1984, we are confronted with the ideological impossibility of Shanti's loss being reconciled with the patriarchal ethos of her community. As the community scapegoats and shames Shanti for having lost her sons and betrayed "the male world," she sees that "a life built around female connections is not … a life worth living," and commits suicide (Das 1990, 346–62).

This brings me to my second point: that judging, in Arendt's sense of the term, is always, in practice, less a question of a person's *intellectual* acuity than of his or her emotional and social capacity. No matter how earnest our intentions, the fact is that whenever we endeavor to accommodate any kind of radical otherness, the habits and dispositions that define our own sense of who we are, are placed in jeopardy. For this reason, people are unlikely to ponder their own worldview as it appears from the standpoint of another unless circumstances compel them to. In reality, understanding is usually a result of *enforced* displacement, of crises that wrench a person out of his or her habitual routines of thought and behavior, rather than a product of philosophical choice or idle curiosity. Understanding others requires more than an intellectual movement from one's own position to theirs; it involves physical upheaval, psychological turmoil, and moral confusion. This is why suffering is an inescapable concomitant of understanding—the loss of the illusion that one's own particular worldview is universally tenable, the pain of seeing in the face and gestures of a stranger the invalidation of oneself. And it is precisely because such hazards and symbolic deaths are the cost of going beyond the borders of the local world that we complacently regard as the measure of *the* world that most human beings resist seeking to know others as they know themselves. By this same token, we find the most compelling examples of how human beings suffer and struggle with the project of enlarging their understanding in those parts of the world where openness has become the unavoidable condition of existence. It is here, in what I call the "migrant imagination," rather than in European salons and seminars, that we may recognize and be reconciled to the often painful truth that the human world constitutes our common ground, our shared heritage, *not as a place of comfortably consistent unity but as a site of contingency, difference, and struggle.*[85]

In reconciling ourselves to this condition, storytelling is crucial, for storytelling provides us not with a means of changing that which we cannot change but with a way of reimagining it. Consider the following ethnographic examples. In his study of the interplay of local and transnational identifications in Belize, Richard Wilk shows that one effect of the increasing presence of foreign goods, television, tourists, money, entrepreneurs, music, language, drugs, gangs, tastes, and ideas in Belize has been the self-conscious creation of localized culture, including the culture of food. This process, Wilk argues, is played out as a narrative or drama that pits the local against the foreign, self against other, and provides Belizeans with a sense of being in control of the "global ecumene" rather than at the mercy of it. "The moral of this story," he notes, "is that the technological apparatus of capitalism, including television and other media, has been turned to very local and anti-hegemonic purposes" (1999, 248). A second example, taken from Andrew Lattas's study of cargo cults in Papua New Guinea, also shows how storytelling enables an imaginative reconfiguring of the relationship of local and global realms. Cargo narratives are grounded in the traditional conviction that journeying across vast distances to unfamiliar places—particularly the land of the dead—is a precondition of enlarging one's understanding and increasing one's power. When Europeans arrived in Papua New Guinea, changing its cultural, economic and political landscapes, this world of empowering otherness became identified with whites. Cargo cult stories accommodated this new focus while remaining preoccupied with "breaking out of contained spaces," transgressing boundaries in order to tap into and move within "the secret space of the other" (1998, 71). Indeed, the Pisin word *stori* means "a narrative about secret and lost forms of power" (82). But these imaginative strategies should not be dismissed as modes of sympathetic magic. Though local metaphors speak of adopting another skin or inhabiting another body (in much the same way that we speak of putting ourselves in another person's shoes), the cult adepts rarely lapse into submissive modes of empathy and imitation, but actively experiment with new imaginative and interpersonal strategies that will provide them with *real* power to control the world.

While cargo narratives are informed by blatantly pragmatic designs, Hannah Arendt's notion of judgment is anchored in the humanistic goals of the Enlightenment. Understanding is its own good. Judgment is "representative" not because one adopts, advocates, or even empathizes with the views of others, still less because one comes into possession of an abstract knowledge that corresponds to some external reality, but simply because the understanding that informs one's judgment is pluralistic rather than monistic, intersubjective rather than subjective (Arendt 1968, 241). Yet, in her insistence that reality lies neither with oneself nor with the Other, but in-between—in the "web of relationships" where self and other are as natively intermingled as love and violence,[86] Arendt unwittingly echoes the communitarian logic of non-Western thought.

Ethnographic Judgment

It is obvious that, for Arendt, judgment can neither invoke nor arrive at any settled position. First, judgment is not a matter of some unreflective, a prioristic, moralistic *condemnation* of difference on the egocentric or ethnocentric grounds that alien beliefs or practices belong outside the pale of what is human. On the contrary, judgment is a way of doing justice to the multiplex and ambiguous character of human reality by regarding others *not as inhuman, but as ourselves in other circumstances*—even though those "others" may include the Adolf Eichmanns of this world. We judge Eichmann, not because what he did or licensed was subhuman and evil, but because he exemplifies a banal mode of human thoughtlessness—as superficial as it is self-interested—in which one assumes a knowledge of others without subjecting this knowledge to the test of putting oneself in the position in which the other has been placed, or in the position in which the other has placed himself or herself.[87] Second, no judgment should claim to bring conversation to a close, for every judgment is itself, in turn, open to the judgment of others (cf. Readings 1996, 134).

Neither of these points imply an argument for moral relativism; they simply make an appeal for strategies that make judgment conditional upon understanding—which is to say, putting oneself in the place of another. And understanding, like storytelling, means beginning with "particulars and things close at hand" rather than with sweeping generalizations (Arendt 1971, 193).

One might argue, for instance, that what is most disturbing about those in the West who raise their voices against the "barbarity" of female genital operations, by declaring clitoridectomy to be an abomination of patriarchy or Islamic medievalism, is not the intrinsic "wrongness" of their point of view but the wrongness of their refusal to understand the phenomenon from any standpoint other than their own, coupled with their bad faith in invoking "human rights" to rationalize a position that they have never risked by putting themselves in the place of the other. In other words, the "universal" should not be either one's own local or particular view projected onto the world at large, or a view from afar, allegedly liberated from social and worldly ties; rather, the word is best used to denote a breadth of experience and an enlarged understanding that come from a sustained *practical and social engagement* in the lifeworld of others (Arendt 1968, 221). In this sense, the assumption underlying Hannah Arendt's theory of judgment is similar to the assumption that underpins ethnography: that it behoves us to put ourselves in the place of others if we are to understand them. It is not that we necessarily stop condemning or condoning; rather that our value judgments are less likely to precede than to follow from our investigations, which rely on a method of suspending our accustomed ways of thinking, not by an effort of intellectual will, but by *a method of displacing ourselves from our customary comfort zones.*

In her essay on Karl Jaspers, Hannah Arendt makes this observation: "Whatever I think must remain in constant communication with everything that has been thought" (1973, 87). Edification, it is here implied, ideally takes the form of a dialogue between the living and the dead— between ourselves and the past. As to which past we may most fruitfully turn, Arendt shares Jaspers's view that this should not be the Christian past, centered on the advent of Christ and focused on the idea of salvation and final judgment; rather it should be defined as the pivotal period between 800 and 200 BC that saw the birth of philosophy simultaneously in several places—Confucius and Lao-tse in China, the Upanishads and Buddha in India, Zarathustra in Persia, the prophets in Palestine, Homer and the philosophers and tragedians in Greece.

As an ethnographer, I question this view on the grounds that this distant "axis of world history" gives us only worldviews to engage with, not lifeworlds in which to sojourn. If one is to actually put oneself in the position of others it is never enough simply to think one's thoughts by way of theirs; one must, at all costs, access and experience directly the lives that others live *in their own place.* In Arendt's words, this need to extend the reach of one's understanding means training "one's imagination to go visiting" (Arendt 1982, 43). However, it may be that anthropology, not history, provides the most challenging terrain for this "visiting imagination." Though it is certainly edifying to enter into "dialogue" with the ancients, it is surely important to learn the languages of those who seem most distant and alien to us in the world *in which we presently live*, and by sojourning among them discover the meaning of the truth that Arendt and Jaspers set such store by—the truth not of abstract knowledge *of* the other but of communication *with* the other, and the meaning not of existence but coexistence.[88]

Ethnography thus provides an antidote to the idealism from which Arendt never completely escapes, for the ethnographic method demands not merely an imaginative participation in the life of the other, but a *practical and social* involvement in the various activities, both ritual and mundane, that articulate and condition the other's worldview (cf. Bourdieu 1996, 22). This imposes great demands not only on an ethnographer's linguistic and conceptual abilities, but on his or her emotional and bodily resources. Ethnography forces the life of the mind from contemplation to experimentation. To paraphrase Foucault, being obliged to live among others on their own terms constitutes a kind of "limit-experience" in which one's identity and sanity are risked in order to explore the possibility of knowing the world other than one has known it before (1990, 8–9). For this reason, anthropological understanding is never simply a cognitive matter, and perhaps no other intellectual discipline combines dispassionate observation and personal ordeal in the way that fieldwork does.

Because it entails a direct, intimate, and practical engagement with the object of one's understanding, ethnographic judgment abolishes the subject-object split of natural science, and replaces it with an intersubjective model of understanding.

This implies a negative dialectic. For while the ethnographer is both influenced by his or her initial preoccupations *and* by the other's self-understandings, the outcome of any intersubjective encounter is never a synthesis of all the various points of view taken together, but an arbitrary closure that leaves both self and other with a provisional and open-ended view that demands further dialogue and engagement.

Although anthropology's foundational methodology—participant-observation—supposedly allows for the coexistence of views from without and views from within, anthropology has always shuttled uneasily between so-called objective and subjective standpoints. At one extreme, there have been numerous methodological and rhetorical inventions to make anthropology a kind of natural science, in which the observer is disengaged from the observed in order to discern the rules and regularities that underlie and explain social reality. At the other extreme there have been a variety of romantic variations on the metamorphic theme of "going native," in which the observer loses his or her identity in the other. The model of intersubjectivity overcomes the false dichotomy between these extremes, for object and subject are no longer construed as having any *a priori*, substantial, or static reality, but seen phenomenologically as words with which we mark moments or modalities of *experience* that reflect the various potentialities that are realized or foregrounded in the course of interactions between persons and persons, persons and things, or persons and beliefs (Jackson 1998a). If ethnographic method is understood to be primarily not some arcane set of techniques we have to acquire but a commonplace body of social skills we already possess (the protocols of hospitality and reciprocity, for instance), then we will be more inclined to accept that subjectivity and objectivity cannot be defined "objectively" and decontextually, since their value is always determined by one's relative position within—and one's particular *experience* of—a particular social field.

Hannah Arendt understood perfectly this relativity of objective and subjective positions. How, she once asked, can one write about totalitarianism without making explicit one's outrage at the injustices and terror it generates? If one is to be "objective" about such phenomena, the lived experiences and consequences of the phenomenon are central, not distorting. Using the example of Nazism, she notes: "To describe the concentration camps *sine ira* is not to be 'objective', but to condone them." She then adds, "I think that a description of the camps as hell on earth is more "objective," that is, more adequate to their essence than statements of a purely sociological or psychological nature" (Arendt, 1953b, 79).[89] In another example, she speaks of excessive poverty in a nation of great wealth. "The natural human reaction to such conditions is one of anger and indignation because these conditions are against the dignity of man. If I describe these conditions without permitting my indignation to interfere, I have lifted this particular phenomenon out of its context in human society and have thereby robbed it of part of its nature … For to arouse indignation is one of the qualities of excessive poverty insofar as poverty occurs among human beings" (78).

The Visiting Imagination[90]

Judging implies journeying, and travel means travail—a succession of changing horizons, arduous digressions, and unsettling perspectives. The art of ethnography is to turn this deterritorialization (Deleuze and Guattari 1991) to good account, to make a virtue out of not being at home in the world.

Aristotle considered homelessness to be one of the blessings of the philosopher's way of life (Arendt 1971, 199–200). In his *Protreptikos* he celebrates the life of the mind (*bios theoretikos*) as the life of a stranger (*bios xenikos*). The intellectual life is best pursued nowhere, doing nothing; it can only be hindered by a preoccupation with particulars, and with local allegiances. True thought, he observed, requires neither tools nor places for their work, for "wherever in the whole world one sets one's thought to work, it is surrounded on all sides by the presence of truth" (Aristotle 1952, 34). I share Hannah Arendt's view that thought cannot free itself from the practical, physical, and sensible immediacies of the world, and imagine she might have shared Merleau-Ponty's view that philosophy is not a matter of rising above the mundane, but of a "lateral displacement" (1964, 119) that enables one to critically reconsider one's views from another vantage point. Rather than a "nowhere" outside of time and circumstance, one seeks an "elsewhere" *within* the world. For an ethnographer, this elsewhere is some other society; for the historian some other time.

For Hannah Arendt, "otherness" had a very personal connotation. As a displaced Jewish German intellectual, her marginal status was both given and chosen. In the latter sense, it meant making a conscious virtue out of her pariah status (Arendt 1944). Like the storyteller, the poet, and the refugee, the conscious pariah may, as a discursive figure, stand for the person who remains unassimilated, ill at ease, and suspect. This estrangement may endow the pariah with an ability to see into and see through the very society from which he or she is ostracized.

Anthropologists call this "stranger value." While insiders find it difficult to see the world from any point of view other than their own, the pariah has no fixed position, no territory to defend, no interest to protect. As a visitor and sojourner, as one who is always being moved on, he is much freer than the good citizen to put himself in the place of another.

It costs him nothing. He can try out a plurality of perspectives without any personal loss of status or identity, because he is already marked as marginal, stateless, and indeterminate. This "visiting imagination" of the pariah implies neither an objective standpoint (the pariah does not seek disinterestedness or distance from the other), nor an empathic one (the pariah is not interested in losing himself in the other); it is, rather, a way of putting himself in the place of another, a way of destabilizing habitual patterns of thinking by thinking his own thoughts in the place of somebody else. The result is neither a detached knowledge of another's world nor an empathic blending with another's worldview. Rather it is a story that switches from one point of view to another without prioritizing any one, yet unsettles in the mind of anyone who reads or hears the story not only his certainties *but his belief in the possibility of certainty.* The *impartial* understanding attained through storytelling is linked, therefore, to the doubts that arise from displacement. It is neither a matter of seeing the world from some privileged "nowhere," nor of aligning oneself with any particular person or group of persons on the sentimental grounds that they are in sole possession of the truth,[91] but of interleaving a multiplicity of particular points of view in a way that calls into question *all* claims for privileged understanding. No matter how abhorrent the view of the other, it represents a logical possibility for one's self. It is in this sense that the difference between self and other is always conditional upon our social interactions, and not predetermined by some genetic, cultural, or moral essence.

THE SINGULAR AND THE SHARED

We are such stuff
As dreams are made on; and our little life
Is rounded with a sleep.

—WILLIAM SHAKESPEARE, *The Tempest*, Act 4, Sc. 1.

In the course of this book, I have sought to demonstrate the strengths of Hannah Arendt's argument that storytelling transforms our lives by enabling us to reshape diffuse, diverse, and difficult personal experiences in ways that can be shared. Through metaphors that merge particular and general subjectivities, storytelling fashions images of a "singular universal": a nation and person are thought of as one, a person becomes a name, an individual exemplifies an idea, and so on. In this closing chapter, however, I argue that storytelling also resists this generalizing and abstracting impulse. Indeed, I want to suggest that without the perennial conversion of cultural narratives into stories that speak to private or idiosyncratic concerns, such narratives lose their viability. My emphasis here is therefore less on the processes that put stories into public circulation than on the ways in which individuals draw on extant narratives to create meanings peculiar to themselves.

This broaches the subject of dreams. For in no other field of human consciousness is experience so overwhelmingly determined by personal preoccupations, and nowhere else is narrative coherence so disabled and compromised.[92] This is not to say that our dreaming takes place outside the social pale; rather it is to emphasize that dreams, like the personal stories that we so often associate with dreams, are charged with such intensely private meanings that we often regard them as too exotic, too shameful, too idiosyncratic, and too antisocial to be publicly voiced or shared.

The Occurrence in Dreams of Material from Fairytales

Let me begin with some examples of how stories in the public domain—in this case familiar Indo-European fairytales—may take on radically idiosyncratic meanings in dreams.

When my daughter, Heidi, was three years old, her mother was hospitalized for ten days. During this time, Heidi would wake in the middle of the night from bad dreams, yet when I asked her what was troubling her, she could not say. A few weeks after her mother returned home from hospital, I broached the question again. Heidi now confided that her nightmares had involved the story of Jack and the Beanstalk—her favorite bedtime reading. In particular, she had associated the giant's castle in the clouds with the hospital to which her mother had been admitted. This prompted me to wonder whether the story's theme of a stolen inheritance might also have helped Heidi objectify her inchoate feelings of personal loss.

Freud touched on this phenomenon in several of his clinical studies where, as in Heidi's case, the symbolic appropriation of folktale imagery occurs in dreams.

Perhaps the most famous of these case histories (*From the History of an Infantile Neurosis* (1918 [1914]) is Freud's account of the "Wolf Man" (Freud 1963). A victim of several childhood traumas—persecuted and seduced by his older sister, shunned by his depressed and indifferent father, sexually molested by his nurse, and disturbed by the behavior of his alcoholic English governess—the Wolf Man's deepest and most painful experience appeared, as a result of Freud's analysis, to have been the "primal scene" of his father copulating violently with his mother *a tergo*. These traumatic experiences seem to have coalesced into a single frightening image of a wolf "standing upright and striding along"—an image that the Wolf Man had unconsciously lifted from a childhood storybook of Little Red Riding Hood (the same picture having been used often by his sister to tease him). Other storybook images of wolves, from Reynard the Fox and the Wolf and the Seven Kids, figured in his dreams and memories, and it was a dream of wolves that enabled Freud to finally trace the Wolf Man's obsessional neuroses to their source.

In another of Freud's case histories (1975a, 281–83), a young married woman confides, in the course of analysis, that she had dreamed of a little manikin that entered and danced around a room that resembled the dining room in her parents' house. On waking, she thought of the story of Rumpelstiltskin, who had danced in the same curious way and in so doing betrayed his name to the Queen, lost his claim to the Queen's child, and in fury tore himself in two. Freud's analysis avails itself of this association. Aware of the woman's ambivalent feelings toward her husband, Freud identified the manikin with a penis, and the manikin's diaphonous grey clothing with a condom. "We may gather," Freud concludes, "that considerations of preventing conception and worries whether this visit of her husband's might not have sown the seed of a second child were among the instigating causes of the dream" (282–83).

One might also add, in support of Freud's reasoning, that Rumpelstiltskin is connected with the dream by a neat antithetical relationship: whereas in the story he comes to take away the Queen's child (only to fail because of a slip of the tongue), in the dream he comes to give the woman a child (only to fail because he is sheathed in a condom). The figure of Rumpelstiltskin thus objectifies the woman's subjective anxieties. Deployed in inverted form, the manikin provides the dreamer with a symbolic disguise for sexual anxieties she was unable to consciously voice or admit.

The Privacy and Publicity of Dreams

The foregoing examples suggest that though the contents of our dreams may be culturally derived, the meaning of our dreams cannot be reduced to cultural determinants. Indeed, as Freud's hermeneutic method shows, dream analysis is an exercise in cultural deconstruction, disclosing the *idiosyncratic* meanings—wishes, desires, fears, reflections, intentions, and frustrations—that a dreamer's unconscious has attached to residues of his or her waking life. "These day residues," Freud notes, "are not the dream itself: they lack the main essential of a dream. Of themselves they are not able to construct a dream. They are, strictly speaking, only the psychical material for the dream-work, just as sensory and somatic stimuli, whether accidental or produced under experimental conditions, constitute the *somatic* material of the dream-work" (1975b, 274). The meaning of dream images is thus seldom isomorphic with the meaning that these images possess in our waking life. In dreams, castles become hospitals, rooms become wombs, and ordinary signs take on esoteric connotations.

Dreams also escape the impress of our everyday, socio-cultural circumstances in yet another way, for, more than any other modality of lived experience, dreams do not obey the logos of everyday life. Accordingly, their contents are contingent and adventitious, their beginnings and ends arbitrary, and they often lack, or seem to lack, any overall or inherent coherence.

In spite of all this, dreams are seldom seen as chaotic and contingent, and in most societies there are elaborate techniques for bringing them into alignment with the social world they seem to have gone beyond. Not only do they get recounted as intelligible narratives, they get interpreted according to cultural codes and conventions.

The gap between dream and waking world is closed in two ways. First, as Freud noted, the dreamer's own "secondary revision" works selectively to transform oneiric experiences into a story that can be communicated, and that can make sense to others—"to fit them for public appearance" as Hannah Arendt puts it (1958, 50). Second, specialist dream interpretation fosters the illusion of a fit between intrapsychic and social realms. Later, I will discuss the relationship between these procedures and censorship. But for the moment I want to adduce some ethnographic examples of how dreams are teased out of the shadows of privacy into the light of day, and transformed into artefacts that belong to the public realm.

In the Kuranko village in northeast Sierra Leone where I lived and worked intermittently in the 1970s I used to record my own dreams and, wherever possible, record and discuss the dreams of my informants. Not only was I curious to know what Kuranko made of their dreams; I hoped, by subjecting my dreams to their scrutiny to deepen my understanding of how culturally relevant and irrelevant elements were sifted and winnowed in the process of dream analysis.

In the dry season of 1979 one of my nearest neighbors was a young man called Abdulai Sisay. After many fruitless months digging and panning for diamonds in the alluvial fields of Kono, he had returned home bewildered and disheartened. Some years before, he had consulted a Qur'anic diviner who had given him good advice. He had then gone to Kono and made enough money to fund his elder brother's pilgrimage to Mecca. Now the same diviner told him that his run of bad luck was about to end, and advised that he should sacrifice a sheep to Allah and share the meat among his neighbors. However, even after dutifully taking the diviner's advice, Abdulai was nagged by doubts, and avid for further insights into the cause of his fluctuating fortunes.

When I told Abdulai I was interested in Kuranko dreams, he immediately confessed a keen interest in how white people interpret dreams. And so, within a few days we were comparing our dreams and dream interpretations.

One morning I told Abdulai that I had dreamed I had been climbing to the top of Senekonke—the great inselberg a few miles from Firawa, where the souls of past chiefs dwelled. Climbing, then falling back, as if a dark force held me in thrall.

When I described this dream to Abdulai he explained that it presaged esteem and prosperity. Then he told me what he had dreamed that same night.

"I was up in the sky, near the moon. I went up like an airplane, and came down to earth again. While I was in the sky I was not afraid, but as I came back to earth I became very frightened, and called out, 'I am falling, I am falling.'"

"In my next dream I was praying. It was the middle of the night. I was praying and counting my beads."

"I think you want to go to Mecca," I said, "just as your elder brother did, but you are afraid that you will not be able to make the journey."

"*A ko sebe!*" Abdulai exclaimed. "That's true. That is what is in my mind."

I did not confide everything that Abdulai's dream suggested to me. His first dream gave me the impression that Abdulai felt less and less in control over his own destiny. The dream seemed to be charged with the same anxieties of powerlessness and marginalization that I discerned around me every day—villagers working through an entire dry season to build a road through the bush, in the expectation that their collective fortunes would improve, only to find that nothing changed; young men, like Abdulai, back from the diamond fields, disappointed and embittered; others back from the cities where they had hoped for a windfall, but found none; students unable to find the money to finish their schooling, or thrown out of college for protesting against the government; men frustrated in their attempts to ally themselves with a powerful mentor and patron. At the same time, Abdulai's dream reminded me of the kinds of fantastic avenues to self-esteem and empowerment that had begun to fill this existential vacuum, particularly among young men. An alliance forged with a powerful bush spirit. The acquisition of powerful medicines, or the ability to transform oneself at will into a powerful animal. Or the hope that Islam and the spiritual authority of the *alhajis*—those who had made the haj to Mecca—would usher in a new age. A generation later, as corrupt governments and coups destroyed the civil state in Sierra Leone, and the patrimonial economy collapsed, these thwarted dreams would assume increasingly violent and vengeful shape, mixing indigenous fantasies of magical power with images from kung fu movies, fixations on invincible trickster heroes like Rambo, and the possession of lethal weaponry.

A few days after his dream of falling from the sky, Abdulai recounted another dream. "I was lying in bed, drawing my wife toward me, when a pale-complexioned woman came up to her and began pulling her away from me."

Assuming that *musu gbe*—pale-complexioned—might, in this context, mean "white woman," I wondered whether Abdulai's dream betrayed a desire to sleep with a European woman, but when I suggested this, Abdulai abruptly clapped his hands together.

"Eh! Not at all. That is not what I had in mind."

"But who," I asked, "is the woman?" For I was thinking of what so many informants had drummed into me—that one never dreams of non-existant things. To dream that one is a witch confirms that one is a witch. To dream of someone who has died is a confirmation that this person still exists, only in some other zone. As is the case among many preliterate peoples, dreams are not considered to be random figments of the imagination, but glimpses into other, parallel, realities, ordinarily invisible and intangible—like things glimpsed in the penumbra of a fire.

"It is not as you say," Abdulai said. "You see, I have two wives. One is pale-complexioned and one is dark. You know that paleness signifies good luck. Well, I had intended taking my dark wife when I went back to the mines. Now I will take the other one, because in the dream she was pulling the dark one away. This means that she will draw the bad luck away and bring me good luck."

"What if things do not go well for you, despite all the good omens?" I asked.

"It all depends on Allah," Abdulai said. "A person's destiny is in the hands of Allah. The Qur'an is Allah's word, and the Qur'an shows us how to understand our dreams."

Such exchanges between Abdulai and me were not uncharacteristic of the way Kuranko discussed dreams amongst themselves, and indicate that the meaning of dreams is both given—in stereotypical interpretations that, for instance, equate dark forests, swamps, and deep water with conspiracy, a pale-complexioned women with good luck, and high places with power and prosperity—as well as negotiated, in conversations upon waking or in consultations with a diviner. My conversations with Abdulai also indicate how "secondary revision" involves foregrounding culturally recognizable and iconic elements, and backgrounding anomalous elements that cannot be fitted into the interpretive repertoire. In both cases, dreams undergo a transformation from being private, internal events into externalized and conventionalized public knowledge. This passage from the intrapsychic to the intersubjective is not, however, merely a matter of conventionalizing dream material, for the social nature of Kuranko dream interpretation mediates—either through consulting an expert, a diviner, or simply talking with close kin or friends—a passage not only from the singular to the social, but from passivity to activity. Accordingly, Kuranko dreams are not escapes *from* reality but ways in which people reorient themselves *to* reality, the better to act in the world with some sense of purpose. Despite Abdulai's fatalistic comments about everything depending on the will of Allah, *in practice* he did everything in his power to ensure that Allah's will was consistent with his own desires.

I now turn to Aboriginal Australia, to explore another set of strategies whereby the semblance of a fit is contrived between the inner world of personal thoughts and feelings (metaphorically associated with "the belly" in both Kuranko and Warlpiri) and the visible, everyday social world.

For Warlpiri, the dream life of individuals is thought to be deeply conditioned by the Dreaming[93]—the field of ultimate being in which all life, human, animal, mineral, and vegetable, is grounded and steeped. Not surprisingly, therefore, it is not uncommon for a person, in her dreams, to glimpse an event or image from the Dreaming that has been momentarily lost to sight. Frequently, this recovered element will be made public, and often publicly performed, so restoring bodily and sensible form to the myth involved (see Jackson 1995 and Dussart 2000 for examples). Such ceremony is likened to "giving birth"; it brings the Dreaming into being—images that bear an uncanny parallel to Heidegger's notion of technology as a "bringing-forth," a "coming to presence," an "unconcealing" or "occasioning" of Dasein (1977, 11–12). There is thus, in Warlpiri life, a continual interplay between what is latent and patent, and dreams, myths, and ceremony are all ways in which the Dreaming is revealed.

Warlpiri compare the relationship between the Dreaming and everyday life to the relation between the invisible and the visible, or sleep and waking. While the Dreaming exists *in potentia*, everyday existence is *in presentia*. In sleep, unconsciousness, or death, the spirit (*pirlirrpa*) is said to go out of the body, often journeying to the country from which it originates—and it is to this same country that the spirit returns when the body dies. This helps us understand the following episode.

In October 1991 I was spending much of my time in "business camp," discussing with older Warlpiri men the circumstances surrounding the destruction of a sacred site by a mining company (Jackson 1995). One afternoon, I was sitting in the shade of some snappy gums, watching a group of men playing cards. Nearby, Zack Jackamarra, renowned and respected for his knowledge of the law, was lying on his back, his head resting on a powdered milk tin, his gaunt face upturned, dead to the world and snoring.

"Thinking about country," one man remarked.

Visiting one's country after many years away may also bring one's Dreaming to mind.

A group of us were camped near Jila. The Nakamarra sisters, Liddy, Lady, and Beryl, had heaped clumps of spinifex to form a windbreak, and laid out their bedding on the exposed earth. My wife, Francine, and I had cleared a space beside them. On the other side of us, also separated by a bolster of spinfex, Jimmy Jampijinpa's elderly mother, Nora, was nursing a smoky fire of mulga sticks into life while cautioning us, in a hoarse voice, against building our fire too close to the spinifex. Not far away, others were also preparing for the night, kindling fires, heating water in blackened pots, preparing damper to cook in the coals. Everyone's space was similarly separated by mounds of spinifex, and by that discrete avoidance of eye contact that gives you an uncanny and immediate sense of privacy in an Aboriginal camp.

I woke next morning with the sky reddening in the east, a dew on the green canvas of my swag, and the air cold. Liddy was softly singing songs of Wapurtali—the Dreaming associated with that place, the Dreaming she had inherited from her father. When Francine greeted her, Liddy said she had dreamed of her aunt Lorna in Lajamanu. Her auntie had also been singing the songs of Wapurtali. "Maybe she is thinking about Wapurtali too," Liddy said.

Clearly, the line between the domain of visible, conscious existence and the ubiquitous, ancestral, and eternal domain of the Dreaming is neither fixed nor impermeable. Realities that are presently invisible may suddenly appear in a dream, while things that are visible today may fade, like the life of a person, into obscurity or latency tomorrow.

For Warlpiri, however, hiddenness, latency, invisibility, and secrecy are not primarily attributes of privacy,[94] as they are in the West; rather they are intrinsic to the ambient Dreaming, which never reveals itself in its entirety at any one time or in any one consciousness. This is not only because the Dreaming is too vast to be comprehended, but because the Dreaming is only ever partially revealed, the operative principle being that what any individual knows is always conditional upon his or her relative position in the social scheme of things—initiated/uninitiated, male/female, old/young, insider/outsider.

Given that the Warlpiri social order depends on people knowing and respecting the boundaries that lie between that which is open to them and that which is closed to them, the question of censorship becomes central. This censorship is both intrapsychic and social. One must exercise great discipline in keeping restricted knowledge to oneself, and one must avoid trespassing in *places* associated with things one has no right to know about.

Censorship and the Episteme

Hannah Arendt observed that when we view the distinction between private and public realms from the standpoint of privacy, rather than that of the body politic, the distinction translates into one between "things that should be shown and things that should be hidden" (1958, 72). Accordingly, privacy implies that most bodily functions and "things connected with the necessity of the life process itself" are sequestered and kept from the gaze of others. More recently, Michel Foucault has shown that a corollary of this habit of censoring certain fields of experience and behavior from public life on the grounds that they belong *by their very nature* to the private realm is that they also get excluded from institutional discourse. Thus, to conventionally designate certain experiences as "private" is to expunge them from public discussion.

However, any account of the workings of the world that tacitly accepted such lines of inclusion and exclusion would fall into the error of identity thinking, inferring reality from the words that name it, and confirming as necessary and "natural" boundaries whose actual function is the protection of vested interests. If critical thought has a unifying goal it is to question and transgress these boundaries, restoring to our awareness the functional and psychic *unity* of the human world that we customarily stake out, both ideologically and epistemologically, as a series of mutually exclusive domains.

But this radically empirical method of pushing back the horizons of what we will admit to our discourse is not only important for the development of scientific understanding; it is, arguably, essential to preserving our humanity against hierarchy.

In the following pages I turn from the "private aspects" of dreams to the "public play-world" that, as David Riesman notes, "has virtually the same economy as that of the dream" (1955, 200). To set the scene, I first consider a case in which the boundary between private fantasy and public reality is transgressed.

As already noted, the boundarylines that define any social order are drawn both intrapsychically and intersubjectively. Just as we ask those with whom we do not identify to keep their distance, we simultaneously expect them to keep their thoughts and feelings to themselves. Considerable anxiety tends to arise in situations where these forms of censorship fail. For when that which we have hidden is made visible, or that which we have spurned comes near, or that which we deem to be "private" becomes public, we feel that society itself is placed in jeopardy.

Celebrity Death

Having noted how the "private" imaginings of an individual may be construed as threats to public order, as harbingers of social chaos, I turn now to a case in which the imagination erodes the boundary between private and public realms without anxiety or alarm. Indeed, in this case, widespread empathic identification with a public figure sets the scene for an extraordinary emotional and moral expression of social solidarity.

August 31, 1997 was a Sunday in Sydney, and I was watching an afternoon television documentary about an Australian physicist who had worked at the Cavendish with Rutherford in the late 1920s. Suddenly, and silently, a message began to move across the top of the screen: *Diana Princess of Wales, has been killed in a car accident in Paris* ...

I was stunned, and two days later, the news still held me in thrall. I found it difficult to focus on my work. I also found it difficult to understand why I was so affected by this event. Diana was nothing to me. Why should I feel grief at her passing? Why should I buy a newspaper every morning, and need to read it alone, to be alone with my thoughts?

About two weeks after Diana's death, I ran into my friend Ghassan Hage in a Glebe coffee bar. He was reading Tina Brown's essay on Diana, based on the last interview she had given. Ghassan confessed he could not stop reading about her and her death. "I'm fascinated by my own fascination," he said.

When I reflected on my own fascination with Diana's life and death, I thought of Plautus's famous phrase: "Whom the Gods love, die young." Celebrities, heroes, and royals are children of the Gods. They participate in the divine. Yet divine favors are never freely bestowed, and so, when a favored mortal falls, we see her fall as the price she paid for soaring so high, a form of hubris.

No less than the Greeks, we are intrigued by how divine gifts—great beauty, strength, intelligence, goodness—may be reconciled with an earthly life.

For every celebrity, the dilemma is how to be extraordinary and ordinary at the same time. How to exist in the public gaze, yet protect one's private life from invasion. How to stay in touch with mundane reality yet preserve one's ethereal status. For royals, the conflict between public duty and private desire may be even more acute. How can one be both a person and an ideal? How can one be a figurehead, an icon, an image, a name, without losing oneself in the abstraction, in the role? Usually, the resolution of these dilemmas involves a splitting of public and private selves. Hence the theatrical partitions between public appearances and private lives, and all the familiar forms of symbolic disguise—the dark glasses against the glare of publicity, the stage-managed interviews, carefully edited press releases, security systems, and bodyguards, and the complaints about the intrusiveness of the press, the expressed desire to be left alone, the anxiety that one's life may be destroyed by the very fans that sustain one's stellar status.

For those who venerate celebrities and royals, a similar ambivalence exists. There is simultaneously a desire to uphold the boundary between public and private domains *and* to see it transgressed. From this arises a paradox. For if the stars are to embody purity, moral perfection, absolute power, and surpassing beauty, then they must appear to belong to another realm, distant, unreachable, and sacrosanct. But if they are to speak to us they must show themselves to be *of* us. Thus, at the same time that we accept and abet their elevation, and extol their virtues, we secretly desire their downfall, to bring them down to earth, to see them as ourselves. Otiose and omnipotent they may be, but we challenge their transcendence, decry their privileges, question their authority, and endorse the tabloid muck-raking that discloses evidence of their fallibility, their ordinary humanity. Undoubtedly, the fan or follower who displays this deep ambivalence toward the object of his or her adoration is no different from anyone in love. In love we risk becoming lost to ourselves, which is why romantic fixations give rise to *both* fantasized images of the other as a god or goddess *and* a desire to recover one's own autonomy by effacing or destroying him/her. "To fall in love," writes Jorge Luis Borges, "is to create a religion that has a fallible god" (1965, 99).

"The problem for the modern monarchy," notes Julian Barnes, "is how to hold in balance the demands of myth and ordinariness" (1995, 143).

Diana came close, if not to achieving this balance then to fostering an image in which elements of a vulnerable humanity were merged with elements of imperishable superiority. She was loved because she was of our common clay, yet outshone the royals among whom she moved. She was an angel who came down to earth, yet remained among the stars. A Goddess who was also human—exposing herself to the squalor and danger of our everyday world by kissing men who were HIV-positive, touching lepers, walking through minefields, and telling the world she wanted her sons to grow up in touch with ordinary people.

John Fitzgerald Kennedy Jr. was also an avatar of these myths in which the human and the divine are brought together. After Kennedy's death, Eric Pooley wrote in *Time* of a man who cultivated "an ordinariness that was his last defense against the extraordinary role life had handed him. He took the subway or rode a bike to work, hanging out mostly with friends who weren't at all famous, using his unparalleled celebrity mostly on behalf of good causes" (Pooley July 26 1999, 34). In the *Guardian* obituary, the headline read "President Kennedy's son remained ordinary and approachable despite intense public scutiny" (*Guardian Weekly*, July 22–28 1999, 16). John Kennedy's and Diana's lives were likened to "fairytales" or "dreams": they appeared not to take refuge in privilege, but to crave the reality of the world in which *we* lived. In Arendt's terms, they mediated between private and public realms.

A week after the death of Diana, Mother Teresa died. But Mother Teresa's death was overshadowed by the public grief for Diana. History repeated itself on July 16, 1999. When John Fitzgerald Kennedy Jr. lost his life off the coast of Massachusetts, a nation mourned, but when, a couple of days later, fifteen "ordinary" people were killed when their plane went down into the Indian Ocean near Christmas Island, the episode hardly rated a mention in the press; the victims were poor Malays, their names of no account.

The difference between our responses to the death of stars and the death of mere mortals hinges on the depth of our attachment, not to them, but to the narratives in which they figure—narratives that hold out the illusory promise that mortals and immortals may merge. And behind this promise lies the idea that our singular subjectivity, our particular selfhood, may be merged with the collective, abstract, universalized, and imagined subjectivities of a nation state, a community, a human family, an enduring idea or transcendent ideal. So deeply do we depend on the master narratives of our culture for the vicarious realization of this dream of uniting our personal existence with some abiding, transpersonal, global reality, that our very lives become fused with the life of the narratives themselves. The widespread grief occasioned by Diana's sudden death disclosed how deeply "my" world, "our" world, and "the" world are coalesced in human consciousness. Today, from my window, I look out onto a cobbled square, a canal, and the curved copper roofs of public buildings—all of which existed long before I became aware of them, all of which will outlast me.

But so familiar is this scene that it is, for the moment, the very integument of my world, and if it suddenly disappeared or was destroyed I would take the loss personally, as though something of myself had been destroyed. It is not that we deliberately identify with the world in which we find ourselves; rather that it contributes the images, objects, and events that our consciousness takes up and uses in giving form to our changing moods, our inchoate thoughts, our fugitive understandings. Though we may not necessarily make it ours, it becomes an inextricable part of our private lives, and with its loss we feel diminished and thrown. This is why any cataclysmic loss of the public realm is experienced viscerally, as an assault on our own integrity. And we are momentarily cast back into privacy and isolation, as though bereaved.

What people mourned when Diana died was in part a person with whom they identified. In her death, the deaths they had known were remembered. But equally, if not more profoundly mourned, was the death of a narrative that had connected our own subjectivity to the wider subjectivity of the world. Other narratives would appear, of course, for all are, at base, narratives of the divine king—in whom the personal and eternal, the particular and general, are coalesced. But for a moment, we had lost the one in whom many had articulated their dream of individual being transfigured by being itself.

Refiguring the Personal

Anyone familiar with Lévi-Strauss's *Mythologiques* will recognize an affinity between my preoccupation with the fusion of particular and general subjectivities, and the structuralist dialectic, in which the unconscious generates and seeks to mediate binary oppositions. But where Lévi-Strauss locates the logic of narrative in innate, synchronous structures of the mind, my focus is on the contradictions, quandaries, and choices that people face, and seek to overcome, in telling stories whose meanings lie in lived space-time and whose consummation and test is how they help us cope with our quotidian lives. The paired contrasts of human and divine, private and public, the one and the many, are, therefore, neither entirely arbitrary nor unconscious. Nevertheless, the existential approach I am using here acknowledges, with structuralism, that many pairs of contrary

terms are mutually interchangeable, their meanings slipping impercep-
tibly, uncannily, and interminably from one formulation to another. Thus,
the "Arendtian" opposition between private and public may find expression as a contrast between visible/invisible, near/far, personal/transper-
sonal, human/divine, and even local/global. This associational or con-
tagious logic is characteristic of storytelling and of dreams. Unlike the
logic of everyday discourse, which depends on fixed relationships between
things and the names we give to things, the terms in narrative lack ontological stability. But whereas structuralism tends to characterize the workings of the unconscious mind as an endless combining and permutating
of terms that offers no final solutions to our existential dilemmas, I take
almost the opposite view, invoking, as I have done in the Introduction to
this book, the imperative human need to strike some balance between
the things over which we have some control and the things over which
we have none. It is neither that we seek to lose ourselves in a crowd, nor
that we seek to make others subservient to our own ambitions; rather that
we hope for a just balance between autonomy and anonymity—between
the need to decide our own lives and the need to assent to that which
we cannot decide, to the forces over which we cannot prevail. We need
heroes, gods, and stars to be sure, but above all we need to feel that *we* participate in the divine and that *they* are within our reach, within the realm
of our own choosing.

NOTES

1. Aristotle's distinction, in the *Nicomachean Ethics*, is as follows: "production (poesis) has an end other than itself, but action (praxis) does not" (1983, 153).

2. Thus Maja Povranović's telling observation that during the Yugoslavian war the "grammar" of nationalism figured significantly in the discourse of international commentators and national leaders *far from the front lines*, but for the "forgotten majority" of civilians, life was a struggle "to defend not primarily their 'national territory' but *the right to continue their lives in terms of gender, occupation, class, and place of residence and not be reduced to their national identities*" (2000, 154, emphasis added).

3. In treating the protean distinction between private and public realms phenomenologically, I might be accused of glossing over the different ways this distinction has been objectified in the course of European history—"the shifting weight," as Richard Sennett calls it, "between public and private life" (1978, 28)—but my intention is to use this distinction as "a point of entry" (Weintraub 1995, 282) into understanding the tensions, present in all societies, between immediate and non-immediate spheres of existence.

4. This point is nicely illustrated in Michael Meeker's study of the linking of heroic deeds and speech among the Bedouin. In a world characterized by "uncertain procedures and uncertain consequences" (1979, 47), ceremonial narratives of raiding and warfare provide a kind of strategic surrogate of actual raiding, enabling Bedouin to rehearse through the poetics of voice the ideals associated with real life. Even a story told about a *failed* raid may open up deep discussion of the values, centered on personal voice and identity, that underlie *successful* raiding (33–41).

5. "My life is a hesitation before birth," noted Kafka in his *Diaries* (cited by Olney 1998, 405). "'I have always sensed that there was within me an assassinated being,' Beckett said. 'Assassinated before my birth. I needed to find this assassinated person again. And try to give him new life. I once attended a lecture by Jung in which he spoke about one of his patients, a very young girl. After the lecture, as everyone was leaving, Jung stood by silently. And then, as if speaking to himself, astonished by the discovery that he was making, he added: In the most fundamental way, she had never really been born. I, too, have always had the sense of never having been born'" (Olney 1998, 325, quoting from Charles Juliet's *Rencontres avec Samuel Beckett* 14, trans. Suzanne Chamier).

6. In her essay on Isak Dinesen (Karen Blixen), Hannah Arendt makes a similar point: "If it is true, as her 'philosophy' suggests, that no one has life worth thinking about whose story cannot be told, does it not follow that life could be, even ought to be, lived as a story, that what one has to do in life is to make the story come true?" (Arendt 1973, 107).

7. My emphasis in this book on the *interplay* between stories that alternately construct and deconstruct the status quo in contexts of situation means that a typology of storytelling genres becomes irrelevant. As Ochs and Capps have demonstrated, building on Bakhtin's crucial insights into the blurred boundaries between "primary" and "secondary" genres, "narrative bows to no simple generic blueprint that sets it apart once and for all from other forms of discourse" (2001, 18).

8. As, for example, in *Tristes Tropiques*, where he argues that "true reality is never the most obvious of realities, and that its nature is already apparent in the care which it takes to evade our detection" (Lévi-Strauss 1973b, 57).

9. Observes Jerome Bruner, "Narrative structure is even inherent in the praxis of social interaction before it achieves linguistic expression" (1990, 77).

10. Pierre Bourdieu speaks of this as the "law of the conservation of violence" (1998, 40).

11. On the "impossibility" of the gift and its paradoxical relation to time, see Derrida 1992, 6–33.

12. Francis Fukuyama emphasizes Hegel's "need for recognition" in arguing against the reductionist view that economic life is driven chiefly by "rational desire" for material gain (1992).

13. Hence the familiar rationalizations of violators: I was only taking what was mine; I was only following orders; I was at the mercy of circumstances beyond my control.

14. A powerful example of this contrast is provided by Allen Feldman's study of political violence in Northern Ireland, where the verb "to do" was used in its active and passive modes to designate any form of aggressive attack, while "being done" or "getting done" signified betrayal, arrest, or death (1991, 99–101).

15. The Nazi reduction of Jews to "Figuren," or "Stücke"—"dolls," "wood," "merchandise," "rags"—and racist reductions of others to skepsels, bugs, geeks, wogs, niggers, etc. are well-known examples, though it should be noted that while racist violence is predicated on such radical othering, it is *motivated* by the rage of recognizing that, despite reducing the other to a mere object, his or her humanity remains obdurately and undeniably recognizable (Michaels 1998, 165–66; Arendt 1979, 190).

16. Consider the comment, characteristic of stories of survivors of the seige of

Sarajevo: "Everything is out of your hands, you are completely helpless, someone else decides over your life and death. You are helpless" (in Macek 2000, 58).

17. Maja Povrzanović has recently commented on this discrepancy and "incompatibility" of "national narratives" and "personal narratives" in the Croatian war (2000, 153).

18. This pattern of forcibly separating mixed descent children from their birth parents and "merging" or "absorbing" them into the European population as menials was established from the earliest days of European occupation, though "merging" only became a national policy of systematic "assimilation" in 1937 (Human Rights and Equal Opportunities Commission [henceforth HREOC] 1997, 27–37). Whether children were "forcibly taken" from their birth parents, "stolen," or simply "given up" for adoption is largely irrelevant, for what is at issue is the entrenched social injustice and deprivation, reinforced by government policies, that turned the childhoods of countless Aboriginal children of mixed descent into living nightmares. Ghassan Hage has explored the homely images that delineate such modalities of structural violence as strategies and logics of "domestication" (1996, 479).

19. Arendt's remark is directly paralleled by Frantz Fanon's comment that colonial violence involves the "systematic negation" of the colonized person, creating a "defensive attitude" in which people are forced "to ask themselves the question constantly: "In reality, who am I?" (1968, 203).

20. As Tim O'Brien observes, recounting his experiences of being a foot soldier in Vietnam, "story-truth is truer sometimes than happening-truth" because only story-truth can convey the experience of what things were like, and in doing so, "make things present" (1990, 203).

21. Of course, many Aboriginal people construct the state as a quasi-parent and turn to it for redress precisely because they were "parented" and raised, as children, in state-run institutions.

22. One of the most poignant and widely publicized examples of this was the refusal of the Biko family to accept the granting of amnesty to the murderers of Steve Biko (Sarkin 1996, 626–28).

23. I am echoing here Hanna Fenichel Pitkin's incisive critique of Hannah Arendt's tendency to hypostacize the social as an alien, monstrous, blob-like entity, inimical to human freedom (1998).

24. Cf. Ranajit Guha's comments (1983a, 157) on the differences between criminal violence (which is partial and singular—the will of an individual) and the violence of insurgency (which is total and integrated—expressing the will of the many).

25. In a 1966 "longitudinal study of the process of adjustment by refugees to

a new environment," the Dutch social psychologist J. Ex noted our lack of scientific knowledge regarding "the experiences and evaluations" of refugees themselves. Writing in 1975, Stephen Keller observed the same dearth of "reports on how the refugee felt during his uprooting, flight, and resettlement" (1975, 40), and more recently Liisa Malkki has expressed concern that our discursive conventions tend to abstract "refugee predicaments from specific political, historical, cultural contexts" and so effectively "silence refugees" (1996, 378).

26. My translation borrows from others: Jane Gary Harris and Constance Link (in Mandelstam 1979, 434), and John Berger and Jean Mohr (1982, 131).

27. The same difficulty obtains with respect to nomadic cultures, where home and belonging are seldom synonymous with being housed and settled (Jackson 1995).

28. One of the most poignant examples of this is "the man with a shattered world"—A. R. Luria's phrase to describe a long-term patient of his, Zazetsky, who suffered massive damage to the left occipital-parietal region of his brain when hit by shell fragments in 1942. Though unable to write connectedly about his life, for twenty-five years Zazetsky painstakingly filled volume after volume of notebooks with accounts of his fragmented world. Writing, observes Luria, "was his one link with life, his only hope of not succumbing to illness but recovering at least a part of what had been lost" (1987, xx). But Zazetsky was under no illusions that his scribblings would constitute a coherent narrative, recover his memory, or be much use to anyone else. Perhaps that is why he referred to his writing as "morbid," though it was something he had to do. "If I shut these notebooks, give it up, I'll be right back in the desert, in that 'know-nothing' world of emptiness and amnesia" (86). What sustained him, then, was a primitive existential imperative—to act rather than be acted upon. "The point of my writing," he said, "is to show how I have been, and still am, struggling to recover my memory ... I had no choice but to try" (84).

29. It is important to note that in some societies, such as the Cham of Cambodia, there is a cultural emphasis on *not* telling or recollecting traumatic stories, but of healing sickness (including the suffering caused by the *mahandori* or "big destruction" of the Pol Pot regime) through a spirit posesssion cult (Trankell 2001).

30. These attitudes and stratagems are sometimes seen among soldiers and survivors returning home from war. Even when the world to which they return is not indifferent, hostile, passionless, or ill-prepared to understand (Parr 1995), soldiers may keep their stories to themselves because they do not trust authority, and because they do not want to burden others with experiences they consider too unspeakable to share, too personal to have social value or relevance.

31. Because it is the lost Aboriginal mother rather than the white father who figures in personal fantasies of reunion, narratives of Aboriginality and sovereignty tend to maternalize its key symbols of land and language.

32. This confirmation of indigenous customary rights is based on British common law dating back to the sixteenth century—the law that underpinned colonial law, and was invoked in the Australian High Court Mabo decision that overturned the doctrine of terra nullius and recognized Aboriginal native title rights.

33. I paraphrase Appadurai (1996a), whose work on postnational social forms and on the phenomenon of the "transnation" is relevant here.

34. I have argued elsewhere that a theory of culture requires a study of crisis—of those contexts and situations in which normative values and customary routines are disrupted, suspended, contested, negotiated, and reshaped (Jackson 1989, 20). Some crises are adventitious—such as wars and calamities of nature, that befall us as bolts from the blue. Other crises are socially contrived and calendrically organized—such as rites of passage. But both modalities of crisis momentarily transform the world from an apparently fixed and finite actuality into a bewilderingly open horizon of possibilities. At such times, people confront the world with which they identify as a world in which they are also alien. Crisis creates a consciousness of that which has been lost—"childhood" in the case of neophytes, "happiness" in the case of the bereaved, "home" in the case of refugees and exiles. But that which has been lost is also seen for the first time as a whole, like the earth seen from space, that excludes oneself, or exists independently of one's being part of it. It is for this reason that holistic concepts of human aggregates, such as "culture," "tradition," and "identity" are, paradoxically, defined not *sui generis* from a position of belonging, but provisionally, from a position of exile and estrangement. Such concepts, arising out of ostracism, separation and loss, are pivotal to healing and reintegration. Their very detachedness makes them potential symbols of transcendence, or powerful means of realigning and revitalizing identity.

35. This may explain why, in New Zealand, Maori sometimes find it difficult to accommodate refugees and migrants who, because they are perceived as uprooted, landless, dislocated, are thought to lack the very attributes of culture that Maori have made icons of their own identity.

36. The antinomy between knowledge and experience goes back to Aristotle: knowing is an attribute of mind, and just as reason resides in the head, so rational knowledge belongs to those who rule, to heads of state. Accordingly, the *hoi poloi* are assigned the traits that reason transcends—raw emotion, base instinct, blind passion. As Dewey has pointed out, Western thought has systematically built its

structures of social inequality out of this simplistic and spurious dichotomy between reason and experience. And we are deeply influenced by it. Which is why so many educated Westerners believe that their ability to reason, to analyze, to know, endows them with an ability to evaluate, assess, and make decisions on behalf of those who allegedly lack these rational skills and are moved merely by emotion, appetite, and instinct. Dewey severely criticized this dichotomy between a transcendental notion of knowledge and a debased notion of experience. Experience, he observed, should not be compared to crude ore which is made useful, intelligible, and valuable by being processed in the crucible of the mind. No human experience is thoughtless, any more than it is devoid of cultural form, and no thinking is free from the determinants of history, culture, and self-interest.

37. Cutting off the hands of women was, in some cases, intended to prevent villagers harvesting their rice, while in other cases amputation of the hands was a symbolic punishment for having voted in the "wrong" way. These metonymic rationalizations—in which individual bodies stand for a diffuse social entity—recall the violence in Rwanda, where mythico-historical fantasies of ethnic difference gave rise to necrographic body maps that provided Hutu and Tutsi alike with symbolic modus operandi for reversing demographic and power inequalities through a systematic and stylized process of dehumanization, dismemberment, disfigurement, and killing (Malkki 1995, 86–96; cf. Taylor 1999, 111).

38. This orientation is anticipated by Rosalind Shaw's elucidation of the ways in which the trauma of slave-trading continues to be inscribed in the "ancestral" practices, images, rumors, and beliefs associated with witchcraft among the Temne of Sierra Leone (Shaw 1997), and by Mariane Ferme's ethnographic demonstration of how the visible, physical violence of warfare in Sierra Leone is grounded in and presaged by the less blatant forms of symbolic violence in everyday life (Ferme 1998, 555–57).

39. *Gbeyekan* means literally "whiteness/pureness of speech." But speaking from the heart without ulterior motives or hidden designs connotes a transparency of intentions that pertains to actions as well as words. Hence the name Gbeyekan suggests honesty, straightforwardness, and openness in one's dealings with others.

40. The phrase suggests goodwill and pure intentions in one's dealings with others.

41. The word *sundan* translates as both stranger and guest. In West African English, the word "stranger" captures the ambiguous status of guests as people to whom one extends the hospitality of one's house or village, but who at the same time remain outsiders and even, possibly, enemies.

42. *M'berin* = "my maternal uncle." That a woman's husband should also be her maternal uncle indicates that avunculate marriages are not uncommon in Kuranko. The vernacular phrase for such marriages—*dogoma sonke* (lit. "handful of rice and sauce-price") carries the connotation that a sister gives her daughter in marriage to her brother as a way of reciprocating his gifts and support to her in her own marriage.

43. Intrapsychic and intersubjective contrasts both find expression in the crucial contrast between private and public space. The socio-spatial distinction that Kuranko make between *kenema* (open to the public gaze) and *duguro* (concealed) suggests the latin distinction between the *res publica* (whatever belongs to or concerns the people as a whole) and the *res privata* (the domain of the domus or house) (Duby 1988, 3–31). At the same time it suggests the European distinction between the open space of the agora (marketplace) and the space of oblique meanings and of allegory (*allos*, "other" + *agoreuin* "speak openly, speak in the assembly or market—the agora"), and thus implies a wide array of differences between activities that take place in the light of day—within the hearing and in sight of others, and are common knowledge—and activities that are clandestine, duplicitous, or veiled by secrecy and darkness. Given these manifold associations, the story of the two Momoris may be said to coalesce several areas of indeterminacy and potential conflict in Kuranko social life—the indeterminate relationships between inward disposition and outward demeanor, self and other, domesticated and wild, and private and public. These three areas implicate three bodies—the body of the person (*morgo*), of the community (*sue*), and of the country (*dugu*).

44. Kenya Fina Mara and Tina Kuyate were both married to the Diang chief, Magba Koroma—Tina being *baramusu* (senior wife) and Kenya Fina *gherinya* (second-married, junior wife).

45. The Senegalese fire finch (*tintingburuwe*) habitually flits and nests around houses, and it is this association with domestic space that may explain why the souls of dead infants are said to inhabit the fire finch while awaiting possible reincarnation, for a small child does not enter the public domain for some time after its birth.

46. This circumlocution conveys the idea that women prepare the best food for their lovers.

47. The Seli is the largest river draining the southern area of Kuranko country. In referring to a local river, the locus of the story ceases to be mythical and is suddenly brought closer to home.

48. *bal'fole*, lit. *balanje* (xylophone)-hitter, by implication a praise-singer, a *jeleba*.

49. The Kuranko phrase *ko manni a nyorgo manni* means literally "something

happened, its partner [i.e. the same thing, its counterpart] also happened."

50. Throughout the telling of this story, Keti Ferenke acted as a kind of second to Kenya Fina, and at this point—responding to Kenya Fina's own aside—he interrupted the story to remind everyone of an incident that had taken place in Kondembaia a few days before. A man had quarreled with another man and inflicted a minor wound with a knife. Uncertain and afraid of the offender, people had kept their distance from him.

51. *kemine gbana*—an unmarried young man, an idler, a drifter. Here the term is used as a synonym for a commoner, someone of inconsequential status.

52. Video and film have increasingly become vital sources of storytelling in even the most remote Sierra Leonean villages, and suggest that the gap between local realities and global identifications is as pressing a concern for the disaffected youth of today as the gap between the favored and the ill-favored, the powerful and the powerless, that lies at the heart of the narratives discussed in this chapter.

53. Mori, or in Krio "mori-man," is the vernacular term for a Muslim.

54. *Sefu* is a vulgarism for vagina.

55. Whenever a visitor takes his leave of a community where he has enjoyed hospitality, it is customary for someone from the community to accompany him halfway on his journey to his next destination. In this story, this custom is made a euphemism for promiscuity.

56. A forty-day quarantine period known as *labinane* follows a death, during which time the immediate bereaved are isolated from the community. Kuranko folk wisdom has it that this is the time it takes for a body to decay under the ground.

57. René Girard takes a similar view, arguing against the structuralist assumption that human reality is intelligible as a *logos*, an incipient logic. "The real structures are intersubjective," he notes (1996, 34–35).

58. Ethnologically, the human laugh is like the threat grimace of higher primates—a characteristic response when two animals meet in the ambiguous space where neighboring home ranges overlap.

59. As early as the mid-sixteenth century, "the civilizing process" that would become central to the self-definition of the European bourgeoisie, had begun to define bodiliness as a sign of shamefulness and barbarity (Elias 1994). As bodily functions were partitioned and censored as impolite, the universal became defined in increasingly ethereal and abstract terms—in notions of equality in the sight of God, notions of equal rights under the law, or intellectual schema worked out by men of vision and genius. And as transcendental designs played up notions of individual identity, redemption, and destiny, the old, earthy ethos of common bodiliness

and community went underground. All this culminated in the rise of the novel—the epitome of possessive individualism and the private life.

60. I have published details of the foregoing episode, slightly fictionalized, in *Barawa* (1986, 130).

61. Women are free to throw boiling water at a man who invades the privacy of a back yard, and supernatural retribution (through the agency of the powerful women's cult *Segere*) may follow if a man infringes the privacy of a woman's room or personal trunk.

62. Kuranko society is composed of four major estates: ruling clans; non-ruling "commoner" clans; traditionally Muslim clans; occupational and hereditary clans, with which rulers may not intermarry, known collectively as *nyemakale*. These clans include the xylophonists and praise-singers (*jelis*), and the bardic keepers of chiefly traditions and genealogies (*finas*). Ranked lowest in the social hierarchy, *finas* or *fin-abas* (*ba*: "big") enjoy the patronage of rulers, whom they serve, though apocryphal stories abound in ruling families that attribute all the catastrophes of the warrior past to the caprice and cunning of *finas* and *jelis* who, exceeding their servile roles, sang the praises of their lord's courageous forebears and so persuaded them, against their better judgment, on foolhardy courses of action.

63. Succession generally follows the principle of primogeniture, though in practice an eldest son will be passed over in favor of a younger brother or even a father's younger brother if he is not capable of shouldering the responsibilities of the office. Moreover, a man's immediate successor is normally the first-born son of his first ("senior") wife—*musu fole*. According to Kuranko naming custom, the first-born son takes the father's father's name; the second-born is named from the mother's side (usually after the mother's father). The successor is thus identified with the patriline, while the second-born is identified with the jurally insignificant matriline. The eldest son's assumption of his father's position formally takes place *after* the father's death. The assumption is signified by the son inheriting and donning his father's cap and gown. "Positions," say the Kuranko, "are like garments."

64. Although a man's fate and fortune are largely determined by his patrilineal forebears and by his membership of a patrilineage, the ancestral blessings are mediated by his mother. Thus, a diviner will often explain a man's misfortune as being a consequence of disrespect shown by the mother towards her husband, while good fortune will be readily attributed to the proper conduct of a man's mother. Partly as a result of these conventional rationalizations, women often blame themselves for their children's misfortunes. But since the blessings of the patrilineal ancestors are a scarce resource, competed for by a man's several wives (each of whom strives for

the prosperity of her own children), a woman may be inclined to blame a co-wife (whose children are well favored) for the failures and misfortunes of her own children. This tension and latent antagonism is most common between junior and senior co-wives, and the status rivalry among half-brothers (sons of the same father but of different mothers) is usually said to derive from it. This relationship between half-brothers or ortho-cousins is known as *fadenye* (lit. "father's child-ship"), and the term *fadenye* may be applied to any relationship marked by rivalry, antagonism, and competition. It is thus directly comparable to the Bambara *fadena* (Griaule 1973, 12) and the Malinke *fadenya* (Bird and Kendall 1980, 14–15; Hopkins 1971, 100)—relationships that Fortes characterizes in terms of "Oedipal fate" (1983).

65. Witchcraft = *suwa'ye*. Usually associated with destructive power, in this context it connotes the extraordinary generative power Sundiata possessed.

66. In the Niane version, Soumaoro Kanté is a powerful sorcerer-king whom Sundiata fights and finally defeats in his conquest and unification of Mali.

67. In the Niane version, the conflict between senior and junior co-wives is even more dramatically pronounced.

68. Among the Lugbara, witchcraft accusations within the minimal lineage are of two kinds: a son against his father, and "brother" against "brother." Apart from indicating the tension and repressed hostility that often exist between father and son, the pattern of witchcraft accusations indicates a trend toward displacement. Thus, accusations between "men of equal generation, 'brothers', tend to occur at later stages in the cycle of development of a lineage." "Accusations by a son against a father … occur mainly during the earlier stages" (Middleton 1960, 227). It should also be noted here that the love-hate relationship between father and son is sometimes exacerbated when senior sons compete with the father for the affections of his junior wives. Such is the case among the Dinka (Deng 1974, 175).

69. I have argued elsewhere (Jackson 1977) that laterally structured cult associations among the Kuranko offset and eclipse tensions and conflicts within the vertically structured field of descent. Neumann has also suggested that the "horizontal organization of age groups obviates personal conflict in the sense of a hostile father-son relationship, because the terms "father" and "son" connote group characteristics and not personal relations … Conflicts, so far as they exist at all, are between the age groups and have a collective and archetypal, rather than a personal and individual, character (Neumann 1954, 141).

70. Herodotus gives three versions, "The Scythian and the Pontic Greek, which are mythological, and a third (c.II seq.) which he adopts as resting on the authority of both nations (12.3), and which he partially confirms by quoting Aristeas (c.13),

who differs only as to the race which drove the Scyths into their new country" (How and Wells 1964, vol. 1, 304).

71. Two of the best clinical biographies, which are relevant here, are Freud's account of parricide in Doestoevsky (Freud 1928) and Erikson's account of William James's relationship with his father (1968, 150–55). In both cases, the son's ambivalence toward the father leads to a form of self-immobilization: in the case of Doestoevsky "neurotic epilepsy," in the case of William James "delayed maturation."

72. As Lévi-Strauss observes, lameness, stuttering, and memory lapses are structurally equivalent in myths from throughout the world. Symbols of ambivalence, they all signify discontinuities in experience, articulating social and psychological hesitancy as physical impediments (1992, 191).

73. In *At Home in the World* (1995, 44) I describe the situation for the Warlpiri of Central Australia, and Jacob Bronowski paints a moving portrait of the same desertion among the nomadic Bakhtari: "What happens to the old when they cannot cross the last river? Nothing. They stay behind to die ... The man accepts the nomad custom; he has come to the end of his journey, and there is no place at the end" (1973, 64).

74. Translated as *Dear Departed* (1991).

75. Elsewhere, she has noted: "It is *very important* that the reader *not* get the impression that the author is greatly or personally interested about her origins, since the whole quest is more sociological and historical than personal" (cited in Beaver 1992, 13).

76. Philosophically, this tension and twofoldness inheres in all human experience; for, as Plato observed, we *simultaneously* apprehend the things of this world in sensuous immediacy *as phenomenon* and in abstract reflection *as ideas*.

77. *Latitudes of Exile: Poems 1965–1975* (John McIndoe: Dunedin).

78. A boaster or braggard.

79. Joe's younger sister Florence Helen Pawelka.

80. It is notable, for instance, that almost all the themes mentioned in Ochs and Capps's 1995 review of narrative theory are anticipated in Arendt's work (though Arendt is not cited in this review).

81. The notion of situatedness is central to the work of both de Beauvoir and Sartre, yet Arendt disliked Sartre because of his evasiveness and "lies" about his role in the resistance, in much the same way as she disapproved of Adorno because he changed his name from Wiesengrund (his Jewish father's name) to his mother's Italian family name, allegedly to hide his Jewishness. Adorno and Sartre have influenced my thinking so deeply that I cannot help but ponder this

paradox of friendship: that those one loves rarely love one another.

82. Lisa Jane Disch puts this very succinctly (citing an undated Arendt typescript "On the Nature of Totalitarianism: An Essay in Understanding"): "The purpose of political theory, as Arendt understands it, is not to make a descriptively accurate report of the world but 'to transcend the limitations of facts and information' to tell a provocative and principled story" (Disch 1994, 140).

83. Seyla Benhabib draws a useful distinction between "agonal action" and "narrative action" in order to highlight Arendt's notion that narrative does not so much reveal some essential meaning that is already in place as bring new understandings into existence through social interaction (1996, 125–26).

84. Arendt's ideas here resemble those of Adorno, for whom thinking demands the abrogation of the ego. "Open thinking points beyond itself," he observed. "What has been cogently thought must be thought in some other place and by other people" (1978a, 168). It is also worth remarking a parallelism with the social phenomenology of Alfred Schutz (possibly because both models have their source in Kant), for whom "the reciprocity of perspectives" and "the interchangeability of standpoints" defined the strategic field of intersubjectivity and "common-sense" thinking (Schutz 1970, 183–84, 1973, 312–16).

85. Georg Groddeck (1977, 132–57) speaks of this forcefield that lies beyond the direct experience and scope of the ego as the It. While the It is impersonal or transpersonal, it nonetheless is felt as a vital presence that shapes and guides our lives, which is why "it" is so often anthropomorphized in theory and theology alike.

86. I see this as Montaigne did—as a mode of understanding that makes metaphor central, for one crosses to and fro between one's own standpoint and the standpoint of another dialogically, availing oneself of common images or tropes to compare one's experiences with the experiences of the other. The result is a rough overlapping that uses the inexactitude of metaphor (the things compared are not exactly alike) to open up conversation, to break an impasse, to close the distance between self and other.

87. Writing in January 1945, Hannah Arendt already anticipates the conclusions she will reach in *Eichmann in Jerusalem* (1963). "Himmler's over-all organization, relies not on fanatics, nor on congenital murderers, nor on sadists; it relies entirely upon the normality of jobholders and family-men" (Arendt 1978, 232). James Baldwin, also writing of the holocaust, says very much the same thing: "A civilization is not destroyed by wicked people; it is not necessary that people be wicked but only that they be spineless" (1970, 77).

88. The history of anthropology has involved a transition precisely from his-

torical to ahistorical modalities of understanding. Thus the late nineteenth century anthropology of Tylor, Frazer, Morgan, and de Coulanges centers its cross-cultural inquiries on antiquity and teleological models of socio-cultural evolution, while the ethnographic method of Malinowski which establishes the modern fieldwork tradition places history in parentheses (as does the later structuralism of Claude Lévi-Strauss).

89. Cf. Devereux (1967) on "subjectivity" as a methodologically essential aspect of "objectivity" in the human sciences, and Adorno on the "reciprocal" need for studies of any abstract "subject" to include accounts of "subjectivity" and vice versa (1978a, 498).

90. In her account of Hannah Arendt's notion of judging, Lisa Jane Disch coins the phrase "the visiting imagination" to capture Arendt's notion of visiting as a way of "constructing stories of an event from each of the plurality of perspectives that might have an interest in telling it and imagining how I would respond as a character in a story very different from my own. It is a kind of representation that arrives at the general through the particular" (Disch 1994, 158).

91. In *Minima Ethnographica* (1998, 194) I question the view espoused by Sartre (1983, 256), Berger (1984, 38), and, more recently, by Said (1994, 44) that critical thought must involve a repositioning of one's viewpoint in such a way that one affiliates oneself with or "bears witness to" the subaltern or the oppressed on the grounds that those most marginal to centers of power, those most unsettled or dislocated by the vicissitudes of history, hold the most authentic insights into the workings of society and history.

92. "No relation of a dream can convey the dream-sensation," writes Joseph Conrad, "that commingling of absurdity, surprise, and bewilderment in a tremor of struggling revolt, that notion of being captured by the incredible which is of the very essence of dreams" (1995, 90).

93. The word *jukurrpa* denotes both dreams and the Dreaming.

94. Aboriginal ethnography challenges our distinction between private and public in another sense too, for in an Aboriginal community many of the traits that we identify with the private individual—personality, emotions, thoughts, quirks, idiosyncracies—are not regarded as fixed essences so much as a repertoire of possibilities that are enacted according to social protocols and demands. Shame consists less in washing one's dirty linen in public than in failing to conform to the rules of public performance.

BIBLIOGRAPHY

Abraham, Karl. 1909. "Dreams and Myths: A Study in Folk-Psychology." In *Clinical Papers and Essays in Psycho-Analysis* (1955), 153–209. London: Hogarth Press.

Abrahamsson, H. 1951. *The Origin of Death*. Uppsala: Studia Ethnographica Upsaliensia no. 3.

Abu-Lughod, Lila. 1993. *Writing Women's Worlds: Bedouin Stories*. Berkeley: University of California Press.

Adorno, Theodor. 1973. *Negative Dialectics*. Translated by E. B. Ashton. New York: Continuum.

———. 1978a. "Resignation." *Telos* 35: 165, 168.

———. 1978b. *Minima Moralia: Reflections from Damaged Life*. Translated by E. F. N. Jephcott. London: Verso.

———. 1998. "Notes on Philosophical Thinking." In *Critical Models: Interventions and Catchwords*. Translated by Henry W. Pickford, 127–34. New York: Columbia University Press.

Amis, Martin. 2001. *Experience*. London: Vintage.

Anderson, Benedict. 1983. *Imagined Communities: Reflections on the Origin and Spread of Nationalism*. London: Verso.

Appadurai, Arjun. 1996a. *Modernity at Large: Cultural Dimensions of Globalization*. Minneapolis: University of Minnesota Press.

———. 1996b. "Sovereignty Without Territoriality: Notes For a Postnational Geography." In *The Geography of Identity*, edited by Patricia Yaeger, 40–58. Ann Arbor: University of Michigan Press.

Arendt, Hannah. 1943. "We Refugees." *The Menorah Journal* 31(1): 69–77.

———. 1944. "The Jew as Pariah: A Hidden Tradition." *Jewish Studies* 6: 99–122.

———. 1953a. "Understanding and Politics." *Partisan Review* 20: 377–92.

———. 1953b. "A Reply." *Review of Politics* 15: 76–84.

———. 1958. *The Human Condition*. Chicago: University of Chicago Press.

———. 1963. *Eichmann in Jerusalem: A Report on the Banality of Evil*. New York: Viking.

———. 1965. *On Revolution*. Harmondsworth: Penguin Books.

———. 1968. *Between Past and Future: Eight Exercises in Political Thought*. Enlarged edition. New York: Viking.

———. 1969. "Reflections on Violence." *New York Review of Books*, February 27.

———. 1971. *The Life of the Mind*. San Diego and New York: Harcourt Brace.

———. 1973. *Men in Dark Times*. Harmondsworth: Penguin.

———. 1977. "The Concept of History." In *Between Past and Future: Eight Exercises in Political Thought*, 41–90. Harmondsworth: Penguin.

———. 1978. *The Jew as Pariah: Jewish Identity and Politics in the Modern Age*. Edited with an introduction by Ron H. Feldman. New York: Grove Press.

———. 1979. *The Origins of Totalitarianism*. New York: Harcourt Brace Jovanovich.

———. 1982. *Lectures on Kant's Political Philosophy*. Edited by Ronald Beiner. Chicago: University of Chicago Press.

———. 1994. *Essays in Understanding, 1930–1954*. Edited by Jerome Kohn. New York: Harcourt Brace & Co.

———. 2000. "Labor, Work, Action." In *The Portable Hannah Arendt*, edited by Peter Baehr, 167–81. Harmondsworth: Penguin.

Aristotle. 1952. *The Works of Aristotle, Volume XII: Select Fragments*. Translated under the Editorship of Sir David Ross. Oxford: Clarendon Press.

———. 1983. *The Nicomachean Ethics*. Translated by David Ross. Oxford: Oxford University Press.

Bakhtin, Mikhail. 1968. *Rabelais and His World*. Translated by Helene Iswolksy. Cambridge, Mass.: The MIT Press.

———. 1981. *The Dialogical Imagination*. Edited by Caryl Emerson and Michael Holquist. Austin: University of Texas Press.

Baldwin, James. 1961. *Nobody Knows My Name: More Notes of a Native Son*. New York: Dell.

———. 1970. *The Fire Next Time*. New York: Dell.

Barnes, Edward. 1999. "The Heart of Darkness." *Time*, January 25: 32–33.

Barnes, Julian. 1995. *Letters from London*. London: Picador.

Basso, Keith. 1979. *Portraits of "The Whiteman": Linguistic Play and Cultural Symbols among the Western Apache*. Cambridge: Cambridge University Press.

———. 1996. "Wisdom Sits in Places: Notes on Western Apache Landscape." In *Senses of Place*, edited by Steven Feld and Keith H. Basso. Santa Fe: School of American Research Press.

Bauby, Jean-Dominique. 1998. *The Diving Bell and the Butterfly*. Translated by Jeremy Leggat. New York: Knopf.

Baumann, Gerd. 1996. *Contesting Culture: Discourses of Identity in Multi-Ethnic London*. Cambridge: Cambridge University Press.

Beaver, Harold. 1992. "Remembering a World She Never Knew." Review of *Dear Departed*, by Marguerite Yourcenar. *New York Times Book Review*, March 1: 13.

Becker, Ernst. 1973. *The Denial of Death*. New York: Free Press.

Beiner, Ronald. 1982. "Hannah Arendt on Judging." In *Lectures on Kant's Political Philosophy*, by Hannah Arendt. Edited by Ronald Beiner, 89–156. Chicago: University of Chicago Press.

Belich, James. 1996. *Making Peoples: A History of the New Zealanders: From Polynesian Settlement to the End of the Nineteenth Century*. Auckland: Allen Lane/Penguin.

Benhabib, Seyla. 1996. *The Reluctant Modernism of Hannah Arendt*. Thousand Oaks and London: Sage Publications.

Benjamin, Walter. 1968. *Illuminations*. Translated by Harry Zohn. New York: Schocken Books.

Berger, John. 1979. *Pig Earth*. London: Writers and Readers Publishing Cooperative.

———. 1983. *Once in Europa*. New York: Pantheon.

———. 1984a. *About Looking*. London: Writers and Readers Publishing Cooperative.

———. 1984b. "Ways of Witnessing." *Marxism Today*, December.

———. 1985. *The Sense of Sight: Writings of John Berger*. Edited with an introduction by Lloyd Spencer. New York: Pantheon.

Berger, John, and Jean Mohr. 1976. *A Fortunate Man: The Story of a Country Doctor*. London: Writers and Readers Publishing Cooperative.

———. 1982. *Another Way of Telling*. London: Writers and Readers Publishing Cooperative.

Bergson, Henri. 1911. *Laughter: An Essay on the Meaning of the Comic*. London: MacMillan.

Bettelheim, Bruno. 1978. *The Uses of Enchantment: The Meaning and Importance of Fairy Tales*. Harmondsworth: Penguin.

Bion, Wilfred R. 1975. *Attention and Interpretation: A Scientific Approach to Insight in Psycho-Analysis and Groups*. London: Tavistock.

Bird, Carmel, ed. 1998. *The Stolen Children: Their Stories*. Sydney: Random House.

Bird, Charles. 1971. "Oral Art in the Mande." In *Papers on the Manding*, edited by C. T. Hodge, 15–25. The Hague: Mouton.

Bird, Charles, and Martha B. Kendall. 1980. "The Mande Hero." In *Explorations in African Systems of Thought*, edited by Ivan Karp and Charles Bird. Bloomington: Indiana University Press.

Borges, Jorge Luis. 1965. *Other Inquisitions*. Translated by Ruth L. C. Simms. New York: Simon and Schuster.

Bottomley, Gillian. 1992. *From Another Place: Migration and the Politics of Culture*. Cambridge: Cambridge University Press.

Bourdieu, Pierre. 1977. *Outline of a Theory of Practice*. Translated by Richard Nice. Cambridge: Cambridge University Press.

———. 1990. *In Other Words: Essays Towards a Reflexive Sociology*. Translated by Matthew Adamson. Stanford: Stanford University Press.

———. 1991. *Language and Symbolic Power*. Edited and introduced by John B. Thompson. Translated by Gino Raymond and Matthew Adamson. Cambridge: Polity Press.

———. 1996. "Understanding." *Theory, Culture and Society* 13(2): 17–37.

———. 1998. *Acts of Resistance: Against the New Myths of our Time*. Translated by Richard Nice. Cambridge: Polity Press.

Boym, Svetlana. 1998. "On Diasporic Intimacy: Ilya Kabakov's Installations and Immigrant Homes." *Critical Inquiry* 24(2): 498–524.

Bozzoli, Belinda. 1998. "Public Ritual and Private Transition: The Truth Commission in Alexandra Township, South Africa 1996." *African Studies* 57(2): 167–95.

Bren, Frank. 1986. *World Cinema 1: Poland*. London: Flicks Books.

Brightman, Carol. 1995. Introduction and epilog to *Between Friends: The Correspondence of Hannah Arendt and Mary McCarthy 1949–1975*. Edited with an introduction by Carol Brightman. San Diego and New York: Harcourt Brace.

Bronowski, Jacob. 1973. *The Ascent of Man*. London: BBC.

Brown, Norman O. 1959. *Life against Death: The Psychoanalytical Meaning of History*. London: Routledge and Kegan Paul.

Bruner, Jerome. 1976. "Nature and Uses of Immaturity." In *Play—its Role in Development and Education*, edited by Jerome Bruner, Alison Jolly, and Kathy Sylva. Harmondsworth: Penguin.

———. 1990. *Acts of Meaning*. Cambridge, Mass.: Harvard University Press.

Bunker, H. A., and B. D. Lewin. 1965. "A Psychoanalytic Notation on the Root

GN, KN, CN." In *Psychoanalysis and Culture,* edited by G. B. Wilbur and W. Muensterberger, 363–67. New York: International Universities Press.

Camara, Sory. 1972. "Introduction à l'Étude des 'TaliMandenka'." Summary of a paper delivered at the Conference on the Manding, School of Oriental and African Studies, London.

Camus, Albert. 1970. *Lyrical and Critical Essays.* Translated by Ellen Conroy Kennedy. New York: Vintage.

Capps, Lisa, and Elinor Ochs. 1995. *Constructing Panic: The Discourse of Agoraphobia.* Cambridge, Mass.: Harvard University Press.

Caruth, Cathy. 1995. "Introduction to Part 2: Recapturing the Past." In *Trauma: Explorations in Memory,* edited with an introduction by Cathy Caruth, 151–57. Baltimore: Johns Hopkins University Press.

Cleveland, Les. 1994. *Dark Laughter: War in Song and Popular Culture.* Westport, Conn.: Praeger.

Conrad, Joseph. 1995. *Heart of Darkness.* Peterborough, Ontario: Broadview Press.

Daniel, E. Valentine. 1996. *Charred Lullabies: Chapters in an Anthropography of Violence.* Princeton: Princeton University Press.

———. 1997. "Suffering Nation and Alienation." In *Social Suffering,* edited by Arthur Kleinman, Veena Das, and Margaret Lock, 309–58. Berkeley: University of California Press.

Daniel, E. Valentine, and Yuvaraj Thangaraj. 1995. "Forms, Formations, and Transformations of the Tamil Refugee." In *Mistrusting Refugees,* edited by E. Valentine Daniel and John Chr. Knudsen, 225–56. Berkeley: University of California Press.

Das, Veena. 1990. "Our Work to Cry: Your Work to Listen." In *Mirrors of Violence: Communities, Riots and Violence in South Asia,* edited by Veena Das, 345–98. Oxford: Oxford University Press.

———. 1991. "Composition of the Personal Voice: Violence and Migration." *Studies in History,* n.s., 7(1): 65–77.

———. 1995. *Critical Events: An Anthropological Perspective on Contemporary India.* Delhi: Oxford University Press.

———. 2007. *Life and Words: Violence and the Descent into the Ordinary.* Berkeley: University of California Press.

Davies, Desmond. 1995–1996. "Sierra Leone: A Human Rights Crisis." *West Africa* (25–31 December 1995–1–7 January 1996): 1994–1995.

———. 1998. "Back to Square One." *West Africa* no. 4193 (6–26 July): 566–69.

Davies, Norman. 1981. *God's Playground: A History of Poland.* Vol. 2. Oxford: Clarendon Press.

Dawood, N. J. 1973. Introduction to *Tales from the Thousand and One Nights.* Translated with an introduction by N. J. Dawood. Harmondsworth: Penguin.

de Certeau, Michel. 1984. *The Practice of Everyday Life.* Translated by Steven Rendall. Berkeley: University of California Press.

Deleuze, Gilles, and Felix Guattari. 1991. *A Thousand Plateaus.* Minneapolis: University of Minnesota Press.

Deng, F. Mading. 1974. *Dinka Folktales.* New York and London: Holmes and Meier.

Derrida, Jacques. 1992. *Given Time: 1. Counterfeit Money.* Translated by Peggy Kamuf. Chicago: University of Chicago Press.

Desjarlais, Robert, Leon Eisenberg, Byron Good, and Arthur Kleinman, eds. 1995. *World Mental Health: Problems and Priorities in Low-Income Countries.* New York: Oxford University Press.

Devereux, George. 1948. "Mohave Coyote Tales." *Journal of American Folklore* 61: 233–55.

———. 1953. "Why Oedipus Killed Laius: A Note on the Complementary Oedipus Complex in Greek Drama." *The International Journal of Psycho-Analysis* 34: 32–41.

———. 1961. "Art and Mythology, Part 1: A General Theory." In *Studying Personality Cross-Culturally,* edited by B. Kaplan. New York: Harper and Row.

———. 1964. "An Ethnopsychiatric Note on Property Destruction in Cargo Cults." *Man* 64: 184–85.

———. 1967. *From Anxiety to Method in the Behavioral Sciences.* The Hague: Mouton.

———. 1970. "La Naissance d'Aphrodite." In *Échanges et Communications.* Vol. 2, edited by J. Pouillon and P. Maranda, 1229–52. The Hague: Mouton.

———. 1972. "Quelques Traces de la Succession par Ultimogéniture en Scythie." *Inter Nord* 12: 262–70.

———. 1978. *Ethnopsychoanalysis: Psychoanalysis and Anthropology as Complementary Frames of Reference.* Berkeley: University of California Press.

———. 1979. "Fantasy and Symbol as Dimensions of Reality." In *Fantasy and Symbol: Studies in Anthropological Interpretation,* edited by R. H. Hook, 18–30. London: Academic Press.

———. 1980. *Basic Problems of Ethnopsychiatry.* Translated by Basia Miller

Gulati and George Devereux. Chicago: University of Chicago Press.

Devisch, René. 1995. "Frenzy, Violence, and Ethical Renewal in Kinshasa." *Public Culture* 7(3): 593–629.

Dewey, John. 1929. *Experience and Nature.* London: Allen and Unwin.

Didion, Joan. 1979. *The White Album.* Harmondsworth: Penguin Books.

Disch, Lisa Jane. 1994. *Hannah Arendt and the Limits of Philosophy.* Ithaca, New York: Cornell University Press.

Dixon, Robert. 1984. *Searching for Aboriginal Languages: Memoirs of a Field Worker.* St. Lucia: University of Queensland Press.

Dobzhansky, T. 1971. *Mankind Evolving.* New Haven: Yale University Press.

Douglas, Mary. 1966. *Purity and Danger: An Analysis of Concepts of Pollution and Taboo.* London: Routledge.

Dresch, Paul. 1995. "Race, Culture and—What? Pluralist Certainties in the United States." In *The Pursuit of Certainty: Religious and Cultural Formulations,* edited by Wendy James, 61–91. London: Routledge.

Drewall, Margaret Thompson. 1992. *Yoruba Ritual: Performers, Play, Agency.* Bloomington: Indiana University Press.

Duby, Georges. 1988. "Private Power, Public Power." In *A History of the Private Life.* Vol. 2, *Revelations of the Medieval World,* edited by Georges Duby. Translated by Arthur Goldhammer. Cambridge, Mass.: Belknap Press of Harvard University Press.

Dussart, Françoise. 2000. *The Politics of Ritual in an Aboriginal Settlement: Kinship, Gender, and the Currency of Knowledge.* Washington: Smithsonian Institution Press.

Edwards, Coral, and Peter Read, eds. 1989. *The Lost Children: Thirteen Australians Taken from their Aboriginal Families Tell of the Struggle to Find their Natural Parents.* Sydney: Doubleday.

Eibl-Eibelsfeldt, I. 1975. *Ethology: The Biology of Behavior.* 2nd ed. New York: Holt, Rinehart and Winston.

Elbert, S. H., and T. Monberg. 1965. *From the Two Canoes: Oral Traditions of Rennell and Bellona Islands.* Honolulu: University of Hawaii Press.

Elias, Norbert. 1994. *The Civilizing Process: The History of Manners and State Formation and Civilization.* Translated by Edmund Jephcott. Oxford: Blackwell.

Erikson, Erik H. 1968. *Identity: Youth and Crisis.* London: Faber and Faber.

Esterson, Aaron. 1972. *The Leaves of Spring: Schizophrenia, Family and Sacrifice.* Harmondsworth: Penguin.

Ex, J. 1966. *Adjustment after Migration: A Longitudinal Study of the Process of Adjustment by Refugees in a New Environment*. The Hague: Martinus Nijhoff.

Fadiman, Anne. 1997. *The Spirit Catches You and You Fall Down: A Hmong Child, Her American Doctors, and the Collision of Two Cultures*. New York: Farrar, Straus and Giroux.

Fanon, Frantz. 1968. *The Wretched of the Earth*. New York: Grove Press.

Fasching, Darrell J., Dell Dechant, and David M. Lantigua. 2011. "Religion, Ethics, and Storytelling." In *Comparative Religious Ethics: A Narrative Approach to Global Ethics*, edited by Darrell J. Fasching, Dell Dechant, and David M. Lantigua. Chichester, West Sussex: Wiley-Blackwell.

Feld, Steven. 1982. *Sound and Sentiment: Birds, Weeping, Poetics, and Song in Kaluli Expression*. Philadelphia: University of Pennsylvania Press.

Feldman, Allen, 1991. *Formations of Violence: The Narrative of the Body and Political Terror in Northern Ireland*. Chicago: University of Chicago Press.

Ferme, Mariane. 1998. "The Violence of Numbers: Consensus, Competition, and the Negotiation of Disputes in Sierra Leone." *Cahiers d'Études Africaines* 150–151: 555–80.

Finkelstein, Norman G. 2000. *The Holocaust Industry*. London: Verso.

Finnström, Sverker. 1999. *Living with Bad Surroundings: War and Uncertainty in Northern Uganda*. Working Papers in Cultural Anthropology, no. 9. Uppsala: Department of Cultural Anthropology and Ethnology.

Fonagy, Peter, and Mary Target. 2003. *Psychoanalytic Theories: Perspectives from Developmental Psychopathology*. New York: Brunner-Routledge.

Fonseca, Isabel. 1995. *Bury me Standing: The Gypsies and their Journey*. New York: Knopf.

Fortes, Meyer. 1983. *Oedipus and Job in West African Religion*. Cambridge: Cambridge University Press.

Foucault, Michel. 1979. *Discipline and Punish: The Birth of the Prison*. Translated by A. Sheridan. Harmondsworth: Penguin.

———. 1990. *The Use of Pleasure*. Vol. 2, *The History of Sexuality*. Translated by Robert Hurley. New York: Vintage.

Frank, A. 1995. *The Wounded Storyteller: Body, Illness, and Ethics*. Chicago: University of Chicago Press.

Freeman, Jane. 1997. "New Faces." In *The Sydney Morning Herald*, January 15: 11.

Freud, Sigmund. 1928. "Dostoevsky and Parricide." In *Standard Edition of the Complete Psychological Works of Sigmund Freud*, translated and edited by James Strachey, vol. 21 (1961), 173–96. London: Hogarth Press.

———. 1963. *Three Case Histories*. Edited by Philip Rieff. New York: Collier-Macmillan.

———. 1975a. "The Occurrence in Dreams of Material from Fairy Tales." In *Standard Edition of the Complete Psychological Works of Sigmund Freud*, translated and edited by James Strachey, vol. 12 (1911–1913), 281–87. London: Hogarth Press.

———. 1975b "An Evidential Dream." In *Standard Edition of the Complete Psychological Works of Sigmund Freud*, translated and edited by James Strachey, vol. 12 (1911–1913), 269–77. London: Hogarth Press.

Fromm, Erich. 1973. *The Crisis in Psychoanalysis: Essays on Freud, Marx and Social Psychology*. Harmondsworth: Penguin Books.

Fukuyama, Francis. 1992. *The End of History and the Last Man*. Harmondsworth: Penguin Books.

Fuller, Graham, ed. 1993. *Potter on Potter*. London: Faber.

Geertz, Clifford. 1973. *The Interpretation of Cultures*. New York: Basic Books.

Gilsenan, Michael. 1996. *Lords of the Lebanese Marches: Violence and Narrative in an Arab Society*. Berkeley: University of California Press.

Girard, René. 1966. *Deceit, Desire, and the Novel: Self and Other in Literary Structure*. Baltimore, Maryland: Johns Hopkins University Press.

———. 1996. "Triangular Desire." In *The Girard Reader*, edited by James G. Williams, 33–34. New York: Crossroad Publishing.

Glaister, Dan. 1999. "Whitbread Completes Clean Sweep for Poet." *Guardian Weekly*, February 7.

Goody, Jack. 1962. ed. *The Developmental Cycle in Domestic Groups*. Cambridge: Cambridge University Press.

———. 1966a. "Introduction." In *Succession to High Office*, edited by Jack Goody, 1–56. Cambridge: Cambridge University Press.

———. 1966b. "Circulating Succession among the Gonja." In *Succession to High Office*, edited by Jack Goody, 142–76. Cambridge: Cambridge University Press.

Gough, David. 1999. "Sect Promotes Village Values: Kenyan Group Sees Salvation in Witchcraft and Circumcision." *Guardian Weekly*, November 18–24: 3.

Graeber, David. 2011. *Debt: The First 5,000 Years*. New York: Melville House.

Graves, Robert. 1955. *The Greek Myths*. 2 vols. Harmondsworth: Penguin Books.

Gray, R. F. 1965. "Some Parallels in Sonjo and Christian Mythology." In *African Systems of Thought*, edited by Meyer Fortes and Germaine Dieterlen. London: Oxford University Press.

Greenberg, Judith. 1998. "The Echo of Trauma and the Trauma of Echo." *American Imago* 55(3): 319–47.

Griaule, Marcel. 1973. "The Mother's Brother in the Western Sudan." In *French Perspectives in African Studies*, edited by Pierre Alexandre, 11–25. London: Oxford University Press.

Groddeck, Georg. 1977. *The Meaning of Illness: Selected Psychoanalytic Writings*. Translated by Gertrud Mander. London: Hogarth Press.

Grossman, David. 2008. *Writing in the Dark*. Translated by Jessica Cohen. New York: Farrar, Straus and Giroux.

Gubbay, Denise. 1989. "ESL: Effective Skills for Living: A Therapeutic Group Approach." In *Refugee Resettlement and Wellbeing*, edited by Max Abbott, 295–305. Auckland: Mental Health Foundation of New Zealand.

Guha, Ranajit. 1983a. *Elementary Aspects of Peasant Insurgency in Colonial India*. Delhi: Oxford University Press.

———. 1983b. "The Prose of Counter-Insurgency." In *Subaltern Studies 2: Writings on South Asian History and Society*, edited by Ranajit Gujha, 1–42. Delhi: Oxford University Press.

Gupta, Akhil, and James Ferguson. 1992. "Beyond 'Culture': Space, Identity, and the Politics of Difference." *Cultural Anthropology* 7(1): 6–23.

Habermas, Jürgen. 1989. *The Structural Transformation of the Public Sphere*. Cambridge, Mass.: The MIT Press.

Hage, Ghassan. 1996. "The Spatial Imaginary of National Practices: Dwelling-Domesticating/Being-Exterminating." *Environment and Planning D: Society and Space* 14: 463–85.

———. 1999. *White Nation: Fantasies of White Supremacy in a Multicultural Society*. Sydney: Pluto Press.

———. 2000. "On the Ethics of Pedestrian Crossings, or Why 'Mutual Obligation' Does not Belong to the Language of Neo-Liberal Economics." *Meanjin* 59(4): 27–37.

Halbwachs, Maurice. 1980. *The Collective Memory*. Translated by Francis J. Ditter Jr. and Vida Yazdi Ditter. New York: Harper and Row.

Hanks, William F. 1990. *Referential Practice: Language and Lived Space among the Maya*. Chicago: University of Chicago Press.

Harrell-Bond, Barbara. 1986. *Imposing Aid: Emergency Assistance to Refugees*. Oxford: Oxford University Press.

Harrell-Bond, Barbara, and Eftihia Voutira. 1992. "Anthropology and the Study of Refugees." *Anthropology Today* 8(4): 6–10.

Hebdige, Dick. 1987. *Cut 'n Mix: Culture, Identity and Caribbean Music.* London: Methuen.

Heidegger, Martin. 1977. *The Question Concerning Technology and Other Essays.* Translated by William Lovitt. New York: Harper and Row.

———. 1978. *Poetry, Language, Thought.* Translated by Albert Hofstadter. New York: Harper and Row.

Herskovits, M. J. 1958. *Dahomean Narrative.* Evanston, Illinois: Northwestern University Press.

Herzfeld, Michael. 1987. *Anthropology through the Looking-Glass: Critical Ethnography on the Margins of Europe.* Cambridge: Cambridge University Press.

———. 1997. *Cultural Intimacy: Social Poetics in the Nation-State.* New York: Routledge.

Hobbes, Thomas. 1978. *Leviathan, of the Matter, Forme and Power of a Commonwealth Ecclesiastical or Civil.* Edited by Michael Oakeshott. New York: Collier.

Hollis, A. C. 1905. *The Masai: Their Language and Folklore.* Oxford: Clarendon Press.

———. 1909. *The Nandi: Their Language and Folklore.* Oxford: Clarendon Press.

Honwana, Alcinda. 1997. "Healing for Peace: Traditional Healers and Post-War Reconstruction in Southern Mozambique." Draft Document submitted to *Peace and Conflict: Journal of Peace and Psychology* 3(3).

Hopkins, N. S. 1971. "Mandinka Social Organization." In *Papers on the Manding,* edited by C. T. Hodge, 99–128. The Hague: Mouton.

Hoskins, Janet. 1998. *Biographical Objects: How Things Tell the Stories of People's Lives.* New York: Routledge.

How, W. W., and J. Wells 1964. *A Commentary on Herodotus.* 2 vols. Oxford: Clarendon Press.

Huband, Mark. 1996. "Africa's Poorest Trapped in War of Mindless Mutilation." *Guardian Weekly,* February 11: 1, 3.

Human Rights and Equal Opportunity Commission. 1997. *Bringing them Home: Report of the National Inquiry into the Separation of Aboriginal and Torres Strait Islander Children from their Families.* Sydney: Commonwealth of Australia.

Innes, Gordon, 1974. *Sunjata: Three Mandinka Versions.* London: School of Oriental and African Studies.

Irwin, Kathie. 1993. "Maori Feminism." In *Te Ao Marama: Regaining Aotearoa:*

Maori Writers Speak Out. Vol. 2, *He Whakaatanga O Te Ao*. Selected and edited by Witi Ihimaera, 299–304. Auckland: Reed.

Jackson, Michael. 1974. "The Structure and Significance of Kuranko Clanship." *Africa* 44: 397–415.

———. 1976. *Latitudes of Exile: Poems 1965–1975*. Dunedin: McIndoe.

———. 1977. *The Kuranko: Dimensions of Social Reality in a West African Society*. London: Hurst.

———. 1978. "Ambivalence and the Last-Born: Birth-Order Position in Convention and Myth." *Man*, n.s., 13: 341–61.

———. 1979. "Prevented Successions: A Commentary upon a Kuranko Narrative." In *Fantasy and Symbol: Studies in Anthropological Interpretation*, edited by R. H. Hook, 95–131. London: Academic Press.

———. 1982. *Allegories of the Wilderness: Ethics and Ambiguity in Kuranko Narratives*. Bloomington: Indiana University Press.

———. 1986. *Barawa and the Ways Birds Fly in the Sky*. Washington: Smithsonian Institution Press.

———. 1989. *Paths toward a Clearing: Radical Empiricism and Ethnographic Inquiry*. Bloomington: Indiana University Press.

———. 1994. *Pieces of Music*. Auckland: Random House.

———. 1995. *At Home in the World*. Durham, North Carolina: Duke University Press.

———. 1996. Introduction to *Things as They Are: New Directions in Phenomenological Anthropology*. Edited by Michael Jackson, 1–50. Bloomington: Indiana University Press.

———. 1997. *The Blind Impress*. Palmerston North: Dunmore Press.

———. 1998a. *Minima Ethnographica: Intersubjectivity and the Anthropological Project*. Chicago: University of Chicago Press.

———. 1998b. "In Extremis: Refugee Stories/Refugee Lives." *Turnbull Library Record* 31: 5–17.

———. 2009. "Where Thought Belongs: An Anthropological Critique of the Project of Philosophy." *Anthropology Theory* 9(3): 235–51.

———. 2011. *Life within Limits: Well-Being in a World of Want*. Durham, North Carolina: Duke University Press.

James, William. 1950. *The Principles of Psychology*. 2 vols. New York: Dover.

———. 1976. *Essays in Radical Empiricism*. Cambridge, Mass.: Harvard University Press.

James, Wendy. 1997. "The Names of Fear: Memory, History, and the Ethnography of Feeling among Uduk Refugees." *Journal of the Royal Anthropological Institute,* n.s., 3(1): 115–31.

Jameson, Fredric. 1984. Foreword to *The Postmodern Condition: A Report on Knowledge,* by Jean-François Lyotard. Translated by Geoff Bennington and Brian Massumi, vii–xxi. Minneapolis: University of Minnesota Press.

Jansen, Adrienne, ed. 1990. *I Have in my Arms Both Ways: Stories by Immigrant Women.* Wellington: Allen and Unwin.

Kahn, Joel S. 1989. "Culture: Demise or Resurrection?" *Critique of Anthropology* 9(2): 5–25.

Kapferer, Bruce. 1988. *Legends of People, Myths of State: Violence, Intolerance, and Political Culture in Sri Lanka and Australia.* Washington: Smithsonian Institution Press.

Karakasidou, Anastasia N. 1997. *Fields of Wheat, Hills of Blood: Passages to Nationhood in Greek Macedonia 1870–1990.* Chicago: University of Chicago Press.

Keesing, Roger M. 1982. "Kasom in Melanesia: An Overview." In *Reinventing Traditional Culture: The Politics of Kastom in Island Melanesia,"* Guest editors Roger M. Keesing and Robert Tonkinson. *Mankind* (Special Issue) 13(4): 297–301.

Keller, Stephen. 1975. *Uprooting and Social Change: The Role of Refugees in Development.* Delhi: Manohar Book Service.

Kerby, Anthony Paul. 1991. *Narrative and the Self.* Bloomington: Indiana University Press.

Kerényi, K. 1959. *The Heroes of the Greeks.* London: Thames and Hudson.

Kermode, Frank. 1967. *The Sense of an Ending: Studies in the Theory of Fiction.* New York: Oxford University Press.

Kernot, B. 1972. *People of the Four Winds.* Auckland: Hicks, Smith.

Kinsley, D. R. 1975. *The Sword and the Flute.* Berkeley: University of California Press.

Kleinman, Arthur. 1982. "Neurasthenia and Depression: A Study of Somaticization and Culture in China." *Culture, Medicine and Psychiatry* 6: 117–89.

Kleinman, Arthur, and Joan Kleinman. 1997a. "The Appeal of Experience; the Dismay of Images: Cultural Appropriations of Suffering in our Times." In *Social Suffering,* edited by Arthur Kleinman, Veena Das, and Margaret Lock, 1–23. Berkeley: University of California Press.

———. 1997b. "'Everything that Really Matters': Social Suffering, Subjectivity, and the Remaking of Human Experience in a Disordering World." *Harvard Theological Review* 90 (3): 315–35.

———. 2000. "The Violences of Everyday Life: The Multiple Forms and Dynamics of Social Violence." In *Violence and Subjectivity*, edited by Veena Das, Arthur Kleinman, Mamphela Ramphele, and Pamela Reynolds, 226–41. Berkeley: University of California Press.

Kleinman, Arthur, Veena Das, and Margaret Lock. eds. 1997. *Social Suffering*. Berkeley: University of California Press.

Knudsen, John Chr. 1995. "When Trust Is on Trial: Negotiating Refugee Narratives." In *Mistrusting Refugees*, edited by E. Valentine Daniel and John Chr. Knudsen, 13–35. Berkeley: University of California Press.

Koestler, Arthur. 1964. *The Act of Creation*. London: Hutchinson.

Krog, Antjie. 1998. *Country of My Skull*. London: Jonathan Cape.

Krulfeld, Ruth M. 1993. "Bridling Leviathan: New Paradigms of Method and Theory in Culture Change from Refugee Studies and Related Issues of Power and Empowerment. In *Selected Papers on Refugee Issues II*, edited by Mary Carol Hopkins and Nancy D. Donnelly, 29–41. Arlington: American Anthropological Association.

Kuper, Hilda. 1947. *An African Aristocracy: Rank among the Swazi*. London: Oxford University Press.

Laing, R. D. 1965. *The Divided Self: An Existential Study in Sanity and Madness*. Harmondsworth: Penguin.

———. 1967. *The Politics of Experience and the Bird of Paradise*. Harmondsworth: Penguin Books.

Lambek, Michael. 2010. *Ordinary Ethics: Anthropology, Language and Action*. New York: Fordham University Press.

Langer, Lawrence L. 1997. "The Alarmed Vision: Social Suffering and Holocaust Atrocity." In *Social Suffering*, edited by Arthur Kleinman, Veena Das, and Margaret Lock, 47–65. Berkeley: University of California Press.

Lattas, Andrew. 1998. *Cultures of Secrecy: Reinventing Race in Bush Kaliai Cargo Cults*. Madison: University of Wisconsin Press.

Laub, Dori. 1995. "Truth and Testimony." In *Trauma: Explorations in Memory*, edited with an introduction by Cathy Caruth, 61–75. Baltimore, Maryland: Johns Hopkins University Press.

Levi, Primo. 1989. *The Drowned and the Saved*. Translated by Raymond Rosenthal. New York: Random House.

Lévi-Strauss, Claude. 1963. *Structural Anthropology*. Vol. 1. Translated by C. Jacobson and B. G. Schoepf. New York: Basic Books.

———. 1970. *The Raw and the Cooked: Introduction to a Science of Mythology 1*. Translated by John and Doreen Weightman. London: Jonathan Cape.

———. 1973a. *From Honey to Ashes: Introduction to a Science of Mythology 2*. Translated by John and Doreen Weightman. London: Jonathan Cape.

———. 1973b. *Tristes Tropiques*. Translated by John and Doreen Weightman. London: Jonathan Cape.

———. 1977. *Structural Anthropology*. Vol. 2. Translated by Monique Layton. London: Allen Lane.

———. 1992. *The View from Afar*. Translated by Joachim Neugroschel and Phoebe Hoss. Chicago: University of Chicago Press.

Liev, Man Lau. 1995. "Refugees from Cambodia, Laos and Vietnam. In *Immigration and National Identity in New Zealand: One People, Two Peoples, Many Peoples?* edited by Stuart W. Greif, 99–132. Palmerston North: Dunmore.

Loizos, Peter. 1981. *The Heart Grown Bitter: A Chronicle of Cypriot War Refugees*. Cambridge: Cambridge University Press.

Luria, A. R. 1987. *The Man with a Shattered World*. Translated by Lynn Solotaroff. Cambridge, Mass.: Harvard University Press.

Lutz, Catherine A. 1988. *Unnatural Emotions: Everyday Sentiments on a Micronesian Atoll and their Challenge to Western Theory*. Chicago: University of Chicago Press.

Lyotard, Jean-François. 1984. *The Postmodern Condition: A Report on Knowledge*. Translated by Geoff Bennington and Brian Massumi. Minneapolis: University of Minnesota Press.

Macek, Ivana. 2000. *War Within: Everyday Life in Sarajevo under Seige*. Uppsala: Uppsala Studies in Cultural Anthropology 29.

MacIntyre, Alasdair. 1984. *After Virtue: A Study in Moral Theory*. 2nd ed. Notre Dame, Indiana: University of Notre Dame Press.

Maclean, Ian. 1995. Introduction to *The Manuscript Found in Saragossa*, xi–xviii. Translated by Ian Maclean. New York: Viking.

Madjar, Vladimir. 1998. *Bosnian Refugees in New Zealand: Their Stories and Life Experiences, Health Status and Needs, and the Implications for Refugee Health Services and Policy*. MBS thesis, Massey University, Palmerston North, New Zealand.

Magnusson, E., and W. Morris. 1869. *Grettis Saga*. London: F. S. Ellis.

Makdisi, Jean Said. 1990. *Beirut Fragments: A War Memoir*. New York: Persea.

Malcolm, Janet. 1994. *The Silent Woman: Sylvia Plath and Ted Hughes*. New York: Alfred A. Knopf.

Malinowski, Bronislaw. 1972. *Argonauts of the Western Pacific*. London: Routledge and Kegan Paul.

———. 1974. *Magic, Science and Religion and Other Essays*. London: Souvenir Press.

Malkki, Liisa. 1992. "National Geographic: The Rooting of Peoples and the Territorialization of National Identity among Scholars and Refugees." *Cultural Anthropology* 7(1): 24–44.

———. 1995a. *Purity and Exile: Violence, Memory, and National Cosmology among Hutu Refugees in Tanzania*. Chicago: University of Chicago Press.

———. 1995b. "Refugees and Exile: From 'Refugee Studies' to the National Order of Things." *Annual Review of Anthropology* 24: 495–523.

———. 1996. "Speechless Emissaries: Refugees, Humanitarianism, and Dehistoricization." *Cultural Anthropology* 11(3): 377–404.

———. 1997. "News and Culture: Transitory Phenomena and the Fieldwork Tradition." In *Anthropological Locations: Boundaries and Grounds of a Field Science*, edited by Akhil Gupta and James Ferguson, 86–101. Berkeley: University of California Press.

Mandela, Nelson. 1994. *Long Walk to Freedom*. London: Abacus.

Mandelstam, Nadezhda. 1975. *Hope against Hope: A Memoir*. Translated by Max Hayward. Harmondsworth: Penguin Books.

Mandelstam, Osip E. 1979. *The Complete Critical Prose and Letters*. Edited by Jane Gary Harris. Translated by Jane Gary Harris and Constance Link. Ann Arbor: Ardis.

Marcuse, Herbert. 1968. *Negations: Essays in Critical Theory*. Translated by Jeremy J. Shapiro. London: Allen Lane, The Penguin Press.

Marquard, Odo. 1991. *In Defense of the Accidental: Philosophical Studies*. Translated by Robert M. Wallace. Oxford: Oxford University Press.

Marx, Karl. 1934. *The Eighteenth Brumaire of Louis Bonaparte*. Moscow: Progress Publishers.

Mauss, Marcel. 1954. *The Gift: Forms and Functions of Exchange in Archaic Societies*. Translated by Ian Cunniston. London: Cohen and West.

McAdams, Dan P. 1993. *The Stories We Live By: Personal Myths and the Making of the Self*. New York and London: Guilford Press.

McGreal, Chris. 1999a. "Enemies Join Forces in Sierra Leone's New Army." *Guardian Weekly*, August 26–September 1: 5.

———. 1999b. "Nigerian Army Called to Account." *Guardian Weekly,* November 4–10: 3.

Meeker, Michael E. 1979. *Literature and Violence in North Arabia.* Cambridge: Cambridge University Press.

Meijl, Toonvan. 1996. "Historicising Maoritanga: Colonial Ethnography and the Reification of Maori Tradition." *Journal of the Polynesian Society* 105(3): 311–46.

Melland, F. H., and E. H. Cholmeley. 1912. *Through the Heart of Africa.* London.

Merleau-Ponty, Maurice. 1964. "From Mauss to Levi-Strauss." In *Signs.* Translated by R. C. McCleary, 114–25. Evanston, Illinois: Northwestern University Press.

———. 1962. *Phenomenology of Perception.* Translated by Colin Smith. London: Routledge and Kegan Paul.

———. 1964. *Signs.* Translated by R. C. McCleary. Evanston, Illinois: Northwestern University Press.

Michaels, Anne. 1998. *Fugitive Pieces.* London: Bloomsbury.

Middleton, John. 1960. *Lugbara Religion: Ritual and Authority among an East African People.* London: Oxford University Press.

Mimica, Jadran. 1993. The Foi and Heidegger. Review of *The Empty Place: Poetry, Space, and Being among the Foi of Papua New Guinea,* by James Weiner. *The Australian Journal of Anthropology* 4(2): 79–95.

Mink, Louis. 1970. "History and Fiction as Modes of Comprehension." *New Literary History* 1: 541–58.

Mohanram, Radhika. 1998. "(In)visible Bodies? Immigrant Bodies and Constructions of Nationhood in Aotearoa/New Zealand." In *Feminist Thought in Aotearoa/New Zealand: Differences and Connections,* edited by Rosemary Du Plessis and Lynne Alice, 21–28. Auckland: Oxford University Press.

Montaigne, Michel de. 1948. *The Essayes of Montaigne.* Translated by John Florio. New York: Modern Library.

Moore, Lorrie. 1998. *Birds of America.* New York: Knopf.

Muecke, Marjorie A. 1995. "Trust, Abuse of Trust, and Mistrust among Cambodian Refugee Women: A Cultural Interpretation." In *Mistrusting Refugees,* edited by E. Valentine Daniel and John Chr. Knudsen, 36–55. Berkeley: University of California Press.

Myerhoff, Barbara. 1975. "Organization and Ecstasy: Deliberate and Accidental Communitas among Huichol Indians and American Youth." In *Symbols and Politics in Communal Ideology: Cases and Questions,* edited by

Sally Falk Moore and Barbara Myerhoff, 33–67. Ithaca, New York: Cornell University Press.

———. 1982. "Life History among the Elderly: Performance, Visibility, and Remembering. In *A Crack in the Mirror: Reflexive Perspective in Anthropology*, edited by J. Ruby, 99–117. Philadelphia: University of Pennsylvania Press.

Myers, Fred R. 1986. *Pintupi Country, Pintupi Self: Sentiment, Place and Politics among Western Desert Aborigines*. Washington: Smithsonian Institution Press.

Nelson, Katherine. 1998. *Language in Cognitive Development: The Emergence of the Mediated Mind*. Cambridge: Cambridge University Press.

Neumann, Erich. 1954. *The Origins and History of Consciousness*. London: Routledge and Kegan Paul.

Niane, D. T. 1965. *Sundiata: An Epic of Old Mali*. Translated by G. D. Pickett. London: Longmans.

Nietzsche, Friedrich. 1973. *Beyond Good and Evil: Prelude to a Philosophy of the Future*. Translated by R. J. Hollingdale. Harmondsworth: Penguin Books.

North, Nicola. 1995. *Crossing the Sea: Narratives of Exile and Illness among Cambodian Refugees in New Zealand*. D. Phil. dissertation, Massey University, Palmerston North, New Zealand.

Nussbaum, Martha C. 1986. *The Fragility of Goodness: Luck and Ethics in Greek Tragedy and Philosophy*. Cambridge: Cambridge University Press.

O'Brien, Tim. 1990. *The Things they Carried*. Boston: Houghton Mifflin.

Ochs, Elinor, and Lisa Capps. 1996. "Narrating the Self." *Annual Review of Anthropology* 25: 19–43.

———. 2001. *Living Narrative: Creating Lives in Everyday Storytelling*. Cambridge, Mass.: Harvard University Press.

O'Flaherty, Wendy D. 1975. *Hindu Myths*. Harmondsworth: Penguin Books.

Olney, James. 1998. *Memory and Narrative: The Weave of Life-Writing*. Chicago: University of Chicago Press.

Olwig, Karen Fog, and Kirsten Hastrup, eds. 1997. *Siting Culture: The Shifting Anthropological Object*. London: Routledge.

Onians, R. B. 1973. *The Origins of European Thought*. New York: Arno Press.

Orsi, Robert A. 1985. *The Madonna of 115th Street: Faith and Community in Italian Harlem, 1880–1950*. New Haven: Yale University Press.

Pageard, R. 1961. "Soundiata Keita and the Oral Tradition." *Présence Africaine* 8: 53–72.

Parr, Alison. 1995. *Silent Casualties*. Birkenhead, New Zealand: Tandem Press.

Peck, Jeffrey M. 1995. "Refugees as Foreigners: The Problem of Becoming German and Finding Home." In *Mistrusting Refugees*, edited by E. Valentine Daniel and John Chr. Knudsen, 102–25. Berkeley: University of California Press.

Person, Yves. 1973. "Oral Tradition and Chronology." In *French Perspectives in African Studies*, edited by Pierre Alexandre, 204–20. London: Oxford University Press.

Peteet, Julie M. 1995. "Transforming Trust: Dispossession and Empowerment among Palestinian Refugees." In *Mistrusting Refugees*, edited by E. Valentine Daniel and John Chr. Knudsen, 168–86. Berkeley: University of California Press.

Pitkin, Hanna Fenichel. 1998. *The Attack of the Blob: Hannah Arendt's Concept of the Social*. Chicago: University of Chicago Press.

Poata-Smith, Evan S. Te Ahu. 1996. "He Pokeke Uenuku i tu ai: The Evolution of Contemporary Maori Protest." In *Nga Patai: Racism and Ethnic Relations in Aotearoa/New Zealand*, edited by Paul Spoonley, David Pearson, and Cluny Macpherson, 97–116. Palmerston North: Dunmore Press.

Pooley, Eric. 1999. "The Art of Being JFK JR." *Time*, July 26: 32–39.

Popper, Karl. 1969. *Conjectures and Refutations*. London: Routledge and Kegan Paul.

Potocki, Jan. 1995. *The Manuscript Found in Saragossa*. Translated by Ian Maclean. New York: Viking.

Pour, Afsané Bassir. 1999. "UN Divided by Sierra Leone Peace Deal." *Guardian Weekly*, August 12–18: 29.

Povinelli, Elizabeth A. 1993. *Labor's Lot: The Power, History, and Culture of Aboriginal Action*. Chicago: University of Chicago Press.

———. 1998. "The State of Shame: Australian Multiculturalism and the Crisis of Indigenous Citizenship." *Critical Inquiry* 24(2): 575–610.

Povrzanović, Maja. 1993. "Culture and Fear: Everyday Life in Wartime." In *Fear, Death and Resistance: An Ethnography of War: Croatia 1991–1992*, edited by Lada Čale Feldman, Ines Prica, and Reana Senjković, 119–50. Zagreb: Institute of Ethnology and Folklore Research.

———. 1997. "Identities in War: Embodiments of Violence and Places of Belonging." *Ethnologia Europaea* 27: 153–62.

———. 2000. "The Imposed and the Imagined as Encountered by Croatian War Ethnographers." *Current Anthropology* 41(2): 151–62.

Ranger, Terence. 1996. "Concluding Reflections on Cross-Mandates." In *In*

Search of Cool Ground: War, Flight and Homecoming in Northeast Africa, edited by Tim Allen, 318–29. London: James Currey.

Rank, Otto. 1959. *The Myth of the Birth of the Hero*. New York: Vintage.

Rapport, Nigel. 2001. "Post-Cultural Anthropology: The Ironization of Values in a World of Movement." In *Realizing Community: Concepts, Social Relationships and Sentiments*, edited by V. Arnit. London: Routledge.

Rattray, Capt. R. S. 1930. *Akan-Ashanti Folk-Tales*. Oxford: Clarendon Press.

Readings, Bill. 1996. *The University in Ruins*. Cambridge, Mass.: Harvard University Press.

Richards, Paul. 1996. *Fighting for the Rainforest: War, Youth and Resources in Sierra Leone*. Oxford: International African Institute, in association with James Currey and Heinemann.

Ricoeur, Paul. 1980. "Narrative Time." In *On Narrative*, edited by W. J. T. Mitchell, 165–86. Chicago: University of Chicago Press.

Riesman, David. 1955. *Selected Essays from Individualism Reconsidered*. New York: Doubleday.

Riesman, Paul. 1977. *Freedom in Fulani Social Life: An Introspective Ethnography*. Translated by Martha Fuller. Chicago: University of Chicago Press.

Rupert, James. 1999. "Machete Terror Stalks Sierra Leone." *Guardian Weekly*, January 3: 12.

Rushdie, Salman. 1995. *Shame*. London: Vintage.

Sacks, Oliver. 1986. *The Man who Mistoook his Wife for a Hat*. London: Picador.

Sahlins, Marshall. 1968. "On the Sociology of Primitive Exchange." In *The Relevance of Models for Social Anthropology*, edited by Michael Banton. A.S.A. Monograph 1. London: Tavistock Press.

———. 1996. "The Sadness of Sweetness: The Native Anthropology of Western Cosmology." *Current Anthropology* 37(3): 395–425.

———. 1999. "Two or Three Things that I Know about Culture." *Journal of the Royal Anthropological Institute* 5(3): 399–421.

Said, Edward. 1994. *Representations of the Intellectual: The 1993 Reith Lectures*. New York: Pantheon.

Salmond, Anne. 1991. *Two Worlds: First Meetings between Maori and Europeans, 1642–1772*. Auckland: Viking.

Sarkin, Jeremy. 1996. "The Trials and Tribulations of South Africa's Truth and Reconciliation Commission." *South African Journal on Human Rights* 12(4): 617–40.

Sartre, Jean-Paul. 1948. *The Emotions: Outline of a Theory*. Translated by Bernard Frechtman. New York: Philosophical Library.

———. 1956. *Being and Nothingness: An Essay on Phenomenological Ontology*. Translated by Hazel Barnes. New York: Philosophical Library.

———. 1968. *Search for a Method*. Translated by Hazel Barnes. New York: Vintage.

———. 1983. *Between Existentialism and Marxism*. Translated by John Matthews. London: Verso.

Scarry, Elaine. 1985. *The Body in Pain: The Making and Unmaking of the World*. New York: Oxford University Press.

Scheper-Hughes, Nancy. 1992. *Death Without Weeping: The Violence of Everyday Life in Brazil*. Berkeley: University of California Press.

Schneider, David. 1968. *American Kinship: A Cultural Account*. Chicago: University of Chicago Press.

Schor, Naomi, and ElizabethWeed, eds. 1994. *The Essential Difference*. Bloomington: Indiana University Press.

Schutz, Alfred. 1970. *On Phenomenology and Social Relations: Selected Writings*. Edited by Helmut R. Wagner. Chicago: University of Chicago Press.

———. 1973. *Collected Papers*. Vol. 1. Edited by Maurice Natanson. The Hague: Martinus Nijhoff.

Sennett, Richard. 1978. *The Fall of Public Man: On the Social Psychology of Capitalism*. New York: Vintage.

Serres, Michel. 1995. *The Natural Contract*. Translated by Elizabeth MacArthur and William Paulson. Ann Arbor: University of Michigan Press.

Shaw, Rosalind. 1997. "The Production of Witchcraft/Witchcraft as Production: Memory, Modernity, and the Slave Trade in Sierra Leone." *American Ethnologist* 24(4): 856–76.

Shipton, Parker. 1989. *Bitter Money: Cultural Economy and Some African Meanings of Forbidden Commodities*. Washington, D.C.: American Anthropological Association.

Silva, Sónia. 2011. *Along an African Border: Angolan Refugees and their Divining Baskets*. Philadelphia: University of Pennsylvania Press.

Skinner, E. P. 1964. *The Mossi of the Upper Volta*. Stanford: Stanford University Press.

Skultans, Vieda. 1997. "Theorizing Latvian Lives: The Quest for Identity." *Journal of the Royal Anthropological Institute* 3(4): 761–80.

Smith, Anthony D. 1971. *Theories of Nationalism*. London: Duckworth.

Southwold, M. 1966. "Succession to the Throne in Buganda." In *Succession to High Office*, edited by Jack Goody, 82–126. Cambridge: Cambridge University Press.

Spinoza, Baruch. 1982. *The Ethics*. Translated by Samuel Shirley. Indianapolis: Hackett Publishing.

St. Cartmail, Keith. 1983. *Exodus Indochina*. Auckland: Heinemann.

Steele, Jonathan. 1998. "A Killer Stalks along Kosovo's Border." *Guardian Weekly* 154(24): 1.

Steen Preis, Ann-Belinda. 1997. "Seeking Place: Capsized Identities and Contracted Belonging among Sri Lankan Tamil Refugees." In *Siting Culture: The Shifting Anthropological Object*, edited by Karen Fog Olwig and Kirsten Hastrup, 86–100. London: Routledge.

Steiner, George. 1973. *After Babel: Aspects of Language and Translation*. London: Oxford University Press.

Stolcke, Verena. 1995. "Talking Culture: New Boundaries, New Rhetorics of Exclusion in Europe." *Cultural Anthropology* 36(1): 1–24.

Taylor, Christopher C. 1999. *Sacrifice as Terror: The Rwandan Genocide of 1994*. Oxford and New York: Berg.

Thomas, Mandy. 1996. *Place, Memory, and Identity in the Vietnamese Diaspora*. Ph.D. dissertation, Australian National University, Canberra.

Todorov, Tzvetan. 1995. *The Morals of History*. Translated by Alyson Waters. Minneapolis: University of Minnesota Press.

Trankell, Ing-Britt. 2001. "Songs of Our Spirits: Memory and Conflict in a Cambodian Cham Community." Paper presented at the AAS Conference, Chicago, 2001.

Trotter, Lieut. Col. J. K. 1898. "An Expedition to the Source of the Niger." *Geographical Journal* 10(3): 386–401.

Turner, Victor. 1970. *The Forest of Symbols*. Ithaca, New York: Cornell University Press.

———. 1985. *On the Edge of the Bush: Anthropology as Experience*. Edited by E. L. B. Turner. Tucson: University of Arizona Press.

Tutuola, Amos. 1952. *The Palm-Wine Drinkard*. London: Faber and Faber.

Van der Kolk, Bessel A., and Onno van der Hart. 1995. "The Intrusive Past: Flexibility of Memory and the Engraving of Trauma." In *Trauma: Explorations in Memory*, edited with an introduction by Cathy Caruth, 158–82. Baltimore, Maryland: Johns Hopkins University Press.

Van de Port, Mattijs. 1998. *Gypsies, Wars and Other Instances of the Wild: Civili-*

zation and its Discontents in a Serbian Town. Amsterdam: Amsterdam University Press.

Wagner, Roy. 1975. The Invention of Culture. Chicago: University of Chicago Press.

Walker, Ranginui. 1995. "Immigration Policy and the Political Economy of New Zealand." In Immigration and National Identity in New Zealand: One People, Two Peoples, Many Peoples? edited by Stuart W. Grief, 282–302. Palmerston North: Dunmore Press.

Weber, Max. 1968. Economy and Society. New York: Bedminster Press.

Weil, Simone. 1952. The Need for Roots: Prelude to a Declaration of Duties towards Mankind. London: Routledge and Kegan Paul.

Weintraub, Jeff. 1995. "Varieties and Vicissitudes of Public Space." In Metroplis: Center and Symbol of Our Times, edited by Philip Kasinitz, 280–319. New York: New York University Press.

Weissman, Stephen M. 1989. His Brother's Keeper: A Psychobiography of Samuel Taylor Coleridge. Madison, Connecticut: International Universities Press.

Werbner, Richard. 1991. Tears of the Dead: The Social Biography of an African Family. London: Edinburgh University Press.

———. 1995. "Human Rights and Moral Knowledge: Arguments of Accountability in Zimbabwe." In Shifting Contexts: Transformations in Anthropological Knowledge, edited by Marilyn Strathern, 99–116. London: Routledge.

Werner, A. 1925. The Mythology of All Races. Vol. 7, Armenian and African. Boston: Marshall Jones.

White, Edmund. 1993. "1983." In 21 Picador Authors Celebrate 21 Years of International Writing, 119–28. London: Picador.

White, Hayden. 1981. "The Value of Narrativity in the Representation of Reality." In On Narrative, edited W. J. T. Mitchell. Chicago: University of Chicago Press.

———. 1987. The Content of the Form: Narrative Discourse and Historical Representation. Baltimore, Maryland: Johns Hopkins University Press.

White, Leslie. 1943. "Autobiography of an Acoma Indian." In New Material from Acoma, 301–60. Bureau of American Ethnology Bulletin 136. Washington, D.C: Smithsonian Institution.

White, Michael. 2007. Maps of Narrative Practice. New York: Norton.

Wikan, Unni. 1999. "Culture: A New Concept of Race." Social Anthropology 7(1): 57–64.

Wilk, Richard. 1999. "'Real Belizean Food': Building Local Identity in the Transnational Caribbean." American Anthropologist 101(2): 244–55.

Winnicott, D. W. 1974. *Playing and Reality*. Harmondsworth: Penguin.

Wolff, Tobias. 1983. Introduction to *Matters of Life and Death: New American Stories*, edited by Tobias Wolff. Green Harbor, Mass.: Wampeter Press.

Young, Michael. 1983. *Magicians of Manumanua: Living Myth in Kalauna*. Berkeley: University of California Press.

Younge, Gary. 1997. "Black, White and Every Shade Between." *Guardian Weekly* 156(222): 23.

Yourcenar, Marguerite. 1991. *Dear Departed*. Translated by Maria Louise Ascher. London: Aidan Ellis.

INDEX

Aboriginals (Australia): and national assimilationist policies, 66; Aboriginality, 110–13; myths among, 265–77; and stolen children, 66–70, 120–22

Abu-Lughod, Lila, 119

Adorno, Theodor, 93, 124, 285n, 264n, 286n, 287n

Agency, 18–19, 23, 29, 32–34, 45, 53, 61, 77–78, 92, 154, 183, 185, 186, 187, 189

Amis, Martin, 40

Anderson, Benedict, 117

Appadurai, Arjun, 119, 132, 133

Arendt, Hannah: on Adorno, 285n; on the banality of evil, 252; on biography and history, 18–20, 226; on the bureaucratic state, 71; on forgiveness and the promise, 19; on the imagination, 21, 146, 171, 249; on judging, 247–49; on Kafka, 71, 79, 82, 97; on objectivity and subjectivity, 262; on natality, 19; on pain, 45, 62; on the pariah, 15, 66–67, 256–57; on plurality, 15; on power, 15, 16, 18, 23; on the relation between public and private realms, 15, 31, 32, 34, 183, 192, 196, 220, 243, 248, 267, 273; on refugees, 15, 79, 82, 91; on Sartre, 285n; on the self-centered (*idion*) and the shared (*koinon*), 58–59; on speech and action, 57; on stories and lives, 276n; on storytelling and critique, 246–47; on the subjective-in-between, 15, 26, 31; on the telling of tales, 245; on the *vita activa* and *vita contemplativa*, 20, 246; on being a "who" and a "what," 15, 32, 115

Aristotle, 256

Auden, W. H., 61, 90

Authorship, 18–19, 35, 41, 45, 66, 186, 225, 228; and authorization, 58, 227, 242, 285n

Bakhtin, Mikhail, 41, 46, 184, 276n

Baldwin, James, 132, 286n

Basso, Keith, 36–37

Bateson, Gregory, 174

Bauby, Jean-Dominique, 24

Baumann, Gerd, 45

Benhabib, Seyla, 45, 286n

Benjamin, Walter, 15, 71, 111, 144, 185, 227, 242, 246

Berger, John, 35–36, 37, 83, 97, 106–7, 227, 242, 278n, 287n

Bergson, Henri: on the comic as a distancing device, 183; on the organic and the mechanical, 181; on the tragic and the comic, 171; on flexible vices and rigid virtues, 172, 180; on laughter as corrective, 180

Bettelheim, Bruno, 24–25

Bion, Wilfrid, 16

Blixen, Karen (Isak Dinesen), 35, 276n